HERALDIC KNITTING

An exquisite example of modern knitting, in fine linen thread, by Paula
Granichstadten; showing how variety of stitch, correctly chosen, and thought-
fully designed, can be used to express form of the most complicated nature.

MARY THOMAS'S
BOOK OF
KNITTING
PATTERNS

DOVER PUBLICATIONS, INC.
NEW YORK

This Dover edition, first published in 1972, is an unabridged republication of the work originally published in 1943 by Hodder and Stoughton, Ltd., London. It is reprinted by special arrangement with Hodder and Stoughton, Ltd., Warwick Lane, London, E.C.4.

International Standard Book Number: 0-486-22818-5
Library of Congress Catalog Card Number: 72-188246

Manufactured in the United States of America
Dover Publications, Inc.
180 Varick Street
New York, N.Y. 10014

DEDICATED
WITH LOVE TO MY CHILDREN
GAVRELLE
AND
RICHARD

PREFACE

The best periods of Knitting have always occurred when yarns have been scarce or expensive, as the desire for better knowledge of the work is stimulated in order that yarn need not be unduly wasted. The urge to knit is satisfied by making a careful collection of stitches and patterns knitted in Sampler form ; and since every work, past-time or hobby must first begin with a collection, so that comparison and selection can be intelligently made, there is no more opportune moment than the present in which to begin this work.

The illustrations in this book are arranged to present a progressive, pictorial story of knitted patterns, to be first enjoyed by turning the pages and watching the designs grow from simple to greater elaboration.

This sensible arrangement serves not only as a story, but as a demonstration of the orderly and scientific methods on which knitting patterns are planned.

Science as applied to knitting puts things in order, and inspires confidence. It does not elaborate, but simplifies the knowledge of knitting. It shows how a pattern is created, and so how it can be elaborated, simplified, or adapted as circumstances require. Such knowledge will greatly elucidate all written directions, and encourage the personal touch, which always adds to the pleasure of knitting.

Each chapter introduces a new motif of design, and the order of the book shows that knitting patterns are first composed of stitches and then stitches and motifs. As each motif can be grouped in a hundred different ways, and then allied to a second or third and grouped in hundreds of other different ways, there can be no possible end to knitting patterns, any more than there can be an end to melody created on the seven notes of the scale. The scope is endless, and this world of fabric lies at the finger-tips for every knitter to enjoy.

All knitting patterns are first planned out on squared paper, in just the same way as Weaving or Embroidery patterns. In fact, in the days of the Guilds there must have been great interchange of designs between workers of all the various applied arts, as each could use the same design with different effect because of different technique. In this way inspirations for knitting patterns could surround us on fabrics, walls, silver or china.

Approaching the work from this angle and noting the old technical, stitch and pattern names, it has been possible to rebuild the old methods of designing knitting patterns such as were known centuries before written descriptions did away with charts, and so the habit of seeing design on paper. Our ancestors could design on paper and with scientific knowledge long before they could write. Indeed, some of the early written recipes now make very curious reading, and these are comparatively late, about early 19th century.

Knitting has a long, sweet, home history, and brief references to this give much of reading interest in the different chapters.

The student should read this book with yarn and needles handy, and test out the different patterns and suggestions as they are described. Any odd scraps of yarn can be used for this purpose, and the lessons learnt will save much valuable time and yarn in the future. After completing a few stitches or a row, the work should be examined so that the visual effect of the technique is appreciated. By this means it becomes possible to recognise at a glance how any fabric is created; moreover, it will also develop a love and knowledge of the work which can be gained in no other way.

The knitter will quickly see how a vertical order of units (stitches or ornamental motifs) will result in a fabric having a width-wise stretch, while the same stitches or motifs in horizontal order will result in a fabric with a depth wise stretch. With this knowledge the designer will choose fabrics and arrange the units in design to obtain their best possible use, not only for their decorative value, but also for their practical value, so that the smartest shapes and style lines can be acquired.

This intimate knowledge of stitch has other practical uses, as it enables one to look at the illustrations of knitted garments, etc., published in printed leaflets and magazines, and so to visualise beforehand how these garments will suit any particular figure, and thus avoid the disappointment of knitting-up a garment which might prove unbecoming. All written directions are general, of necessity, like ready-made garments, and unless the figure is Stock Size, some adjustment is always necessary, so the advice to cut and keep your own Master Pattern, and check the size and shape of a garment as the work progresses, is a sensible and economical plan.

Yet another helpful suggestion is to make a Knitted Sampler of all the different recipes given in each chapter. A separate sampler for each chapter, which should then be labelled. A " family group " of stitches recorded in this way will provide a reference of great value when seeking different fabrics or effects for designing garments. The sampler could be about 20 stitches wide, and each different pattern about 12 rows in depth. Before changing from one pattern to the next, knit 2 rows of Garter Stitch, so that each specimen is separate and easily recognisable.

Many knitted samplers of rare beauty are shown in this book, and these should serve to inspire the modern student. A sampler has a dual value. It is a record and also a means of learning a new stitch.

For those who desire a reference book only, without considering the ways and origin of design, each pattern is independently described, so that all can take just what they want and how they want. Also any pattern or stitch can be found immediately under its own name by referring to the index, and when the name is unknown, by its principle of technique—Slip, Cross, Eyelet, etc.—given at the top of each page.

In addition to showing the methods of creating each stitch or pattern, little sketches are shown throughout the book suggesting appropriate use of special fabrics or motif for garment use.

Two chapters, contrasting the old and modern methods of making knitted garments, are given, so that the difference between the two can be compared and appreciated.

The fact is often overlooked that a knitter in making a garment, or any article for that matter, is really doing two things at the same time :—

1. Making a garment. (A dressmaker's job.)
2. Making a fabric. (A weaver's job.)

It is this which makes it so necessary to consider each job separately. First shape, then fabric, and afterwards unite them in the simplest possible way. To do this it is essential to know how each fabric is designed, so that several patterns can be successfully amalgamated in pleasing effect.

The designing charts will aid in this objective, but the greatest inspiration will be found in the order of the book, and the arrangement of the different repeating motifs in family groups presented under their own headings of Crossed, Slip, Ladder, Eyelet, Faggot, etc. In this way two or more members of the same family can be selected and blended successfully. (See, for example, Fig. 68, which is composed entirely of patterns chosen from the Crossed Motif " family ").

A second or third attempt at designing will permit of greater adventure, and the uniting of different family groups. For this purpose the broader classification of fabrics and motifs in Vertical and Horizontal will be found useful.

Soon the knitter herself will visualise a thousand other ways in which a motif can be used, and so have at her disposal an inexhaustible variety of fabrics.

Thick fabrics or thin fabrics, patterned fabrics or plain fabrics, those blazing in colour † or decorated with beads.† She can make fabric to imitate fur (Looped Knitting),† Lace, Picot, Filet, or Crochet, and even cloqué and woven fabric, by a mere change of technique. Every ornament known to dressmaking can be imitated, even hemstitching and buttons !

There is no work in the world more ingenious than Knitting, and this is why its appeal has lasted over so many centuries.

MARY THOMAS.

△ This mark is used throughout the book to stress points of importance, which a beginner might pass lightly over. It is there to say " Look out. Watch this point, or you will go wrong ! "

† This mark, used through the book, means see Mary Thomas's Knitting Book for greater detailed and illustrated directions. This first book deals exclusively with the different forms and technique of knitting, details of garment making, knitting history, etc.

ACKNOWLEDGMENTS

I would like to acknowledge with my sincere thanks the brilliant work of the artists, Miss H. Lyon-Wood, Miss Dorothy Dunmore, and Miss Margaret Agutter, who is also responsible for all the little humorous caricatures.

My thanks are also due to the many kind people who have so willingly forwarded me valuable information and help, and especially to Mrs. Edith M. Walker, for the loan of her many books; also to Miss Dorothy Moss for typing the MS.

The great kindness of various people and museums who have loaned articles for illustration is acknowledged with thanks beneath the various pictures respectively reproduced.

MARY THOMAS.

CONTENTS

LIST OF ILLUSTRATIONS

Whenever you see this sign
STOP !
CAUTION ! !
GO ! ! !

THE A.B.C. OF DESIGN

Knitting begins with one foundation fabric, and from this all patterns originate. This fabric has two names, because it has two views, a FRONT and a BACK. The front is known as Knit Fabric, commonly called Stocking Stitch, while the back is known as Purl Fabric. It is also known as White and Black Fabric, because this is how Knit and Purl Fabric appears in chart form (*see* Figs. 6 and 18).

Both sides are used as a basis of design, so it is more convenient to assume there are two separate foundation fabrics, just **as two** stitches are assumed, whereas Purl Stitch is really only a back view of Knit Stitch, just as Purl Fabric is the back view of Knit Fabric. (The Dictionary meaning of Purl is to " Invert a stitch ".)

On this slender foundation, one stitch, one fabric, but dual in name and reversible, and so opposite as black and white in every characteristic, the whole structure of Patterned Knitted Fabrics is built up. The Knit side provides a vertical line of design, and the Purl side a horizontal line of design, and each order has its own peculiar elasticity, as follows :—

KNIT OR FRONT FABRIC. *Fig. 1 (Classification Warp or Vertical Fabric).*

Also known as WHITE FABRIC, RIGHT FABRIC, SMOOTH FABRIC, JERSEY FABRIC, STOCKING STITCH and PLAIN FABRIC (because it is represented by a Plain Chart, *see* Fig. 6).

This is the front of the fabric, and each new stitch, as shown, is drawn through and to the FRONT of the stitch on the needle, in the same way as a chain is looped, so that the fabric presents an appearance of chain loops ascending in *vertical lines* (*see* Fig. 1). The side elevation (A, Fig. 1) shows this quite clearly, and gives the

FIG. 1.—Knit or Front Fabric.

reason why it can be classified as Vertical, or, in textile language, as Warp Fabric. Warp threads are the long vertical threads on the loom, and thinking in terms of these gives the designer a long vertical line more easily built into pattern than stitches. The elasticity of the fabric is width-wise, and so it tends to Take-in and cling.

PURL OR BACK FABRIC. *Fig. 2 (Classification Weft or Horizontal Fabric).*

Also known as ROUGH FABRIC, REVERSED FABRIC, BACK FABRIC, WRONG FABRIC (as it is the wrong side) and BLACK FABRIC (as in Chart, Fig. 18).

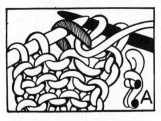

This is the back of the foundation fabric, and the actions are inverted, so each new loop is drawn through away from the knitter as shown. The stitch on the needle is then dropped so that the head of the chain loop—the part invisible from the front—now shows (*see* side elevation A, Fig. 2). These

FIG. 2.—Purl or Back Fabric.

"heads" in total form a *horizontal line* of bent over stitches across the fabric, and so classify Purl as a Horizontal or Weft Fabric, Weft being the loom threads which travel from left to right. This provides a second long designing line, sweeping horizontally across the fabric. The elasticity is depth-wise and so the fabric tends to Take-up.

FABRIC CONSTRUCTION.

As shown, Knitted Fabric is composed of a series of loops, and according to which way the loop faces—front view (Knit) or back view (Purl)—and according to its order in design—Vertical or Horizontal—so is the depth or width of the fabric varied, and its elasticity changed. This is apparent even in the foundation fabric, and experiment will show that a Jersey knitted in Stocking stitch, if worn with the Purl side outermost, is slightly shorter and broader than when worn with the Knit side outermost, because the stitches take the opposite bend when encircling the body. Thus in one fabric it is possible to have two different elastic pulls.

The first variations of Knit and Purl Fabric are detailed to show how the method works. Both are pure types, one an all-vertical or Warp Fabric, and the other an all-horizontal or Weft Fabric, so the peculiar depth, or width, and elasticity of each fabric is accentuated.

FIRST VARIATION OF KNIT FABRIC. *Fig. 3 (Classification Warp or Vertical Fabric).*

Designed on the front of the foundation fabric.

The chain loops ascend vertically, one Knit Stitch facing to the front and one facing to the back.

In this order they pull in opposite directions, and so "take-in" the WIDTH, as in accordion pleating. The depth of the Purl stitch in vertical arrangement remains unaltered, as it is only "reversed". This is an extra narrow fabric, and so extremely elastic in width.

Both sides are alike, and the pattern described as 1 and 1 Rib, made by alternating the two STITCHES. The Knit rib stands out boldly, because Knit stitches in vertical arrangement appear embossed, while Purl stitches recede, because they

Fig. 3.—First Variation of Knit Fabric.

are looking the other way. A strong vertical line, long or short, narrow or broad, can always be obtained by a vertical order of Knit stitches. (*See* Figs. 7 to 14 for designing sequence.)

FIRST VARIATION OF PURL FABRIC. *Fig. 4 (Classification Weft or Horizontal Fabric).*

Designed on the back of the foundation fabric.

The Fabric is designed horizontally and in rows, one row of Purl stitches followed by one row of Knit stitches, so that one row shows the back of all the stitches and one row the front.

FIG. 4.—First Variation of Purl Fabric.

This opposing action bends and broadens the stitches, and so shortens the depth of the fabric. In knitting terminology the fabric "takes up", and consequently the elastic pull is depthwise. △ All patterns, where the Stitches or Motifs are arranged in rows, always "take up".

Both sides of the fabric are alike, and the pattern is described as 1 and 1 Welt, or 1 and 1 Horizontal Rib, or, more commonly, as Garter Stitch.

The Purl row, being on its own fabric, stands out boldly

because Purl stitches arranged horizontally appear embossed, while Knit stitches recede and form a background. This is exactly the opposite to Fig. 3. A strong horizontal line, of design long or short, broad or narrow, can always be obtained by a horizontal order of Purl stitches. (*See* Figs. 19 to 22 for further development.)

DESIGN

These two lines, vertical and horizontal, can therefore be regarded as hypothetical Weft and Warp lines when designing, and Figs. 7 to 39 were designed in this way, as the charts reveal. Again, for garment designing, either can be used to emphasise style-lines.

The amalgamation of the vertical and horizontal lines begin in Fig. 35, and the natural progress of pattern follows.

It is also shown that Motifs respond to this vertical and horizontal arrangement, and so to the Knit and Purl classification and elasticity, to greater or lesser degrees, according to the way the motif is used—spaced or close together. Motifs, like stitches, are free agents, and can be used in repeat exactly as required.

Suitability of purpose will naturally govern the designer's choice of stitch, motif, or fabric.

When articles such as shawls, scarves, etc., are required, some fabric selected from the Purl family is better, as a horizontal arrangement of stitches or motifs will keep the fabric better extended in width, so that it will lie flatter, and without curl at the edges. As most lace fabrics belong to the Knit group, Shetland knitters, in using these for shawls, will correct any curl by introducing a row of Purl at intervals across the fabric, as in Fig. 189; or on single-width scarves by using a Garter Stitch Selvedge.

ELASTICITY

Knitted fabrics, as just shown, have width and depth plus elasticity, and it is this latter quality which distinguishes them so much from woven fabrics. This is a consideration to designers who will use the order of the Knit and Purl stitches in design, according to width or depth requirements, and note also that Ornamental Motifs, in repeat, have much the same effect.

Knit Fabric, and its many variations, has a width-wise elasticity. Also motifs in vertical arrangement tend to " take-in ", and so permit of width-wise stretch.

Purl Fabric, and its many variations, has a depth-wise elasticity. Also motifs in horizontal arrangement tend to "take-up", and so permit of depth-wise stretch.

These rules apply to both circular and single fabrics.

Elasticity correctly used is a means of shaping a fabric. The best known is the choice of Ribbing for cuffs, collars, stocking tops, etc., but more subtle use can be made of this quality for better fit to garments for fuller figures.

Because of the depth-wise elasticity of all Horizontal Fabrics, they can, if desired, be designed for use across the figure—*i.e.*, knitted from armhole to armhole, instead of being knitted from bottom upwards. In this way the horizontal lines appear as vertical lines on the figure, and rows of different colours added at intervals, thus become vertical stripes, and with good effect. Garter Stitch is the favourite, but motifs in Horizontal arrangements can be used in the same way.

A fabric which combines both the vertical and horizontal lines, as in Fig. 39, has a two-ways stretch, so in a single-width fabric it is balanced. For this reason it was so often used for old knitted bedspreads, etc., as the old workers understood the use of this elastic quality so well. Indeed, before the advent of elastic, knitted strips took its place, the last surviving relic of this use being the knitted Highland garter and the knitted bandage.

THE STOCKING AND THE GARTER. *Fig. 5.*

A simple picture-memory of the Vertical and Horizontal principles of Knitted Fabric is aptly supplied in the Stocking and the Garter, which was hung as a Trade Sign over the door of a professional knitter's home or workshop.

The Gartered Stocking has always featured in the Heraldic devices of all Knitting Guilds, and, for this reason, it symbolised the knitters Warp and Weft. It did not necessarily denote their occupation, as they might knit gloves, hats, coats, breeches, either in addition to or without knitting stockings at all.

Fig. 5.—The Stocking and the Garter.

KNITTING CHARTS

Knitting Charts present a picture of the pattern on paper, and so show what written directions can never do—how patterns are created, and, once accustomed to charting, it becomes quite easy to knit directly from the Chart without bothering to write directions.

In creating new designs it is better to chart more than one repeat, in order to see how the pattern will work out, but in knitting or writing out the pattern, △ one repeat only is described for Round Knitting. On △△ two knitting-pins an extra half repeat may be necessary, varying according to design, in order to make both selvedge sides symmetrical. So in Flat Knitting one repeat plus half for garment or even finish may be necessary. Example, Ribbed Fabrics, Figs. 7, etc.

Study first the design you have created, and then enclose the full repeat in a square, and knit this portion only, either reading directly from the chart or, if preferred, write out the directions and then knit.

CHART READING

The Chart shows the △ front of the fabric. Each line represents a Row or Round. The same chart serves for either technique, but the reading differs, as the chart is read in the same order and direction as the row or round is being knitted. Note this carefully, when knitting on two pins :—

Front Rows (front of fabric facing knitter). Read chart from right to left. (Front rows are also knitted from △ right to left.)

Back Rows read from △ left to right, as back rows are knitted from left to right. Also, when knitting with the back of work facing knitter, the stitches must be made as they will appear on the △ front. To do this the Knit symbol must be read as Purl and the Purl symbols as Knit. They are TRANSLATED. Example : in Stocking Stitch, all back or even rows are purled so that they appear knit on the right side.

When the fabric is knitted round and on four or several needles, read the chart as follows :—

Rounds. The front of fabric △ always faces the knitter, and the work always proceeds in the same direction, each needle being knitted from right to left. So, every line on the chart is read from right to left, beginning first line with first round, second line with second round, △ reading one repeat only as pattern (*see also* page 192).

6

SOLID FABRICS

Designing Units—Knit and Purl Stitches

Solid fabrics are composed of Knit and Purl stitches only, and these in designing symbols are represented as black and white squares.

WHITE Squares = *Knit stitches.*
BLACK Squares = *Purl stitches.*

The story begins with an all-white chart, depicting Knit Fabric or Stocking Stitch, followed by its vertical variations, or Ribbing. The fabric is then reversed, and discovered as an all-Purl Fabric, and so in symbols on an all-black chart (*see* Fig. 18). The sequential variations are this time horizontal, and so known as Welts, Welting or Horizontal Ribbing. It is these two lines, Vertical and Horizontal which provide the main structure of all design, either in repeat as all-over fabrics, or singly for special effects (*see* page 277). Every pattern is made up of some repeating motif, simple or elaborate, and seeing familiar patterns in design as charts, will inspire their freer and more graceful use, because they can be so obviously varied to suit taste and requirements.

All fabrics can be either knitted Round, using 4, 5 or more needles, in which case the fabric is circular, or they can be knitted Flat, using two needles only, producing an opened or Single fabric with two selvedge sides.

The method of charting is the same for both, but the method of reading the chart differs (*see* page 6). As the Single Fabric, knitted in rows, is the most popular, directions are mainly given for this method, with a few hints at the beginning about Round Fabrics in order to call attention to the difference in the number of stitches cast on. Also *see* page 46.

7

KNIT FABRICS

The first fabric is Knit Fabric, Warp Fabric, Vertical Fabric, Jersey Fabric, Smooth Fabric or Stocking Stitch, which, being comprised of all Knit stitches, shows a " Plain " chart, and so is again known as " Plain " Fabric, just as Knit Stitch is commonly known as " Plain " Stitch, and for this reason.

Knit Fabrics are classified as Warp or Vertical Fabrics (*see also* page 1).

KNIT FABRIC OR STOCKING STITCH. *Fig. 6.*

Round Fabric

Cast On any number of stitches, and arrange on three needles and knit with a fourth.

Round I, and all succeeding rounds: Knit.

Single Fabric

Cast On any number of stitches.
Row I: Knit.
Row 2: Purl.

Repeat these 2 rows throughout.

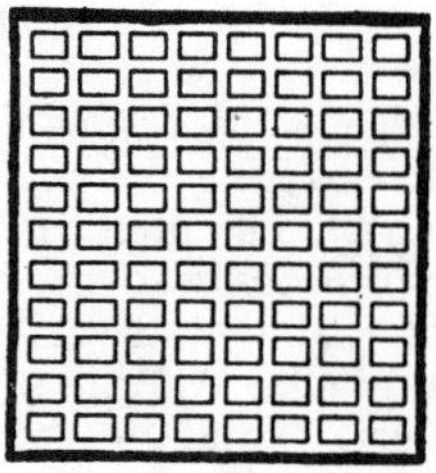

Fig. 6.—Stocking Stitch.

DOUBLE KNIT FABRIC

Also known as DOUBLE KNITTING, DOUBLE STOCKING STITCH or just DOUBLE FABRIC.

The fabric is double but knitted on two knitting-pins. There is no opening at the base, but one end can be left open when casting off if desired by dividing the stitches on two needles, taking one stitch alternately on to each needle and casting off with a third as for a Round Fabric.

Cast On an even number of stitches.
Row I: Knit.
Row 2: K.2 * Insert needle into 3rd stitch and throw yarn twice round point of pin and draw through a double loop. Pass the yarn between the needles to front and slip the 4th stitch purlwise. Take yarn to back again. * Repeat these two movements from * to *. K. last 2 stitches.

Row 3: K.2. * Insert needle into 3rd stitch, throw yarn twice round point of needle. Yarn to front and slip next stitch, slipping the double loop as one stitch. Take yarn to back again. * Repeat * to *. K. last 2 stitches.

Repeat Row 3 only for length required. Knit the last row plain and then cast off.

Important Note.

To make a closer and firmer fabric, drop out the Double Throw in each alternate stitch, and use an ordinary Knit Stitch, otherwise directions are the same.

Row 1 : Knit.
Row 2 : K.2. * K.1. Yarn Fd. S.1. (p.w.) *. Repeat * to *, ending K.2. Repeat Row 2 throughout.

USES. To make double heel flaps. For silk ties, scarves, belts, etc.

RIBBED PATTERNS

Ribbed Patterns are the first variations of Knit Fabric. They are made by alternating the two stitches, Knit and Purl, keeping each vertically above its kind. Knit stitches arranged vertically above each other appear embossed, while Purl stitches in vertical arrangement sink and form a background.

The number of stitches forming a Rib can be even or uneven, *i.e.*, 2 and 2 even, the Rib being composed of 2 Knit and 2 Purl, or 2 and 3 uneven—2 Knit and 3 Purl.

NOTE.—In Garment Knitting it is usual to finish with an extra half repeat, so that the ribbing balances either side. This is done when casting-on. In Round Knitting this is not necessary, as shown below.

RIBBED FABRICS (EVEN)

Even ribbing of any width can be designed; the number of stitches to be cast on is obtained by the addition of the two units. Example: For a rib of 7 and 7, cast on 14 stitches, plus 7 for garment finish when making a single fabric.

ONE AND ONE RIB (EVEN). *Fig. 7.*

Round Fabric

Cast On stitches divisible by 2.
   Round 1: * K.1, P.1. * Repeat.
   Round 2 and all succeeding rounds the same.

Single Fabric

Cast On stitches divisible by 2 plus 1.
   Row 1: * K.1, P.1. * Repeat, ending K.1.
   Row 2: P.1. * K.1, P.1. * Repeat * to *.

Repeat these 2 rows.

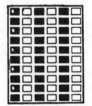

Fig. 7.—1 & 1 Rib.
Even.

TWO AND TWO RIB (EVEN). *Fig. 8.*

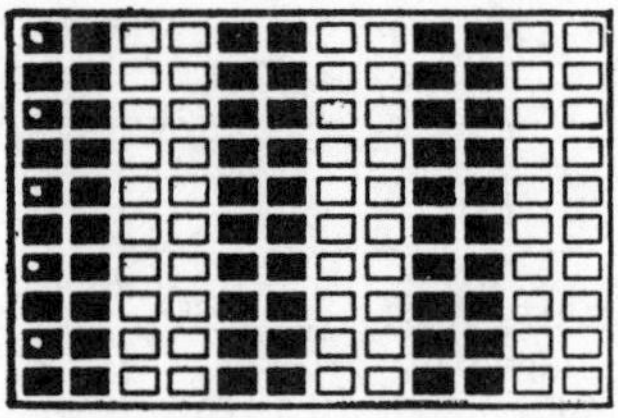

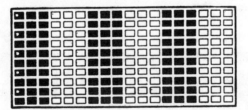

FIG. 8.—2 & 2 Rib. Even.

Round Fabric

Cast On stitches divisible by 4.
   Round 1: * K.2, P.2. * Repeat.
   Round 2 and all succeeding rounds the same.

Single Fabric

Cast On stitches divisible by 4 and 2 over.
   Row 1: * K.2, P.2. * Repeat, ending K.2.

Row 2: P.2. * K.2, P.2. * Repeat * to *.

Repeat these 2 rows throughout.

THREE AND THREE RIB (EVEN). *Fig. 9.*

FIG. 9.—3 & 3 Rib. Even.

Cast On stitches divisible by 6 and 3 over.

   Row 1: * K.3, P.3. * Repeat, ending K.3.

   Row 2: P.3. * K.3 P.3. *

Repeat these 2 rows.

FIVE AND FIVE RIB (EVEN). *Fig. 10.*

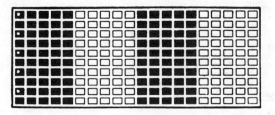

FIG. 10.—5 & 5 Rib. Even.

Cast On stitches divisible by 10 and 5 over.

Row 1: * K.5, P.5. * Repeat, ending K.5.
Row 2: P.5. * K.5, P.5. *

Repeat these 2 rows.

USE. Even ribbing increases the length but reduces the width of the fabric, as in accordion pleating. It is very elastic in width, and so particularly effective for cuffs, polo collars, stocking tops and basques of jumpers, or to give waisted effect to a dress (*see* Fig. 11).
Also slimming for undergarments.

FIG. 11.—Use of Ribbing.

RIBBED PATTERNS (UNEVEN)

Uneven Ribs of any width can be designed as required. The number of stitches to be cast on is obtained by the addition of the two units forming the complete repeat. Example: In 5 and 3 Rib, cast on 8 stitches, plus 5 for even or garment finish.

ONE AND TWO RIB. *Fig. 12.*

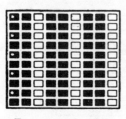

FIG. 12.—1 & 2 Rib. Uneven.

The background is wider than the rib, and so gives better prominence to the rib of Knit stitches.

Cast On stitches divisible by 3 and 1 over.
    Row 1: * K.1, P.2. * Repeat, ending K.1.
    Row 2: P.1. * K.2, P.1. * Repeat * to *.
Repeat these 2 rows.

Further variations : 1 and 3 Rib or 3 and 1 Rib, 5 and 1 Rib, and so on.

THREE AND TWO RIB. *Fig. 13.*

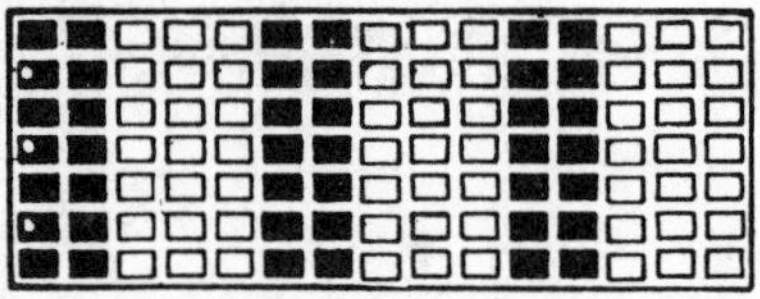

FIG. 13.—3 & 2 Rib. Uneven.

Cast On stitches divisible by 5 and 3 over.
    Row 1: * K.3, P.2. * Repeat, ending K.3.
    Row 2: P.3. * K.2, P.3. * Repeat * to *.

Repeat these 2 rows.

Variations : 5 and 2 Rib, 7 and 2 Rib.

FIVE AND THREE RIB. *Fig. 14.*

Cast On stitches divisible by 8 and 5 over.
    Row 1: * K.5, P.3. * Repeat, ending K.5.

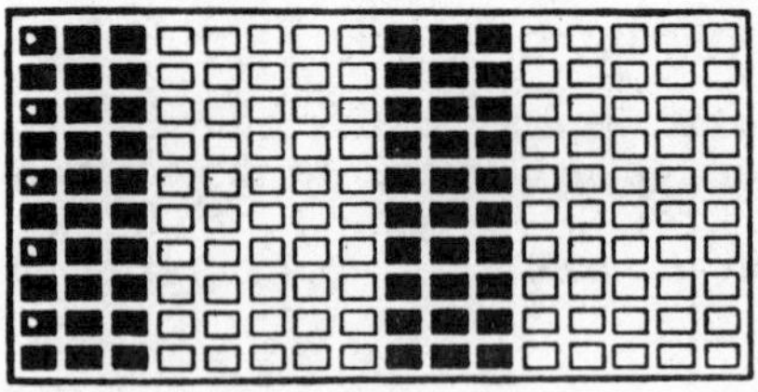

Row 2: P.5. * K.3, P.5. * Repeat * to *.

Repeat these 2 rows.

Variations : 7 and 3 Rib, 9 and 3 Rib.

Uses. Uneven-ribbed fabrics have a tailored effect, smart for knitted sports wear. Both sides of the fabric are decorative.

FIG. 14.—5 & 3 Rib. Uneven.

FIG. 15A.—Knife Pleating.

RIBBED PLEATING

By introducing a wider rib of Knit and Purl between narrower ribs (*see* Fig. 15A), or other fabrics, the wide Knit rib will roll over the Purl, and so form a pleat (*see also* Fig. 45).

KNIFE PLEATING.   *Figs. 15A and* B.

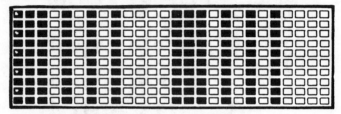

FIG. 15B.—Knife Pleating.   Chart.

Cast On stitches divisible by 13.
> Row 1: * K.4, P.1, K.1, P.1, K.1, P.1, K.1,
> P.3. *   Repeat.
> Row 2: * K.3, P.1, K.1, P.1, K.1, P.1, K.1,
> P.4. *   Repeat.

Repeat these 2 rows.

△ For Round Knitting, repeat 1st row only for all rounds.

BROKEN RIBBING

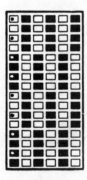

All evenly ribbed patterns of any width can be " broken " and so create some very charming fabrics.   As the rib grows wider, so must greater proportionate depth be given to the ribbing before the break occurs.

ONE AND ONE BROKEN RIB.   *Fig. 16.*

Cast On stitches divisible by 2.
> Rows 1 to 4: * K.1, P.1. *   Repeat.
> Rows 5 to 8: * P.1, K.1. *   Repeat.

Repeat these 8 rows.

FIG. 16.—1 & 1 Broken Rib.

Variation :   Knit 2 rows plain between each break.   Then known as MACARONI RIB.

TWO AND TWO BROKEN RIB. *Fig. 17.*

Cast On stitches divisible by 4.
    Rows 1 to 6:   * K.2, P.2. *   Repeat.
    Rows 7 to 12:   * P.2, K.2. *   Repeat.

    Repeat these 12 rows.

    Variation : Knit 4 rows plain between each break or 4 rows of Purl Fabric (a Welt). Then known as WINDOW-PANES.

USES. Broken-ribbed fabrics do not possess the same clinging elastic quality as evenly-ribbed fabrics, because the accordion-pleated effect has been partly eliminated. The result is a flatter fabric, to be used for any garment or article as needed.

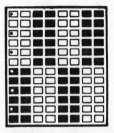

FIG. 17.—2 & Broken Rib.

PURL FABRICS

The first Purl Fabric, which is the back of the foundation fabric (*see* page 2), is represented by an all-black chart, as it is comprised entirely of Purl or Black stitches, and so is the opposite of Fig. 6. Purl or Rough Fabric is also known as Reverse, Back, Wrong and Black Fabric, and for this reason. Purl Fabrics are classified as Weft or Horizontal Fabrics (*see also* page 2).

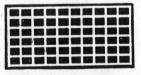

PURL FABRIC. *Fig. 18.*

Round Fabric

Cast On any number of stitches and arrange on three needles.
    Round 1: Purl.
    Round 2 and all succeeding rounds alike.

Single Fabric

Cast On any number of stitches.

    Row 1: Purl.
    Row 2: Knit.

    Repeat these 2 rows throughout.

FIG. 18.—Purl Fabric.

WELT PATTERNS

Welts are the first variation of Purl Fabric.

△ They consist of horizontal ridges running across the width of the fabric, and are formed by alternating Knit and Purl rows, either singly or in groups. The result is Horizontal Ribs or Welts of Purl Fabric on a background of Knit Fabric.

Welt is the old name for horizontal ribbing, and, being short and descriptive, it is retained. Purl stitches arranged in rows present an embossed appearance, which is the opposite to their effect when arranged vertically (compare in Fig. 24). A Welted Fabric has a horizontal corrugated effect, and the elastic stretch is vertical, but not so yielding as ribbing.

A Welt, like a rib, can be even or uneven.

The first Welt is Garter Stitch, which, viewed from the front, consists of one row Purl (embossed) and one row Knit (background). △△ In Round Knitting this is the method of work as shown in the single example, Fig. 19. In Flat Knitting all rows are either all Knit or all Purl, which arrives at the same result. Strictly speaking, all rows should be Purl, and as this links the series in better sequence on the diagrams, the directions here are given as Purl.

WELT PATTERNS (EVEN)

As these fabrics are designed in rows, the number of stitches to cast on is not decided by a repeat, but by width of fabric required. Four examples are given, but a Welt can be of any depth, and the sequence continued as required. Note the repetition of the row where the fabric changes from Purl to Stocking Stitch. Directions are given for Single Fabrics; if Round Fabrics are required, read directly from the charts.

ONE AND ONE WELT, OR GARTER STITCH. *Fig. 19.*

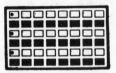

FIG. 19.—1 & 1 Welt.
Even.

Round Fabric.

Cast On any number of stitches.

Round 1: Purl.
Round 2: Knit.

Repeat these 2 Rounds.

Single Fabric.

Cast On any number of stitches.

    Row 1: Purl.
    Row 2: Purl.

Repeat these 2 rows.

TWO AND TWO WELT. *Fig. 20.*

Cast On any number of stitches.

    Row 1: Front of fabric.   Purl.
    Row 2: Knit.
    Row 3: Knit.
    Row 4: Purl.

Repeat these 4 rows.

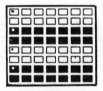

FIG. 20.—2 & 2 Welt.
Even.

THREE AND THREE WELT. *Fig. 21.*

Cast On any number of stitches.

    Row 1: Purl.
    Row 2: Knit.
    Row 3: Purl.
    Row 4: Purl.
    Row 5: Knit.
    Row 6: Purl.

Repeat these 6 rows.

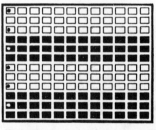

FIG. 21.—3 & 3 Welt.   Even.

FOUR AND FOUR WELT.
    Fig. 22.

Cast On any number of stitches.

    Row 1: Purl.
    Row 2: Knit.
    Row 3: Purl.
    Row 4: Knit.
    Row 5: Knit.
    Row 6: Purl.
    Row 7: Knit.
    Row 8: Purl.

Repeat these 8 rows.

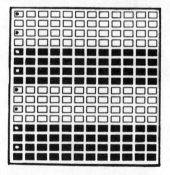

FIG. 22.—4 & 4 Welt.   Even.

DECORATIVE USE OF WELTS

Welts extend the fabric width-wise and diminish the depth, being corrugated in appearance.   They have a contrary effect to ribbing, and so are effective :—

FIG. 23A.—Use of Welts.
"Tucking."

FIG. 23B.—Use of Welts.
Scarf.

FIG. 23C.—Use of Welts.
Frilling.

1. To form horizontal "tucked" effects across the front and sleeves of a jumper (*see* Fig. 23A).

2. To extend the base of a scarf or a Bell cuff (*see* Fig. 23B).

3. To make a narrow kilted frill which has a goffered effect. This can be done by "Turning," † or knitted in separate strips and attached afterwards (*see* Fig. 23C).

FIG. 25.—Ribs and Welts.

COMPARISON RIBS AND WELTS

This photograph (Fig. 24) shows an interesting comparison of a Ribbed and a Welted Fabric.   Both contain the same number of rows and stitches, yet compare the difference in height and width.   (See what happened to the twins' pullovers !   Fig. 25.)

One is a Knit Fabric and the other a Purl Fabric, and according to the effect desired, broad or narrow, so can these fabrics be best used in garment designing. The front and back of either fabric is similar.

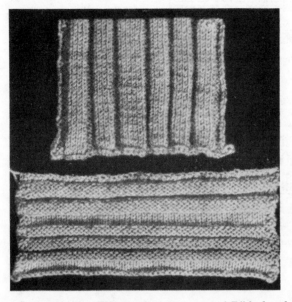

Fig. 24.—Comparing the difference in appearance of Ribbed and Welted Fabrics. The same number of rows and stitches is used for both fabrics. The Ribbed Fabric "Takes-in" while the Welted Fabric "Takes-up".

WELTED FABRICS (UNEVEN)

Welts, like Ribs, can be even or uneven, but because of the dominating roll of the Purl Welt, it is better to allow an extra row or rows to the background fabric of Knit, or the irregularity does not show to any effect. Two examples are given, but the sequence can be developed as required.

ONE AND TWO WELT. *Fig. 26.*

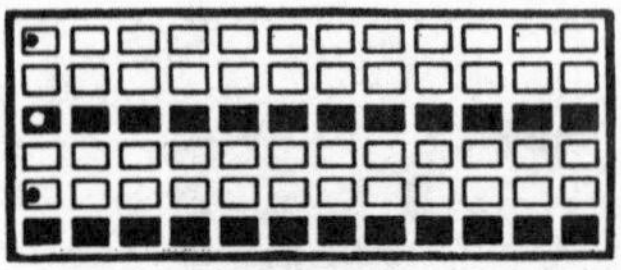

Cast On any number of stitches.
Row 1: Purl.
Row 2: Purl.
Row 3: Knit.
Row 4: Knit.
Row 5: Knit.
Row 6: Purl.

FIG. 26.—1 & 2 Welt.   Uneven.

Repeat these 6 rows.

TWO AND THREE WELT. *Fig. 27.*

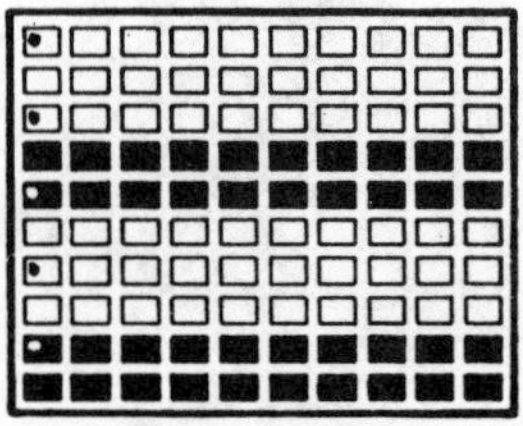

Cast On any number of stitches.
Row 1: Purl.
Row 2: Knit.
Row 3: Knit.
Row 4: Purl.
Row 5: Knit.
Row 6: Knit.
Row 7: Purl.
Row 8: Purl.
Row 9: Knit.
Row 10: Purl.

FIG. 27.—2 & 3 Welt.   Uneven.

Repeat these 10 rows.

BROKEN WELTS

Figs. 28 to 30 show that Welts can be broken just as Ribbed Fabrics, and the effect is very charming and resembles designings in brick building.   The Welts can be of any width or depth.

ONE AND ONE BROKEN WELT (SINGLE). *Fig. 28.*

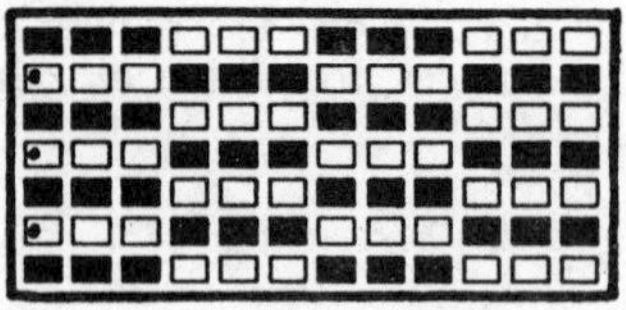

Cast On a number of stitches divisible by 6.
Row 1: * K.3, P.3. *   Repeat.
Row 2: * P.3, K.3. *   Repeat.

Repeat these 2 rows.

FIG. 28.—1 & 1 Broken Welt.

TWO AND TWO BROKEN WELT (DOUBLE). *Fig. 29.*

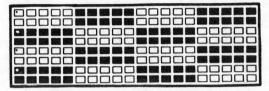

FIG. 29.—2 & 2 Broken Welt.

Cast On stitches divisible by 10.
 Rows I and 2: * K.5, P.5. *   Repeat.
 Rows 3 and 4: * P.5, K.5. *   Repeat.

Repeat these 4 rows.

THREE AND THREE BROKEN WELT (TREBLE). *Fig. 30.*

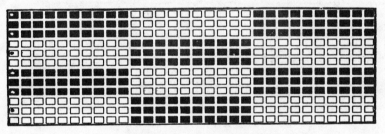

FIG. 30.—3 & 3 Broken Welt.

Cast On stitches divisible by 20.
 Rows I to 3: * K.10, P.10. *   Repeat.
 Rows 4 to 6: * P.10, K.10. *   Repeat.

Repeat these 6 rows.

USES. Broken Single Welts (1 and 1) are still width fabrics, like ordinary Welts, but are flatter and without the corrugated effect. Double and Treble Broken Welts have a smart blistered effect (Cloqué), suitable for sporting fabrics (*see* Fig. 31B)

WELTS, IRREGULAR AND BROKEN

The planning must be done on graph paper. The embossed effect is very striking, as shown in Fig. 31B, Bric-à-brac Cloqué Pattern.

△ In designing these fabrics it is often advisable to arrange more rows in the Knit Welt than in the Purl, as the Knit rows get hidden beneath the roll of the Purl. If a space of 3 Knit rows is desired to show, allow 5 rows between each Welt, which permits one either side to be hidden beneath the Purl. The sequence can be developed, as before, using larger or smaller Welts as required.

FOUR AND SIX WELT. *Figs. 31A and B.*
BRIC-A-BRAC CLOQUÉ PATTERN.

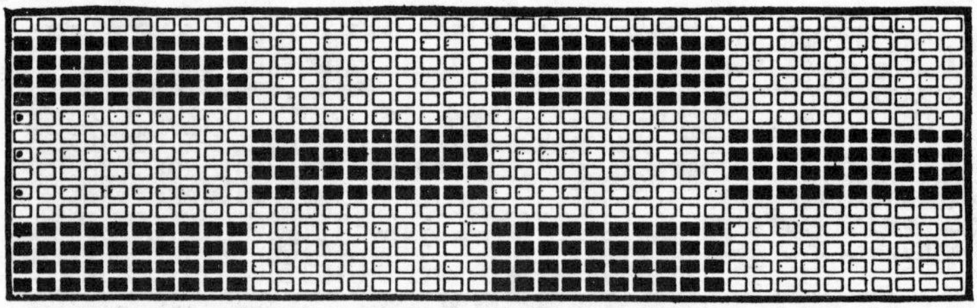

FIG. 31A.—Welt 4 & 6.   Irregular and Broken.

Cast On stitches divisible by 20.
    Rows 1 to 4: * K.10, P.10. * Repeat.
    Row 5:   Knit.
    Rows 6 to 9: * P.10, K.10. * Repeat.
    Row 10:   Purl.

Repeat these 10 rows.

USES. In common with all other Welt fabrics, this is a width fabric with a sporting quality, and satisfactory for all garment use.

FIG. 31B.—Welt 4 & 6. Bric-à-brac Cloqué Pattern.

GARTER WELTS

A Welt of Garter Stitch can be alternated with Stocking Stitch, and either can be of any depth by increasing the number of rows contained in the Stocking Stitch Fabric or those contained in the Garter Stitch Fabric. Example : 5 rows of Stocking Stitch followed by 7 or 9 rows of Garter Stitch, and so on.

Fig. 32A is an effective pattern known as Wager Welt, the game being to wager that no one will guess the number of rows to be purled in the receipt (*see* Fig. 32B). It is a safe bet. No one ever guesses correctly. The answer is " One " when the fabric is knitted single. The old English name is ALL FOOLS' WELT. The French call it PUZZLE STITCH, the Germans, DISPUTE STITCH—so wide is its fame as the sport of the knitting world.

The reverse side, when knitted, will reveal a delightful fabric of SHADOW WELTS.

WAGER WELT OR ALL FOOLS' WELT. *Figs. 32A and* B.
(*See also* GARTER WELTS, page 23.)

FIG. 32A.—Wager or All Fools' Welt.

Cast On any number of stitches.
  Row 1: Knit.
  Row 2: Purl.
  Row 3: Knit.
  Row 4: Knit.
  Row 5: Knit.
  Row 6: Knit.
  Row 7: Knit.
  Row 8: Knit.

  Repeat these 8 rows.

  USES. Both sides of the fabric are decorative. Effective for sports wear, sweaters, etc.

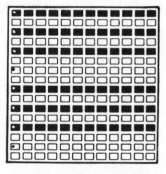

FIG. 32B.—Wager or All Fools' Welt.

GARTER WELTS (BROKEN)
WAGER OR ALL FOOLS' WELT (BROKEN). *Fig. 33.*

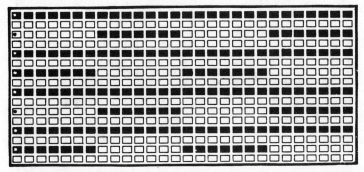

FIG. 33.—Wager Welt (Broken).

Cast On stitches divisible by 14.
    Row 1: Knit.
    Row 2: K.7, P.7.
    Row 3: Knit.
    Row 4: Knit.
    Row 5: Knit.
    Row 6: P.7, K.7.
    Row 7: Knit.
    Row 8: Knit.

The sequence continues in this way, the chart showing the method of designing. The back is a shadow cloqué.

ANCIENT DECORATIVE USE OF WELT

The photograph (Fig. 34) shows the tops of four old white cotton socks, the bottom one being dated 1814.

Top. Five Welts are used as a decoration.

Second. A Welt is used either side of a narrow diaper pattern, and so converts it into a little ribbon effect.

The third is Fig. 106.

The fourth is a wide diaper pattern, again separated from the Stocking Stitch fabric by a Welt.

This suggests many uses in design, as the embossed effect of the Welt has a definite finish as an enclosure.

See also King Charles's Vest (Fig. 59), where the pattern is again enclosed between a border of Welts.

By courtesy of Mr. Fritz Iklé.

FIG. 34.—Old Sock Tops, showing Decorative Use of Welts (*see* page 25).

RIBS AND WELTS COMBINED

These patterns combine the use of Ribs and Welts, or the Vertical and Horizontal line. They are reversible and really fascinating in appearance. The first design alternates one row of 1 and 1 Rib, followed by a Purl Welt.

Fig. 36 is a 2 and 2 Rib, divided by a 2 and 2 Welt (two rows of each). Fig. 37 is a 3 and 3 Rib, and 3 and 3 Welt, divided in the same way. The units are an even number of each fabric, but an uneven number can be designed in the same way.

RIB 1 AND 1. WELT 1. *Fig. 35.*

Also known as GARTER RIBBING, " TUFTED MOSS STITCH " and " WAISTCOAT STITCH ". Reverse side, FANCY RIBBING.

Cast On an even number of stitches.
Row 1: * K.1, P.1. * Repeat.
Row 2: Knit.

Repeat these 2 rows.

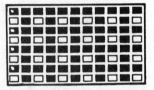

FIG. 35.—Rib 1 & 1. Welt 1.

Variation I

Row 1: * K.1 B., P.1. * Repeat.
Row 2: Purl.

Repeat these 2 rows.

Variation II

(Fabric the same both sides.)
Row 1: * K.1, P.1. * Repeat.
Row 2: Knit.
Row 3: * K.1, P.1. * Repeat.
Row 4: Purl.

Repeat these 4 rows.

RIB 2 AND 2. WELT 2. *Fig. 36.*

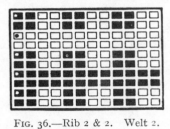

FIG. 36.—Rib 2 & 2.   Welt 2.

Cast On stitches divisible by 4.
Rows 1 and 2: * K.2, P.2. *
     Repeat.
Row 3: Purl.
Row 4: Knit.
Rows 5 and 6: * K.2, P.2. *
     Repeat.
Row 7: Knit.
Row 8: Purl.

Repeat these 8 rows.

Variation

Omit Rows 3 and 4.   Then known as THREADED RIB (*see also* Fig. 53).

RIB 3 AND 3. WELT 3 AND 3. *Figs. 37A and B.*

Also known as HARRIS TWEED PATTERN.

FIG. 37A.—Rib 3 & 3.   Welt 3 & 3.   Harris Tweed Pattern.

Cast On stitches divisible by 6.
    Rows 1 to 3: * K.3, P.3. *
        Repeat.
    Row 4: Knit.
    Row 5: Purl.
    Row 6: Knit.
    Rows 7 to 9: * K.3, P.3. *
        Repeat.
    Row 10: Purl.
    Row 11: Knit.
    Row 12: Purl.

Repeat these 12 rows.

The sequence continues in this way.

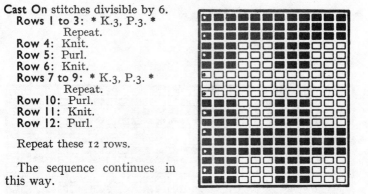

Uses. Sports Fabrics.

Fig. 37B.—Rib 3 & 3. Welt 3 & 3.

RIB-WELT FABRICS (BROKEN)

These patterns show the vertical and horizontal (Ribbing and Welting) crossing each other, as in weaving, to produce all the many and different varieties of Basket pattern.

RIB 1 AND 1. WELT 1 AND 1 (BROKEN). *Fig. 38.*

Also known as DOUBLE BASKET, FINE.

The Rib is 5 stitches high, the Welt 5 stitches in width.

FIG. 38.—Fine Double Basket Pattern.
(Irregular.)

Cast On stitches divisible by 10.
    Rows 1, 3 and 5:   * P.6, K.1, P.1, K.1, P.1. *   Repeat.
    Rows 2 and 4:   * K.1, P.1, K.1, P.1, K.1, P.5. *   Repeat.
    Rows 6, 8 and 10: * K.6, P.1, K.1, P.1, K.1. *   Repeat.
    Rows 7 and 9:   * P.1, K.1, P.1, K.1, P.1, K.5. *   Repeat.

Repeat these 10 rows.

RIB 2 AND 2. WELT 2 AND 2 (BROKEN). *Figs. 39*A *and* B. (IRREGULAR.)

Also known as DOUBLE BASKET, HEAVY.

Ribs are 8 stitches high and Welts 8 stitches in width.

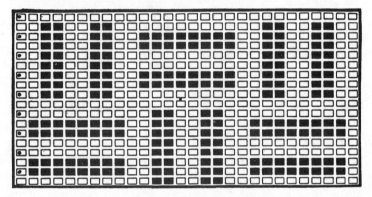

FIG. 39A.—Heavy Double Basket Pattern.

FIG. 39B.—Heavy Double Basket Pattern.

Cast On stitches divisible by 18 and 10 over.
Row 1: * K.11, P.2, K.2, P.2, K.1. * Repeat, ending K.10.
Row 2: P.1, K.8, P.1. * P.1, K.2, P.2, K.2, P.2, K.8, P.1. * Repeat * to *.
Row 3: * K.1, P.8, K.2, P.2, K.2, P.2, K.1. * Repeat, ending K.1, P.8, K.1.
Row 4: P.10. * P.1, K.2, P.2, K.2, P.11. * Repeat * to *.
Rows 5, 6, 7, 8. Repeat Rows 1, 2, 3, and 4.
Row 9: Knit.
Row 10: P.2, K.2, P.2, K.2, P.2. * P.10, K.2, P.2, K.2, P.2. * Repeat * to *.
Row 11: * K.2, P.2, K.2, P.2, K.2, P.8. * Repeat, ending K.2, P.2, K.2, P.2, K.2.
Row 12: P.2, K.2, P.2, K.2, P.2. * K.8, P.2, K.2, P.2, K.2, P.2. * Repeat * to *.
Row 13: * K.2, P.2, K.2, P.2, K.10. * Repeat, ending K.2, P.2, K.2, P.2, K.2.
Rows 14, 15, 16, 17: Same as Rows 10, 11, 12, 13.
Row 18: Purl.

Repeat these 18 rows.

The designing sequence continues in this way.

CHECKS

DESIGNING WITH UNITS.

In the following patterns, the two Stitches are considered as repeating units and arranged singly or in groups to take some geometrical shape. To such patterns there is no end. The most successful designs show an equal distribution of both units, and so a balanced fabric such as Moss Stitch. If one unit predominates, then the classification, Vertical and Horizontal, becomes apparent.

The smallest check is the ever-popular Moss Stitch, also known as Huckaback Stitch, since at one time it was the custom to knit hand-towels in cotton or linen yarns using this stitch. The cushion in Fig. 40 B is in Moss Stitch.

CHECKS 1 AND 1. *Figs. 40A and* B.

Also known as MOSS STITCH and HUCKA-BACK STITCH.

Cast On an △ uneven number of stitches.
Row 1: * K.1, P.1. * Repeat, ending K.1.

Repeat this row.

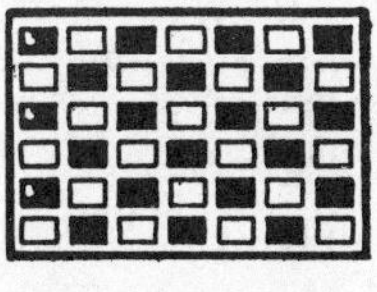

FIG. 40A.—Checks 1 & 1. Moss Stitch.

KNITTED CUSHION

NEEDLES size 10.   Standard size 6.

YARNS.   8 oz. each of Oyster and Pale Fawn.   4-ply.   Knit using the wool double, one of each colour to give "Tweed" effect.

Can be knitted as a circular fabric, or as a single fabric and seamed at the sides.

FIG. 40B.—Knitted Cushion in Moss Stitch using Double Yarn.

ROUND FABRIC.

CAST ON 173 stitches.   Odd number.   Divide on three needles. Knit in Moss Stitch for depth of 19 inches.   Divide on two needles and join the bag together and cast-off at the same time. Insert pad in opposite end.   Finish with knitted Faggot fringe as on page 158, using both colours as before.

SINGLE FABRIC.

CAST ON 87 stitches.   Knit Moss Stitch for 19 inches.   Make second side to match.   Join together and finish with fringe (*see* page 158).

CHECKS 2 AND 2. *Fig. 41.*

Also known as DOUBLE MOSS STITCH.

Cast On stitches divisible by 4.
Row 1: * K.2, P.2. * Repeat.
Row 2: Same as Row 1.
Row 3: * P.2, K.2. * Repeat.
Row 4: Same as Row 3.

Repeat these 4 rows.

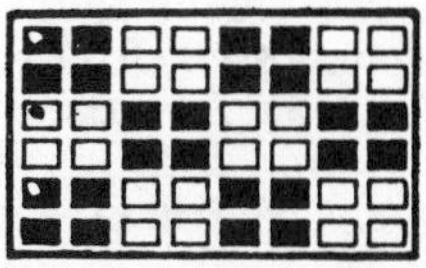

FIG. 41.—Checks 2 & 2.
Double Moss Stitch.

CHECKS 3 AND 3 (OBLONG SHAPE). *Figs. 42A and B.*

Also known as LOZENGE PATTERN and sometimes as BASKET PATTERN, but *see* Figs. 38 and 39 for basket technique.

Cast On stitches divisible by 6.
Rows 1 to 3: * K.3, P.3. *
Repeat.
Rows 4 to 6: * P.3, K.3. *
Repeat.

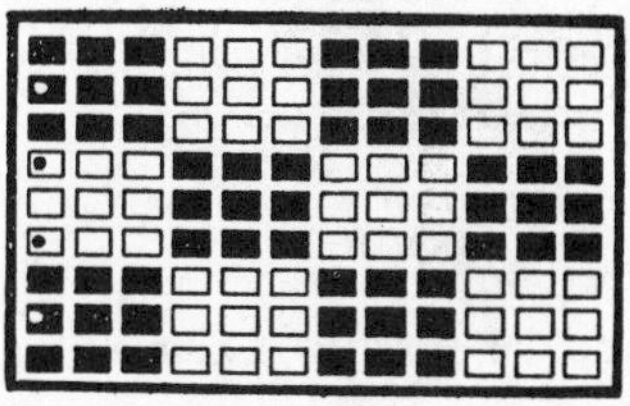

FIG. 42A.—Checks 3 & 3. Oblong.

FIG. 42B.—Oblong Checks 3 & 3 and 6 & 6.

PADDED CHECK

One row of Knit stitches spaced between the checks will give an embossed effect to the squares.   In a 3 and 3 check (Fig. 42) this would be the 4th row, which, to make it knit on the right side, would be Purled.   In an even check, 6 and 6, the 7th row would be a Knit row.   In round knitting always Knit.

CHECK 3 AND 3 (SQUARE SHAPE). *Figs. 43A and B.*

Also known as DICE PATTERN.

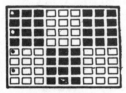

FIG. 43A.—Checks 3 & 3. Square.

Cast On stitches divisible by 6.
  Rows I to 4: * K.3,
       P.3. *   Repeat.
  Rows 5 to 8: * P.3,
       K.3. *   Repeat.

NOTE.—Compare Figs. 42 and 43. Knitting stitches are oblong in shape, and NOT square. When a cube shape is required, this difference must be taken into consideration and corrected by the extra row, as in Fig. 43. This check is 3 stitches wide, but 4 rows high, and so square in shape, compared with Fig. 42, which is 3 stitches wide but only 3 rows high, and so works out as an oblong. The diagrams are scaled as accurately as possible to show the proportions of rows and stitches. The difference averages about 3 stitches wide to 4 rows in depth for a square as follows :—

FIG. 43B.—Square Checks 3 & 3 and 6 & 6.

CHECK 6 AND 6 (SQUARE). *Fig. 43B* (Top).

Also known as CHESSBOARD CHECK.

Cast On stitches divisible by 1.
   Rows 1 to 8: * K.6, P.6. * Repeat.
   Rows 9 to 16: * P.6, K.6. * Repeat.

Repeat these 16 rows.

CHECK 12 AND 12 (SQUARE)

Also known as GIANT CHECK.

Cast On stitches divisible by 24.
   Rows 1 to 16: * K.12, P.12. * Repeat.
   Rows 17 to 32: * P.12, K.12. * Repeat.

Repeat these 32 rows.

CHECKS, BROKEN

Method consists of dividing the square diagonally, and can be applied to checks of any size. A single example is given here, and permits of further variation by working one half of the diagonal in Moss Stitch, preferably the Purl half.

VARIATION : To design a more slender wedge shape repeat every row twice. This will make the pattern change every other row, instead of on every row, as in Fig. 44.

BROKEN CHECK. *Fig. 44.*

Cast On stitches divisible by 5.
   Row 1 : Purl.
   Row 2 : * K.4, P.1. * Repeat.
   Row 3 : * K.2, P.3. * Repeat.
   Row 4 : * K.2, P.3. * Repeat.
   Row 5 : * K.4, P.1. * Repeat.
   Row 6 : Purl.

Repeat these 6 rows.

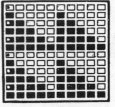

FIG. 44.—Broken Check.

BROKEN CHECKS AND RIBS

The direction of the diagonal line shown in Fig. 44 is reversed in the next repeat above, so that the two black parts come together and form a pennant. By introducing a vertical rib of 2 and 2 between the pennants the famous Pennant Pleating Pattern is formed.

PENNANT PLEATING.   *Figs. 45A and* B.

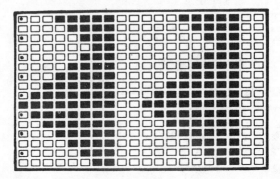

FIG. 45A.—Chart (Pennant Pleating).

FIG. 45B.—Pennant Pleating.

Cast On stitches divisible by 10.

Row 1:	* K.2, P.2, K.6. *	Repeat.
Row 2:	* P.5, K.3, P.2. *	Repeat.
Row 3:	* K.2, P.4, K.4. *	Repeat.
Row 4:	* P.3, K.5, P.2. *	Repeat.
Row 5:	* K.2, P.6, K.2. *	Repeat.
Row 6:	* P.1, K.7, P.2. *	Repeat.
Row 7:	* K.2, P.8. *	Repeat.
Row 8:	* P.1, K.7, P.2. *	Repeat.
Row 9:	* K.2, P.6, K.2. *	Repeat.
Row 10:	* P.3, K.5, P.2. *	Repeat.
Row 11:	* K.2, P.4, K.4. *	Repeat.
Row 12:	* P.5, K.3, P.2, *	Repeat.

Repeat these 12 rows.

To reverse the pleat, reverse the directions, *i.e.*, read: Row 1, * K.6, P.2, K.2, * and so on throughout.

DIAGONAL RIB OR HALF CHEVRON PATTERNS

Method consists of moving a rib of Knit stitches either one stitch right or left, travelling always in the same direction, according to diagonal (right or left), as required. For a steeper angle the rib moves left or right every other row—*i.e.*, every knit row. The rib can move over any background, Purl, Welted or Fancy. Fig. 46 shows a left diagonal, and the smallest unit (2 and 2) suitable in a diagonal rib movement.

The principle presents fascinating developments, as the Knit Rib or the background can be of any width—even, as in Fig. 46, or uneven. Example: 5 Knit stitches and 2 Purl (5 and 2) or 7 and 3, etc. The Purl is usually the lesser. If wide background effects are required, then instead of Purl use Moss Stitch, as in Fig. 40, as it has more character. The Patterns are also effective when broken with wide vertical Ribs.

For garment use, the opposite diagonal should be used for one half of the front and back.

DIAGONAL RIB 2 AND 2. *Fig. 46.*

Knit rib of 2 stitches, moving diagonally one stitch to left in **every row.**

Cast On stitches divisible by 4.

    Row 1: * K.2, P.2. * Repeat.

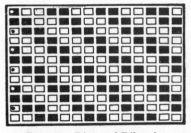

Fig. 46.—Diagonal Rib 2 & 2.

Row 2: P.1. * K.2, P.2. *
Repeat * to *, ending
K.1.
Row 3: * P.2, K.2. *
Repeat, ending P.2.
Row 4: K.1. * P.2, K.2. *
Repeat * to *, ending
P.1.

Repeat these 4 rows.

STEEP DIAGONAL OR SPIRAL RIBBING

Any Diagonal Pattern, when knitted Round, becomes spiral. This pattern is designed in blocks, as in Fig. 52, right half of Chevron, but consists of six blocks instead of four, and these move one stitch to right every 6th round. If knitted as a Single Fabric in Rows, instead of Rounds, the pattern is then a Steep Diagonal Rib.

Cast On stitches divisible by 6.
Rounds 1 to 6:   K.3, P.3.
Rounds 7 to 12:   K.2. * P.3, K.3. *   Repeat * to *, ending K.1.
Rounds 13 to 18: K.1. * P.3, K.3. *   Repeat * to *, ending K.2.
Rounds 19 to 24: * P.3, K.3. *   Repeat.
Rounds 25 to 30: P.2. * K.3, P.3. *   Repeat * to *, ending P.1.
Rounds 31 to 36: P.1. * K.3, P.3. *   Repeat * to *, ending P.2.

Repeat from Round 1.

USES. For heel-less stockings, bed or hospital socks and sea-boot stockings. Knitted as follows :—

SPIRAL RIBBING BED-STOCK-ING (HEEL-LESS)

When worn, the spiral ribbing should be adjusted round the leg so that it appears straight. This shapes it to the ankle, and the heel adjusts itself. Also used by Cornish knitters for fishermen's jerseys when the figure is corpulent.

Cast On stitches divisible by 12. Arrange on 3 needles.
Rounds 1 to 30. Rib. * K.2, P.2. * Repeat. This forms the top of sock, then change to Spiral Ribbing as above, and knit this for a depth of 16½ inches. Divide stitches on two needles and shape toe.

DIAGONAL RIB CROSSING TREBLE WELTS

Any diagonal movement over a Welted Fabric permits of many charming developments (*see* Escalator Pattern).

ESCALATOR PATTERN. *Figs. 47A and B.*

The Rib of 5 Knit stitches moves diagonally 4 stitches to the left every 6th row over a background of 3 and 3 Welt Fabric. All diagonal movements tend to lengthen the written directions. The effect is of a threaded Welt.

The photograph shows the fascinating appearance of Escalator Pattern.

FIG. 47A.—Escalator Pattern or Diagonal Rib Crossing Treble Welt.

Cast On stitches divisible by 32.
>**Row 1:** * K.5, P.11. * Repeat.
>**Row 2:** * K.11, P.5. * Repeat.
>**Row 3:** * K.5, P.11. * Repeat.
>**Row 4:** Purl.
>**Row 5:** Knit.
>**Row 6:** Purl.
>**Rows 7 and 9:** P.4. * K.5, P.11. * Repeat * to *, ending K.5, P.7.
>**Row 8:** K.7. * P.5, K.11. * Repeat * to *, ending P.5, K.4.
>**Rows 10 and 12:** Purl.
>**Row 11:** Knit.

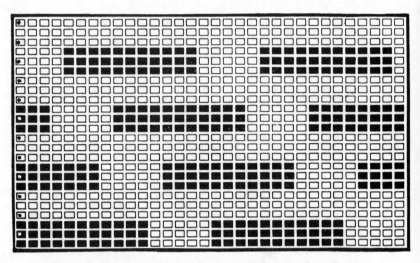

FIG. 47B.—Diagonal Rib Crossing Treble Welts (Escalator Pattern).

Rows 13 and 15: P.8. * K.5, P.11. * Repeat * to *, ending K.5, P.3.
Row 14: K.3. * P.5, K.11. * Repeat, * to *, ending P.5, K.8.
Rows 16 and 18: Purl.
Row 17: Knit.
Rows 19 and 21: K.1, P.11. * K.5, P.11. * Repeat * to *, ending K.4.
Row 20: P.4. * K.11, P.5. * Repeat * to *, ending K.11, P.1.
Row 22: Purl.
Row 23: Knit.
Row 24: Purl.

Repeat from Row 1.

DIAGONAL RIB FANCY. *Fig. 48.*

The rib of 3 Knit stitches moves diagonally over a background of Moss Stitch. The sequence of design continues in this way, and can be given greater variety by increasing the size of the checks and the width of the rib, making it 4 or 5 stitches wide instead of 3. For garment use these diagonals form a left or right, the opposite diagonal being used for the other half of the front. In this way they meet as a chevron in the middle.

Cast On stitches divisible by 10.
Row 1: * K.3, (P.1, K.1) 3 times, P.1. *   Repeat.
Row 2: * (P.1, K.1) 3 times, P.3, K.1. *   Repeat.

Row 3: * K.1, P.1, K.3, (P.1, K.1) twice, P.1. * Repeat.
Row 4: * (P.1, K.1) twice, P.3, K.1, P.1, K.1. * Repeat.
Row 5: * (K.1, P.1) twice, K.3, P.1, K.1, P.1. * Repeat.
Row 6: * P.1, K.1, P.3, (K.1, P.1) twice, K.1. * Repeat.
Row 7: * (K.1, P.1) 3 times, K.3, P.1. * Repeat.
Row 8: * P.3, (K.1, P.1) 3 times, K.1. * Repeat.
Row 9: * (K.1, P.1) 4 times, K.2. * Repeat.
Row 10: * (P.1, K.1) 4 times, P.2. * Repeat.

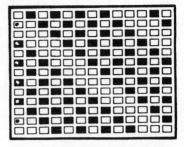

FIG. 48.—Diagonal Rib Fancy.

DIAGONAL RIB AND CHECK COMBINED. *Fig. 49.*

Method embraces the use of ribbing and blocks of stitches, the simplest being the square. Any geometric form, triangles, oblongs, etc., large or small, can be treated in the same way.

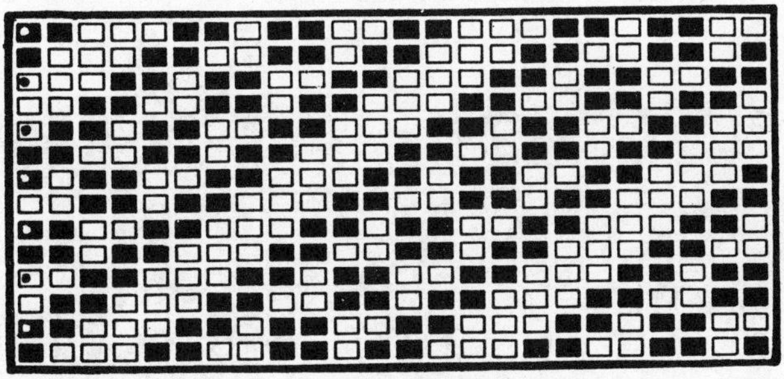

FIG. 49.—Diagonal Rib and Check.

Cast On stitches divisible by 12.

Row 1:	* P.1, K.1, P.2, K.2, P.2, K.3, P.1. *	Repeat.
Row 2:	* K.2, P.3, K.2, P.1, K.2, P.2. *	Repeat.
Row 3:	* P.2, K.2, P.2, K.3, P.2, K.1. *	Repeat.
Row 4:	* P.2, K.2, P.3, K.2, P.1, K.2. *	Repeat.
Row 5:	* K.2, P.2, K.3, P.2, K.1, P.2. *	Repeat.
Row 6:	* K.2, P.2, K.2, P.3, K.2, P.1. *	Repeat.
Row 7:	* P.2, K.3, P.2, K.1, P.2, K.2. *	Repeat.
Row 8:	* K.1, P.1, K.2, P.2, K.2, P.3, K.1. *	Repeat.
Row 9:	* K.3, P.2, K.1, P.2, K.2, P.2. *	Repeat.
Row 10:	* P.1, K.2, P.1, K.2, P.2, K.2, P.2. *	Repeat.
Row 11:	* K.1, P.2, K.1, P.2, K.2, P.2, K.2. *	Repeat.
Row 12:	* P.3, K.2, P.1, K.2, P.2, K.2. *	Repeat.

Repeat these 12 rows.

ZIG-ZAG OR CHEVRON PATTERNS

Two diagonal lines or ribs meeting at a given point will produce the Chevron and in repeat a Zig-zag Pattern. These Chevrons can be :—

> 1. Small, as in Fig. 50B, where they are 3 stitches wide, and mount every 2nd row, over a Purl background (*see* diagram).
>
> 2. Broad, as in Fig. 51, where a Chevron of 3 stitches alternates with another of Moss Stitch and mounts every row.
>
> 3. Steep, as in Fig. 52, where the Chevron mounts every 4th row.

These three examples permit of great development.

LITTLE CHEVRON.   *Figs. 50A and* B.

Cast On stitches divisible by 12 and 1 over.
    Row I: * P.1, K.3, P.5, K.3. *   Repeat, ending P.1.
    Row 2: K.1.   * P.3, K.5, P.3, K.1. *   Repeat * to *.

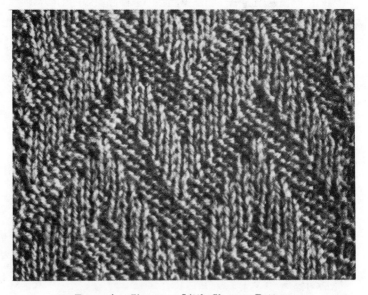

FIG. 50A.—Zig-zag or Little Chevron Pattern.

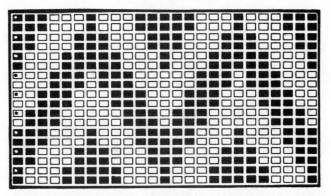

Fig. 50B.—Zig-zag or Little Chevron Pattern.

Row 3: P.2. * K.3, P.3. * Repeat * to *, ending K.3, P.2.
Row 4: K.2. * P.3, K.3. * Repeat * to *, ending P.3, K.2.
Row 5: P.3. * K.3, P.1, K.3, P.5. * Repeat * to *, ending K.3, P.1, K.3, P.3.
Row 6: K.3. * P.3, K.1, P.3, K.5. * Repeat * to *, ending P.3, K.1, P.3, K.3.
Row 7: * K.1, P.3, K.5, P.3. * Repeat, ending K.1.
Row 8: P.1. * K.3, P.5, K.3, P.1. * Repeat * to *.
Row 9: K.2. * P.3, K.3. * Repeat * to *, ending P.3, K.2.
Row 10: P.2. * K.3, P.3. * Repeat * to *, ending K.3, P.2.
Row 11: K.3. * P.3, K.1, P.3, K.5. * Repeat * to *, ending P.3, K.1, P.3, K.3.
Row 12: P.3. * K.3, P.1, K.3, P.5. * Repeat * to *, ending K.3, P.1, K.3, P.3.

Repeat these 12 rows.

FANCY CHEVRON (BROAD). *Fig. 51.*

Cast On stitches divisible by 22.
Row 1: * P.1, K.1, P.3, (K.1, P.1) twice, K.1, P.5, (K.1, P.1) twice, K.1, P.2. * Repeat.
Row 2: * K.3, P.1, (K.1, P.1) twice, K.3, P.1, (K.1, P.1) twice, K.3, P.3. * Repeat.
Row 3: * K.4, P.3, (K.1, P.1) 5 times, K.1, P.3, K.1. * Repeat.
Row 4: * P.2, K.3, P.1, (K.1, P.1) 4 times, K.3, P.3, K.1, P.1. * Repeat.
Row 5: * P.3, K.3, P.3, (K.1, P.1) 3 times, K.1, P.3, K.3. * Repeat.
Row 6: * K.1, P.3, K.3, P.1, (K.1, P.1) twice, K.3, P.3, K.4. * Repeat.
Row 7: * P.1, K.1, P.3, K.3, P.3, K.1, P.1, K.1, P.3, K.3, P.2. * Repeat.

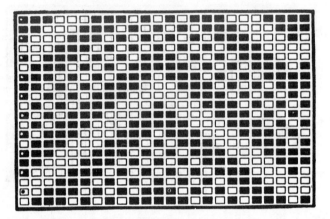

FIG. 51.—Fancy Broad Chevron.

Row 8: * K.3, P.3, K.3, P.1, K.3, P.3, K.3, P.1, K.1, P.1. * Repeat.

Row 9: * (P.1, K.1) twice, P.3, K.3, P.5, K.3, P.3, K.1. * Repeat.

Row 10: * K.1, P.1, K.3, P.3, K.3, P.3, K.3, P.1, (K.1, P.1) twice. * Repeat.

Row 11: * (P.1, K.1) 3 times, P.3, K.3, P.1, K.3, P.3, K.1, P.1, K.1. * Repeat.

Row 12: * K.1, P.1, K.1, P.1, K.3, P.5, K.3, P.1 (K.1, P.1) 3 times. * Repeat.

Row 13: * P.3, (K.1, P.1) twice, K.1, P.3, K.3, P.3 (K.1, P.1) twice, K.1. * Repeat.

Row 14: * (K.1, P.1) 3 times, K.3, P.1, K.3, P.1, (K.1, P.1) twice, K.4. * Repeat.

Repeat these 14 rows.

CHEVRON PATTERN (DEEP). *Fig. 52.*

PINNACLE CRÊPE PATTERN.

This pattern has a pretty crêpe-like rib.

Cast On stitches divisible by 18.

Rows 1 and 3: * K.1, (P.2, K.2) twice, P.1, (K.2, P.2) twice. * Repeat.

Rows 2 and 4: * (K.2, P.2) twice, K.1, (P.2, K.2) twice, P.1. * Repeat.

Rows 5 and 7: * (P.2, K.2) twice, P.3, K.2, P.2, K.2, P.1. * Repeat.

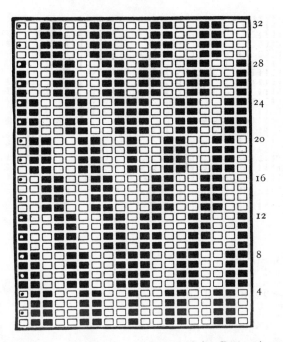

FIG. 52.—Deep Chevron (Pinnacle Crêpe Pattern.)

Rows 6 and 8: * K.1, P.2, K.2, P.2, K.3, (P.2, K.2) twice. * Repeat.

Rows 9 and 11: * P.1, (K.2, P.2) twice, K.1, (P.2, K.2) twice. * Repeat.

Rows 10 and 12: * (P.2, K.2) twice, P.1, (K.2, P.2) twice, K.1. * Repeat.

Rows 13 and 15: * (K.2, P.2) twice, K.3, P.2, K.2, P.2, K.1. * Repeat.

Rows 14 and 16: * P.1, K.2, P.2, K.2, P.3, (K.2, P.2) twice. * Repeat.

Repeat these 16 rows.

ZIG-ZAG CHECKS. *Fig. 53.*

Checks and other symbols besides ribs can be used and arranged in zig-zag forms. A single example is given in Fig. 53—Checks, divided by 4 rows of Stocking Stitch, which makes a very pretty fabric.

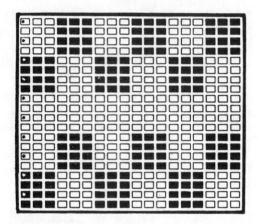

Fig. 53.—Zig-zag Checks.

Cast On stitches divisible by 6.
    Rows I to 4: * K.3, P.3. *   Repeat.
    Rows 5 to 8: * P.3, K.3. *   Repeat.
    Rows 9 and 11: Knit.
    Rows 10 and 12: Purl.

Repeat these 12 rows.

DIAMOND PATTERNS

Two long diagonal lines crossing in opposite directions produce the ever-popular Diamond patterns. These, like all other patterns, can be very simple or extremely complicated, and offer endless scopes for new effects. There are two designing methods :—

    1. The diamond can be given in outline, as in Figs. 54 and 55.
    2. The intersection of the lines can be used as positions for spot designs, as in Figs. 56 and 57, producing what is technically known as half-drop patterns.

All Diamond patterns are built on the half-drop principle, and for this reason written directions for Flat Knitting and garment finish must be given for one complete pattern and a half, or according to convenient division (*see also* page 9).

SINGLE DIAMOND PATTERN. *Fig. 54.*

Cast On stitches divisible by 6
    and 1 over.
    Row 1: K.3. * P.1, K.5. *
            Repeat * to *, ending
            P.1, K.3.
    Row 2: P.2. * K.1, P.1, K.1,
            P.3. * Repeat * to
            *, ending K.1, P.1,
            K.1, P.2.
    Row 3: * K.1, P.1, K.3, P.1. *
            Repeat, ending K.1.
    Row 4: * K.1, P.5. *
            Repeat, ending K.1.
    Row 5: Same as Row 3.
    Row 6: Same as Row 2.

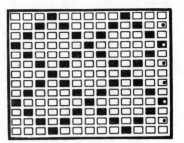

Fig. 54.—Single Diamond Pattern.

Repeat these 6 rows.

DOUBLE DIAMOND PATTERN. *Fig. 55.*

For effect, see the yoke of the vest worn by King Charles, Fig. 59.

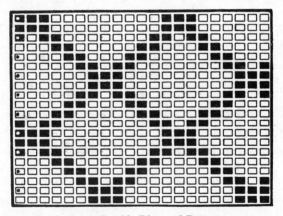

Fig. 55.—Double Diamond Pattern.

Cast On stitches divisible by 12 and 1 over.
    Row 1: P.2. * K.9, P.3. * Repeat * to *, ending K.9, P.2.
    Row 2: K.2. * P.9, K.3. * Repeat * to *, ending P.9, K.2.
    Row 3: * K.1, P.2, K.7, P.2. * Repeat, ending K.1.

Row 4: P,2. * K.2, P.5, K.2, P.3. * Repeat * to *, ending K.2, P.5, K.2, P.2.

Row 5: K.3. * P.2, K.3, P.2, K.5. * Repeat * to *, ending P.2, K.3, P.2, K.3.

Row 6: P.4. * K.2, P.1, K.2, P.7. * Repeat * to *, ending K.2, P.1, K.2, P.4.

Row 7: K.5. * P.3, K.9. * Repeat * to *, ending P.3, K.5.

Row 8: P.5. * K.3, P.9. * Repeat * to *, ending K.3, P.5.

Row 9: K.4. * P.2, K.1, P.2, K.7. * Repeat * to *, ending P.2, K.1, P.2, K.4.

Row 10: P.3. * K.2, P.3, K.2, P.5. * Repeat * to *, ending K.2, P.3, K.2, P.3.

Row 11: K.2. * P.2, K.5, P.2, K.3. * Repeat * to *, ending P.2, K.5, P.2, K.2.

Row 12: P.1. * K.2, P.7, K.2, P.1. * Repeat * to *.

Repeat these 12 rows.

SPOT-PATTERNS

HALF-DROP PRINCIPLE. These patterns still claim the Diamond as foundation, since the places where the lines intersect are used as positions for the spots (*see* Fig. 56, which shows how Figs. 57 and 58 are designed). The principle permits of great

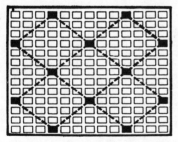

FIG. 56.—Foundation of Spot Design.

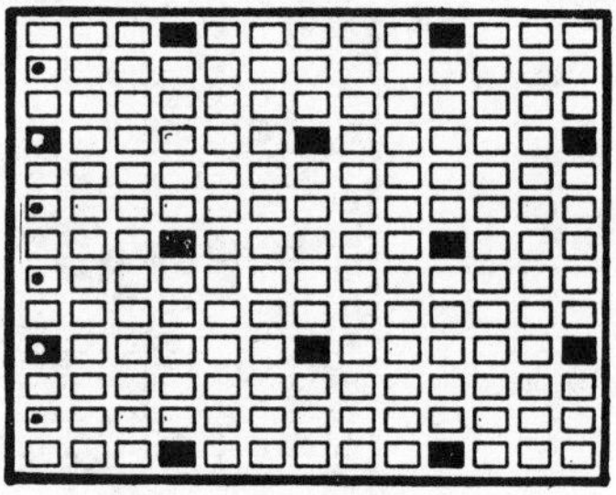

FIG. 57.—Spot Pattern.

elaboration, as the repeating motif can be either geometric or floral, instead of a spot. Such elaborations are beyond the scope of this work, though they offer every possibility to the designer.

SPOT PATTERN. *Fig. 57.*

Cast On stitches divisible by 6 and 1 over.

Row 1: K.3. * P.1, K.5. * Repeat * to *, ending P.1, K.3.

Row 2: Purl.

Row 3: Knit.
Row 4: K.1.   * P.5, K.1. *   Repeat * to *.
Row 5: Knit.
Row 6: Purl.

Repeat these 6 rows.

SPOT PATTERN (CROSS MOTIF).

Fig. 58.

For principle of designing this pattern, *see* Fig. 56.

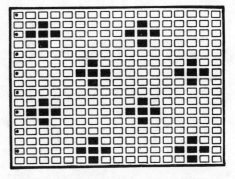

FIG. 58.—Spot Pattern.   Cross Motif.

Cast On stitches divisible by 8 and 5 over.
Row 1: K.2.   * P.1, K.7. *   Repeat * to *, ending P.1, K.2.
Row 2: P.1.   * K.3, P.5. *   Repeat, ending K.3, P.1.
Row 3: Same as Row 1.
Row 4: Purl.
Rows 5 and 7: * K.6, P.1. *   Repeat * to *, ending K.6.
Row 6: P.5.   * K.3, P.5. *   Repeat * to *.
Row 8: Purl.

Repeat these 8 rows.

BROCADE PATTERNS

These fabrics can be developed into the most exquisite designs, as shown in Fig. 59A, a knitted vest of blue silk, worn on the scaffold by Charles I on the day of his execution, 1649.

Figs. 59B and 59C show in chart form the pattern as it is knitted. The written directions are too long for inclusion in this book.

Fig. 59B is the yoke in a Double Diamond Pattern (*see also* Fig. 55), while the narrow border beneath of Diamonds and Crosses is enclosed between a Double Welt. The Double Diamond Pattern is repeated at the cuff and the hem.

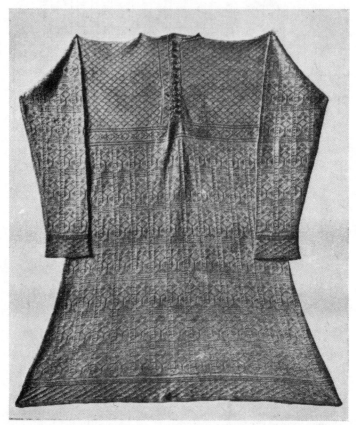

FIG. 59A.—Knitted Vest in Blue Silk, worn by Charles I on day of his execution, 1649. A wonderful example of knitted Brocade Patterns.

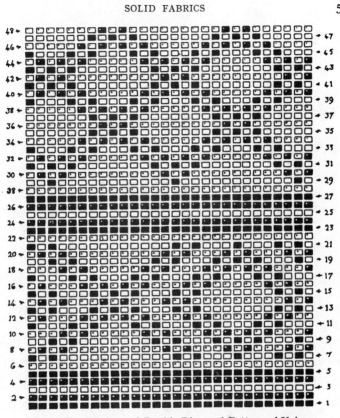

FIG. 59B.—Border and Double Diamond Pattern of Yoke.

Fig. 59C is the Brocade Motif, which is repeated some 80 odd times on the front only, not to mention the sleeves and the back, and without a single mistake!

It is a prodigious piece of work, and probably knitted by a Master Guildsman of that date, though no name has been recorded.

Silk knitting was then a speciality, and it is found in the Prague records that a "man called Hans Werder of Gorlitz, who on 13 August, 1593 gives evidence, describes himself as a 'silk-knitter'", thereby differentiating himself from the wool-knitters.

The necessity for specialising can be appreciated, as it is recognised that once accustomed to knitting with wool, it needs

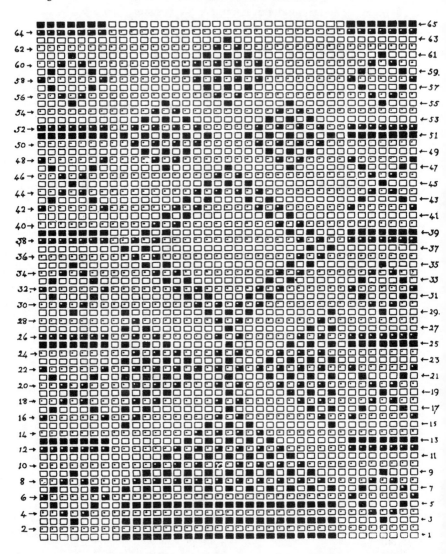

FIG. 59C.—Brocade Pattern on King Charles's Vest.

a little adjustment of tension before acquiring strict regularity with a silk yarn. Silk-knitting of this period was at a very high standard of perfection.

To assist in reading the pattern from the chart dots are added, to indicate back rows, as follows :

WHITE SQUARES bearing a BLACK SPOT show that this is a Knit Stitch on the front of the fabric, and so on back rows will be Purled.

BLACK SQUARES bearing a WHITE SPOT show that this is a Purl Stitch on the front of the fabric, and so on back rows will be Knitted.

INITIALS AND MONOGRAMS

Initials and Monograms are designed on squared paper in the same way as other knitted fabrics (*see* Fig. 60). Any alphabet designed for embroidery will serve as a model, though it must be remembered that knitting stitches are not square, but oblong, and extra rows should be allowed for depth—about one every 4th row.

Also note that any horizontal or diagonal line of a letter needs extra width, as the stitches (unless they are Purl) are inclined to sink. In Fig. 60 the chevron forming the middle of the M is 3 stitches, whereas the vertical lines are only 2 stitches wide. Also note cross bar to the letter T.

The Initial can be worked out in Moss Stitch on a Stocking Stitch background, or in a contrasting colour.

In adding initials to gloves, socks, bags, etc., the letters must

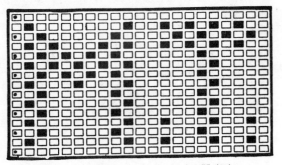

FIG. 60.—Initials as designed for Knitting.

be knitted upside down, so that they appear correctly placed when the article is worn or carried.

Fig. 61 shows a sampler of letters and figures, from which the knitter would choose her letters and figures as required, and mark her knitted socks and gloves in the same way as she marked her linen.   Four samplers are shown, two of which are Round samplers.

See also Fig. 34 for a knitted date, and Fig. 227 for initials in fine bead knitting.

By courtesy of Mrs. Hermann Tragy

FIG. 61.—Knitted Samplers No. 3, dated 1776, shows a collection of Knitted Letters and Figures.

ORNAMENT

In all the previous designs only Knit and Purl stitches have been used. Ornament is something △ additional to these. Knitted Ornament is always simple, such as a Slipped Stitch, *i.e.*, just slipping a stitch instead of knitting it, or a Dropped Stitch, *i.e.*, dropping a stitch instead of knitting it, but, however simple the change may be, it must be considered as Ornament, and so classified as a Motif. In design this Motif becomes the repeating unit, and can be used on the same designing principles, Vertical, Horizontal, Diagonal, etc., as in Solid Fabrics.

A Motif can consist of one or more Units, but however many units are needed to make a Motif, that same number must be repeated each time the Motif is required. The most Ornamental Units are the Over and the Decrease.

The charts throughout the book show the designing methods, and Fig. 62 shows all the symbols used to express the different Motifs.

The plain chart representing Stocking Stitch (Fig. 6) now becomes a kind of background on which the new Motif is arranged. In the same way, if black paper were used, Purl Fabric (Fig. 18) would also be a background. As it is, the squares must be blackened to represent Purl.

For speedy charting the " dot " and " hoop " symbols used to express " Knit the Over " or " Purl the Over " in Fig. 62 make good " shorthand " symbols for Knit and Purl stitches.

All subsequent designs will now employ some Ornamental Motif, in addition to stitches, and each chapter will be devoted to one Motif and its variations. It is the repetition of the Motif which will create the design, and this to be pleasing must be systematically planned.

HOW TO CHART

△ Each Ornamental Symbol occupies one square only of the chart, even if it is a Decreasing symbol indicating that 2 or 3 stitches are knitted together, as the complementary Increase (Over or Made Stitch) will then occupy the vacant square. This may be adjacent or some nearby square; according to pattern,

55

ORNAMENTAL SYMBOLS

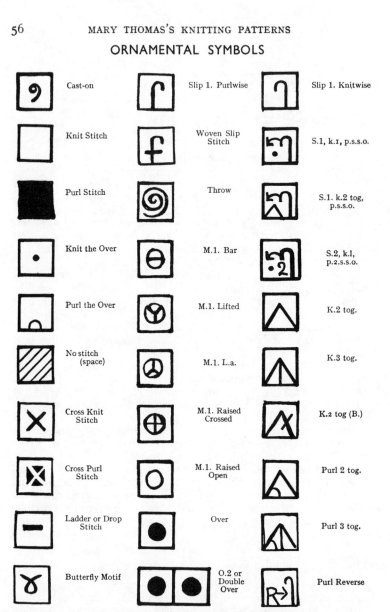

FIG. 62.—Ornamental symbols as used to express the different repeating Motifs and Units, as charted on the following pages. *See* page 290 for detailed description of Ornamental Increases and Decreases.

as shown. In this way the pattern is kept balanced and the correct number of stitches are retained on the needle.

Exception occurs to this rule in Fancy Stitch patterns, as there explained.

△ For full explanation of all the different Increasing and Decreasing methods as used in Ornament *see* pages 290 to 301. These claim the star rôle in Ornament, and to appear at their best the Decrease must be strictly paired. *See* Key Chart (Fig. 297) prepared for this purpose.

All manner of increasing and decreasing is used in designing, but the principal ornamental Increase is the " Over ".

In design it needs one Over and one Decrease to make △ one complete Motif, as one unit, the Over, makes an Increase, while the other takes the extra stitch away. This duel Motif is used to make four different types of pattern : Eyelets, Faggot, Bias (sometimes) and Lace, and each employs the Motif differently.

In Eyelet pattern the motif is spotted at regular intervals. In Faggot pattern it is arranged either vertically or diagonally. In making Bias, the Motif is divided, one unit being on the left and the other on the right of the fabric. In Lace patterns both units are independent, but complementary to each other (*see* page 170). This independent Over, as used in Lace Patterns, is often described as a Lace Space, or Lace Stitch.

The methods are carefully explained chapter by chapter.

PATTERNS IN CROSS AND CROSS-OVER MOTIFS

Designing Units—Cross and Cross-over Stitches

The first Ornamental Motif is a Cross Stitch, made by knitting through the Back of the stitch instead of the front (Fig. 63). In repeat this Motif is single, and occupies only one square on the Chart.

In all, there are seven different Motifs, the most popular Cross-Over Motif being Cable Rib Pattern. Here we begin with the simplest, a Cross Stitch, and then proceed to the more elaborate Cross-Over Motifs.

MOTIF I. A CROSS STITCH

A stitch can be Crossed on the front of the fabric, as in Fig. 63, or on the back of the fabric, as in Fig. 64, when it is purled, but shows crossed on the front. Such being the case, it is possible, though hardly expedient, to knit all the different patterns shown in Solid Fabrics anew, by substituting Cross stitches (Knit and Purl) instead of ordinary Knit and Purl stitches.

Eastern knitted fabrics made in this way number amongst the oldest known of knitted textiles, and date from the second and third centuries, but their method of knitting round (*see* page 268) made this easy.

When knitted on two needles, the back rows are decidedly awkward, which no doubt explains why the fabric has fallen from favour. A compromise is often made, using Cross stitches

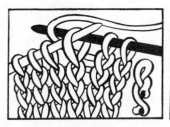

Fig. 63.—Cross Stocking Stitch. Knit Motif. (K.1 B.)

Fig. 64.—Cross Stitch. Purl Motif. (P.1 B.)

on the Knit row and ordinary Purl on the back rows, but the effect, though attractive, is not the same, as the width-wise " pull " of the fabric, which is such a feature, is lost.   Knit a square of 4 inches in Cross Stocking Stitch and test this out.

Cross stitches are now used mainly as repeating Motifs, but since they can be made on either front or back rows, they permit of playful use as a third Knitting Stitch.

ABBREVIATIONS :

K.I B.—Knit through the back of the stitch.
P.I B.—Purl through the back of the stitch.

CROSS STOCKING STITCH. *Fig. 63.*

Round Fabric

Cast On any number of stitches and divide on three needles.
  Round 1 : * K.1 B. *   Repeat.
  Round 2 and all succeeding rounds the same.

Single Fabric

Cast On any number of stitches.
  Row 1 : * K.1 B. *   Repeat.
  Row 2 : * P.1 B. *   Repeat.

Repeat these 2 rows.

VERTICAL DESIGNS

The motif (Cross stitches) can be arranged vertically as ribs and follow the same grouping as in Solid Fabrics.

CROSS CORD RIB

Only the Knit stitches are crossed on the front of the fabric, but on the back row the Purl Stitches must be crossed, and not the Knit.

Cast On stitches divisible by 6 and 3 over.
  Row 1 : * K.3 B., P.3. * Repeat, ending K.3 B.
  Row 2 : P.3 B.   * K.3, P.3 B. * Repeat * to *.

Repeat these 2 rows.

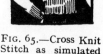

USES. In Vertical arrangement, Cross stitches stand out with a cord-like prominence, and are particularly valuable as ribs to separate different patterns (*see* Fig. 211).   Arranged in groups of 5 or 7 stitches, they also make an excellent imitation of tucks (*see* Fig. 65).   (*See also* Fig. 68.)

FIG. 65.—Cross Knit Stitch as simulated tucks.

HORIZONTAL DESIGNS

The Motif can be alternated with either Knit or Purl stitches. Many delightful fabrics are created by grouping these in different orders.

FANCY CROSS GARTER STITCH

Cast On an even number of stitches.
    Row 1: Knit.
    Row 2: * K.1, K.1 B. *   Repeat.

Repeat these 2 rows.

WAFFLE STITCH. *Fig. 66.*

FIG. 66.—Waffle Stitch.

Cast On stitches divisible by 2.
    Row 1: * K.1 B., P.1. *   Repeat.
    Row 2: * P.1 B., K.1. *   Repeat.

Repeat these 2 rows.

Both sides of fabric are decorative.

VARIATION : Knit Row 1 using needle two sizes larger.

RICE STITCH. *Fig. 67.*

FIG. 67.—Rice Stitch.

Cast On an even number of stitches.
 Row 1: Knit.
 Row 2: * K.1 B., P.1. * Repeat.

Repeat these 2 rows.

CROSS-OVER MOTIFS

The second and subsequent Motifs are composed of two or more stitches which are crossed-over each other, as follows :—

MOTIF 2. One stitch is crossed over another, giving a repeating unit of 2 stitches for each Motif and so will occupy 2 squares on the Chart.

MOTIF 3. The stitches are crossed in pairs, giving a unit of 4 stitches for each Motif and so will occupy 4 squares on the Chart.

MOTIF 4. The stitches are crossed in threes, giving a unit of 6 stitches for each Motif and so will occupy 6 squares on the Chart, and so on, the unit increasing as required. A vertical arrangement of this Motif is known as Cable Rib.

MOTIF 5. The stitches can be crossed and " travelled " to form lattice effects, with a unit of 6 stitches (or as required) for each Motif which in repeat will occupy 6 squares on the Chart.

MOTIF 6.   The stitches can be crossed 2 over 2 over 2, making a
          Plait with a unit of 6 stitches for each Motif which
          will again occupy 6 squares on the Chart. This
          also can vary in size as required.

MOTIF 7.   The stitches can be lengthened by Throws and then
          be crossed, giving a unit of 4 stitches, or as required.

TWIN MOTIFS

Each of the above six Motifs can be crossed in two different
ways and so make two different diagonals as follows :—

    1. Cross left over right.⎫ Twin Motifs.
    2. Cross right over left.⎭

△ In this way we have related or " Twin " Motifs, and it is
this contrary movement of making the Cross-over which creates
design.   Each of these motifs and their Twin Actions or technique are shown separately, and afterwards shown arranged in
design.

Cross-over Motifs make very beautiful patterns, a classic
example of their use being shown in Fig. 68, where the larger
Motifs are considerably enhanced by being formed of Cross Knit
stitches.

SWEATER FROM ARAN

Fig. 68 is a magnificent example of Cross-Over Motifs
arranged in pattern.   It is a classical choice, every pattern being
of the same Cross-Over family.   The knitting is intricate, but
traditional of Aran, and worn by the Irish fishermen of that
island.

The central panel is composed of a Travelling Rib (see Fig. 87),
made of Cross Knit stitches (2 over 2), each diamond space
between being alternated Purl and Moss Stitch.   The panel is
enclosed either side by a Cable Rib of 5 stitches (3 over 2).
Beyond this either side is a small Travelling Rib of one Cross Knit
stitch, travelling to form small diamond shapes filled with four
Cross Knit stitches.   Next, a zig-zag line composed of two Cross
Knit and Travelling stitches on a background of Purl Fabric.

FIG. 68.—Fisherman's Sweater from Aran, Ireland, in traditional
Cross-over Patterns.

The fancy ribbing at the base of the sweater shows an unusual
crossed pattern composed as follows :—

Cast On stitches divisible by 8.
  Row 1: * K.3, P.1, K.1 B., P.1, K.1 B., P.1. * Repeat.
  Row 2: * K.1, P.1 B., K.1, P.1 B., K.1, P.3. * Repeat.

Repeat these 2 rows twice. Knit every 7th row as follows, making
the 2 Crossed stitches exchange places:—

  Row 7: * K.3, P.1. Slip next 2 stitches on match and drop to
       front. K.1 B., P.1 (the purl stitch off match), K.1B.
       (off match), P.1. * Repeat.
  Row 8: Same as Row 2. Repeat these 8 Rows.

On the sleeve, the central panel is composed of a Travelling
Rib of one Cross K. Stitch forming a lattice on a background of
Purl Fabric. Either side is a Cable Rib of 4 Cross K. stitches, and
this shows how very distinctive ribs of Cross Knit stitches appear.

MOTIF 2 (ONE OVER ONE)

This small second Motif can Cross right-over-left and left-over-right, as in Figs. 69 and 70, and without the aid of a third needle, as is necessary for larger Motifs. So the twins can be called Knit and Purl Motif.

KNIT MOTIF. *Figs. 69A and B.* **Right-over-Left Cross.**

△ △ **Abb :** K.I over I.

FIG. 69A.—Knit Motif
I over I. Working
method.

△ Front of fabric (Fig. 69A). Take the needle behind the first stitch and insert it knitwise into the second. Knit this stitch and leave it on the left needle, and then knit the first stitch (Fig. 69B). Slip both stitches off the needle together.
Result: The first stitch crosses over the second, forming a "right-over-left" cross (*see* Fig. 71).

PURL MOTIF. *Fig. 70.* **Left-over-Right Cross.**

△ △ **Abb :** (P.I over I).

△ Back of fabric. Insert the needle purlwise into the second stitch, and purl it

FIG. 69B.—Knit Motif
I over I. Working
method.

FIG. 70.—Purl Motif I over I.
Working method.

(Fig. 70). Leave it on the left needle, and purl the first stitch. Slip both stitches off the needle.
Result: △ On the FRONT of the fabric this will produce a "left-over-right" cross (*see* Fig. 72).

VERTICAL DESIGN

Either Motifs, Knit or Purl, can be used singly or as a pair.
In vertical arrangement either Motif will produce a Knotted Rib. The number of stitches between the ribs can vary as required, and be Purl or Lace, such as Faggot Stitch, etc. The background must contrast, or the effect is lost (*see* Figs. 71 and 72, where Purl Fabric is used).

KNOTTED RIB. *Fig. 71A and* B.

Using Knit Motifs on front row (*see* chart).

Cast On stitches divisible by 5 and 3 over.
    Row 1: * P.3, (K.1 over 1). *
        Repeat, ending P.3.
    Row 2: K.3. * P.2, K.3. *
        Repeat * to *.

Repeat these 2 rows.

FIG. 71A *and* B.—Knotted Rib (Right over Left) and Chart.

KNOTTED RIB. *Fig. 72A and* B.

Using Purl Motifs on back row (*see* chart).

Cast On stitches divisible by 5 and 3 over.
    Row 1: * P.3, K.2. *
        Repeat, ending P.3.
    Row 2: K.3. * (P.1 over 1), K.3. *
        Repeat * to *.

Repeat these 2 rows.

FIG. 72A *and* B.—Knotted Rib (Left over Right) and Chart.

FIG. 73A.—Wheat-Ear Rib.

WHEAT-EAR RIB. *Figs. 73A and* B.

In this pattern both Motifs, Knit and Purl, are used, but alternate on a rib of 3 stitches. Arrows in chart show how the stitches cross.

Cast On stitches divisible by 9.

    Row 1: P.4. * (K.1 over 1), P.7. *   Repeat * to *, ending (K.1 over 1), P.3.

    Row 2: K.4. * (P.1 over 1), K.7. *   Repeat * to *, ending (P.1 over 1), K.3.

Repeat these 2 rows.

FIG. 73B.—Chart.

ZIG-ZAG KNOTTED RIB. *Fig. 74.*

The same Twin Motifs are alternated on 3 stitches, but in reverse order. This small change makes a considerable difference, and patterns can be elaborated on this principle.

Cast On stitches divisible by 9.

    Row 1: P.3. * (K.1 over 1), P.7. *   Repeat * to *, ending (K.1 over 1), P.4.

Row 2: K.3. * (P.1 over 1), K.7. * Repeat * to *, ending (P.1 over 1), K.4.

FIG. 74.—Zig-zag Knotted Rib. Chart.

Repeat these 2 rows.

MINIATURE CROSS-OVER RIB (SIMPLE). *Fig. 75.*

The Knit Motif (Fig. 69) is used every fifth row only, as shown in chart. Edge stitches also shown.

Cast On a multiple of 10 stitches and 5 over.

    Rows 1 and 3: K.2. * P.1, K.2, P.2, K.1, P.2, K.2. *   Repeat * to *, ending P.1, K.2.

    Rows 2 and 4: P.2, K.1. * P.2, K.2, P.1, K.2, P.2, K.1. *   Repeat * to *, ending P.2.

    Row 5: K.2. * P.1, (K.1 over 1), P.2, K.1, P.2, (K.1 over 1). *   Repeat * to *, ending P.1, K.2.

    Row 6: Same as Row 2.

Repeat these 6 rows.

FIG. 75.—Miniature
Cross-over Rib.
Chart.

MINIATURE CROSS-OVER RIB (HALF DROP).

*Figs. 76*A *and* B.

Also known as MINIATURE CABLE.

The Knit Motifs are alternated on the half-drop principle. The photo reveals a well-known pattern, while the chart shows how simply it is designed. No edge stitches are shown.

Cast On stitches divisible by 14 and 5 over.

Row 1: P.2. * K.1, P.2, (K.1 over 1), P.2, K.1, P.2, K.2, P.2. * Repeat * to *, ending K.1, P.2.

Row 2: K.2, P.1. * K.2, P.2, K.2, P.1. * Repeat * to *, ending K.2.

Row 3: P.2. * K.1, P.2, K.2, P.2, K.1, P.2, (K.1 over 1), P.2. * Repeat * to *, ending K.1, P.2.

Row 4: K.2, P.1. * K.2, P.2, K.2, P.1. * Repeat * to *, ending K.2.

Repeat these 4 rows.

FIG. 76A.—Chart.

FIG. 76B.—Miniature Cross-over Rib. Half Drop.

HORIZONTAL DESIGN

The Twin Motifs (Figs. 69 and 70) are arranged in rows and can be used to the exclusion of all ordinary stitches as in Fig. 77, or the units can be arranged geometrically, or broken by a vertical rib.

PLAITED BASKET STITCH. *Figs. 77*A *and* B.

Both Motifs are arranged in rows and alternated to give an all-over plaited effect, obtained by casting-on an odd number of stitches (*see* chart).

Cast On an odd number of stitches.
    Row 1: K.2.   * (K.1 over 1). *   Repeat * to *, ending K.1.
    Row 2: P.2.   * (P.1 over 1). *   Repeat * to *, ending P.1.

Repeat these 2 rows.

USES.   A close sporting fabric for garments, gloves or cushions.

FIG. 77**A**.—Chart.

FIG. 77**B**.—Plaited Basket Stitch.

MOTIFS 3 AND 4 (TWO OVER TWO AND THREE OVER THREE)

When two or more stitches cross over in pairs or threes they cannot be knitted, as in Figs. 69 and 70, but must be crossed, as in Figs. 78 and 79. This shows a unit of 3 over 3, but 2 over 2 or larger Motifs are made in the same way.

A third two-pointed needle is necessary (or an orange stick or match will serve).   △ The Cross " left over right " or " right over left " is now varied by dropping the spare needle either to the FRONT or to the BACK.   △ Both Motifs are made on the front of the fabric, so they cannot be known as Knit and Purl but as " Left-over-Right " and " Right-over-Left " Motifs, or the two referred to as TWIN Motifs.

LEFT-OVER-RIGHT CROSS. *Figs. 78*A *and* B.

   △ △ **Abb :**   (K. 2 over 2 Back) or (K. 3 over 3 Back).

Slip three stitches on to a spare needle, and drop to the △ BACK (Fig. 78A). Knit the 4th, 5th, and 6th stitches (A, B, C). After this knit D, E, F, or the 1st, 2nd, and 3rd stitches.
Fig. 78B shows the result, △ a Left-over-Right Cross, which is the correct CABLE CROSS. △ This is referred to as (K.3. over 3 BACK) or, when the Motif is only four stitches, as (K.2 over 2 BACK).

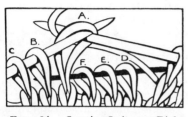

FIG. 78A.—Crossing Left over Right
(2 over 2) or (3 over 3) Units.

FIG. 78B.—Resulting
Left over Right Motif.
(Drop to back.)

RIGHT-OVER-LEFT CROSS. *Figs. 79A and* B.

△ △ **Abb :** (K. 2 over 2 Front) or (K. 3 over 3 Front).

Slip three stitches on to a spare needle and drop to the △ FRONT (Fig. 79A). Knit the stitches A, B, C, and then knit the stitches off the spare needle lettered D, E, and F.

Fig. 79B shows the result, △ a Right-over-Left Cross. (This is a more convenient method of crossing in Round Knitting.)

Referred to as (K.3 over 3 FRONT) or (K.2 over 2 FRONT).

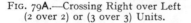

FIG. 79A.—Crossing Right over Left
(2 over 2) or (3 over 3) Units.

FIG. 79B.—Resulting
Right over Left Motif.
(Drop to front.)

NOTE.—Any convenient number of stitches can be chosen as a unit, and these can be even (2 over 2, 3 over 3), or odd (3 crossed over 2).

△ Old knitting patterns invariably use an uneven number (3 over 2), making one less stitch on the needle dropped to the back (*see* Fig. 68, where the Cable consists of 5 stitches only). This lessens the pull, and so allows the twist to lie flatter. When knitting in cotton yarns which are void of elasticity, this pull is an important consideration. Another method is to knit the stitches off the spare needle in the following row or round (*see* Old Scottish Stitch, Fig. 91). A third method is to knit the whole Cable Rib in Cross Knit stitches. This also gives a more distinguished appearance (*see* cable on sleeve, Fig. 68, *also* Fig. 85).

DESIGN (TWO OVER TWO) AND (THREE OVER THREE)

These Motifs can be arranged vertically, horizontally, or as spot designs.

Fig. 78 is generally assumed as Cable Stitch, but this is only one of its many arrangements, so the name Cable should only be used when describing this particular pattern. This consists of a vertical arrangement of Fig. 78 only, bordered either side by Purl stitches, or by some other contrasting effect as in Fig. 113. So it is really a rib pattern or Cable Rib Stitch. If the Purl stitches are omitted, the pattern is merely a vertical arrangement of Crossed Motifs, and not Cable at all.

A vertical arrangement of Twin Motifs (Figs. 78 and 79), made to alternate, will produce a Waved Rib (see Fig. 86). Twin Motifs are also necessary in forming a Travelling Rib Lattice (Fig. 87), or a Plait (Fig. 91).

Both Motifs, large or small, can be arranged horizontally, and as all-over repeating spot designs. The smaller Motif, 2 over 2, is shown in this form (Figs. 80–82), while the larger Motif, 3 over 3 (Figs. 84–86), is shown in the more familiar vertical patterns, though both can be used in either way.

DOUBLE-PLAITED BASKET STITCH. *Figs. 80A and B.*

The designing principle is the same as Fig. 77, only the Motif has a unit of 4 stitches as shown in chart instead of 2. *See* Figs. 78 and 79 for technique.

FIG. 80A.—Double-Plaited Basket Stitch.

FIG. 80B.—Double-Plaited Basket Stitch.   Chart.

Cast On stitches divisible by 4.
   Row 1: Knit.
   Row 2: Purl.
   Row 3: K.1.   * (K.2 over 2 BACK). *   Repeat * to *, ending K.3.
   Row 4: Purl.
   Row 5: K.3.   * (K.2 over 2 FRONT). *   Repeat * to *, ending K.1.
   Row 6: Purl.

Repeat from Row 3.

ZIG-ZAG PLAITED RIB. *Figs. 81A and* B.

The Twin Motifs are arranged in rows and alternated as before (Fig. 80), but now spaced 3 rows apart, as shown in chart, instead of only one.

Cast On stitches divisible by 4.
Row 1: Knit.
Row 2: Purl.
Row 3: K.1. * (K.2 over 2, BACK). Repeat * to *, ending K.3.
Row 4: Purl.
Row 5: Knit.
Row 6: Purl.
Row 7: K.3. * (K.2 over 2, FRONT).* Repeat * to *, ending K.1.
Row 8: Purl.
Row 9: Knit.
Row 10: Purl.

Repeat from Row 3.

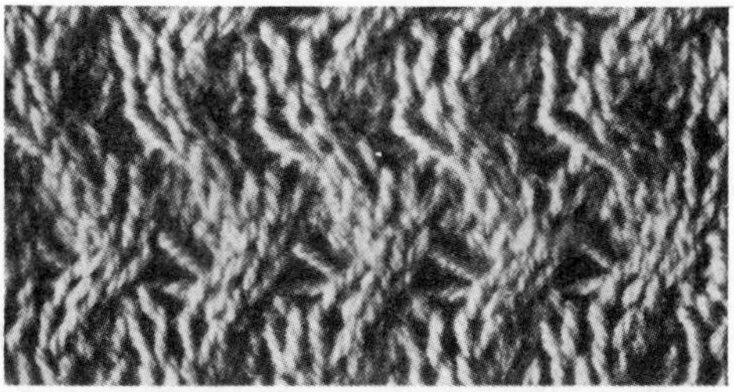

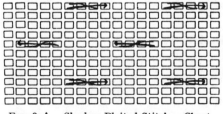

FIG. 81A.—Zig-zag Plaited Rib.

FIG. 81B.—Zig-zag Plaited Rib Chart.

SHADOW PLAITED STITCH. *Figs. 82A and* B.

The Twin Motifs 2 over 2 are here divided by 3 rows as in Fig. 81, but also divided by an interval of 4 Knit stitches (*see* Spot Pattern, Fig. 57). This makes an all-over Shadow Plaited Fabric. The number of intervening stitches can be more than 4, in which case the number of intervening rows should be correspondingly increased.

Cast On stitches divisible by 8 and 2 over.
Row 1: Knit.

FIG. 82A.—Shadow Plaited Stitch. Chart.

Row 2: Purl.
Row 3: K.1.   * (K.2 over 2 BACK), K.4. *   Repeat * to *, ending K.1.
Row 4: Purl.
Row 5: Knit.
Row 6: Purl.
Row 7: K.1.   * K.4 (K.2 over 2 FRONT) *   Repeat * to *, ending K.1.
Row 8: Purl.
Row 9: Knit.
Row 10: Purl.

Repeat from Row 3.

FIG. 82**B**.—Shadow Plaited Stitch.

FIG. 83.—Plaited Four Stitch.

PLAITED FOUR STITCH.   *Fig. 83.*

The Twin Motifs have a Unit of 8 (4 over 4) ; four stitches are slipped on the spare needle and dropped to the front in one row, and to the back on the next crossed row (*see* Figs. 78 and 79).   This and Figs. 77 and 80 are all of the same designing principle, but using graded Motifs.   The charting is similar to Fig. 80.

Cast On stitches divisible by 8 and 4 over.

Row 1: Knit.

Row 2: Purl.

Row 3: K.2.   * S.4 on spare needle, drop to FRONT, K.4.   Knit
4 stitches off spare needle. *   Repeat * to *, ending K.2.

Row 4: Purl.

Row 5: Knit.

Row 6: Purl.

Row 7: K.6.   * S.4 on spare needle, drop to BACK, K.4.   Knit 4
stitches off spare needle. *   Repeat * to *, ending K.6.

Row 8: Purl.

Row 9: Knit.

Row 10: Purl.

Repeat from Row 3.

Leave the yarn loose when stranding across the back.

MOTIF 4 (THREE OVER THREE)

Showing vertical arrangements of
Motif.

CABLE RIB REPEAT. *Figs. 84*A
and B.

Chart.   One Motif Left over Right is
repeated in vertical order.

FIG. 84A.—Cable Rib Repeat.
(Chart.)   Unit 6 stitches.

FIG. 84B.—Cable Rib
Repeat.

Cast On a multiple of 10 stitches and 4 over.

Row 1: * P.4, K.6. *   Repeat, ending P.4.

Row 2: K.4.   * P.6, K.4. *   Repeat * to *.

Rows 3 and 5: As Row 1.

Rows 4 and 6: As Row 2.

Row 7: * P.4, (K.3 over 3, BACK). *   Repeat * to *, ending P.4.

Row 8: K.4.   * P.6, K.4. *   Repeat * to *.

Repeat these 8 rows.

To alternate this pattern in the Half Drop principle, make the Cable
Cross in the 3rd and 7th throw on each alternate Rib as in Fig. 85.

CABLE IN CROSS KNIT STITCH. *Fig. 85.*

The Motif is composed of 5 Cross Knit stitches (3 over 2) and alternated.

Pattern can be varied by increasing width of fabric between the cable; instead of P. 2 there can be 4 or 5 Purl stitches, or a Ladder Stitch, or Purl fabric centred with Faggot Insertion.

Cast On stitches divisible by 14 and 2 over.

Rows I and 3: * P.2, K.5 B. * Repeat, ending P.2.

Rows 2 and 4: K.2. * P.5 B., K.2. * Repeat * to *.

Row 5: * P.2, S.2 on spare needle, drop to back. Knit (B.) next 3 stitches, and then knit (B.) the 2 slipped stitches, P.2, K.5 B. * Repeat, ending P.2.

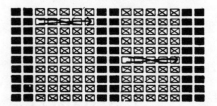

FIG. 85.—Cable Rib in Cross Knit Stitch. Chart.

Row 6: K.2. * P.5 B., K.2. * Repeat * to *.

Row 7: * P.2, K.5 B. * Repeat, ending P.2.

Row 8: Same as Row 6.

Row 9: * P.2, K.5 B., P.2, (S.2 stitches on spare needle and drop to back. Knit (B.) next 3 stitches. Knit (B.) the 2 stitches on spare needle). * Repeat, ending P.2.

Row 10: K.2. * P.5 B., K.2. * Repeat * to *.

Repeat from Row 3.

WAVED RIBBON RIB. *Figs. 86A and B.*

The Twin Motifs (3 over 3 right and left) are alternated and vertically arranged. The spare needle is dropped to the back for the first, and to the front for the next (*see* arrows in chart, Figs. 86 A and B, also Figs. 78 and 79). The effect is a vertical Waved Rib, and not a Cable. Can be used singly or as an all-over pattern.

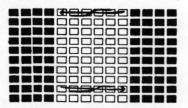

FIG. 86A.—Waved Ribbon Rib. Chart.

FIG. 86B.—Waved Ribbon Rib.

Cast On stitches divisible by 10 and 4 over.
Knit 2 rows and then begin pattern.
Row 1: * P.4, (K.3 over 3 Back). * Repeat, ending P.4.
Rows 2, 4, 6, and 8: K.4. * P.6, K.4. * Repeat * to *.
Rows 3, 5, and 7: * P.4, K.6. * Repeat, ending P.4.
Row 9: P.4. * (K.3 over 3 Front), P.4. * Repeat * to *.
Rows 10, 12, 14, and 16: K.4. * P.6, K.4. * Repeat * to *.
Rows 11, 13, and 15: * P.4, K.6. * Repeat, ending P.4.

Repeat these 16 rows.

WAVED RIBBON RIB IN CROSS STITCH.

The Rib is knitted in Cross Knit Stitches and the Motifs are alternated (*see* Fig. 85).

Cast On stitches divisible by 16 and 2 over.
Rows 1 and 3: * P.2, K.6 B., P.2, K.6 B. * Repeat, ending P.2.
Rows 2 and 4: K.2. * P.6 B., K.2, P.6 B., K.2. * Repeat * to *.
Row 5: * P.2, (K.B. 3 over 3, Front), P.2, K.6 B. * Repeat, ending P.2.
Rows 6 and 8: K.2. * P.6 B., K.2, P.6 B., K.2. * Repeat * to *.
Row 7: * P.2, K.6 B., P.2, K.6 B. * Repeat, ending P. 2.
Row 9: * P.2, K.6 B., P.2, (K.B. 3 over 3, Front). * Repeat, ending P.2.
Rows 10 and 12: K.2. * P.6 B., K.2, P.6 B., K.2. * Repeat * to *.
Row 11: * P.2, K.6 B., P.2, K.6 B. * Repeat, ending P.2.
Row 13: * P.2, (K.B. 3 over 3, Back), P.2, K.6 B. * Repeat, ending P.2.
Rows 14 and 16: K.2. * P.6 B., K.2, P.6 B., K.2. * Repeat * to *.
Row 15: * P.2, K.6 B., P.2, K.6 B. * Repeat, ending P.2.
Row 17: * P.2, K.6 B., P.2, (K.B. 3 over 3, Back). * Repeat, ending P.2.
Row 18: K.2. * P.6 B., K.2, P.6 B., K.2. * Repeat * to *.

Repeat from Row 1.

MOTIF 5 (TRAVELLING DIAGONAL CROSSED RIB). *Fig. 87.*

These patterns form an Embossed Trellis all over the fabric, and for a knitted example, *see* the centre panel of Fisherman's Sweater (Fig. 68).

Both Motifs, left and right (*see* Figs. 78 and 79), are used, and these cross and " travel " diagonally and in contrary directions to form a lattice of diamonds (*see* chart, Fig. 87). In this pattern the Motif (3 over 3) starts from the centre of 6 stitches, these then divide, 3 travelling to the right and 3 to the left, crossing every seventh row, and in so doing △ exchange places with the background stitches.   It is always the △ same 3 stitches which travel and cross over on top.   The diamond space between the trellis can be Purl as shown, Moss or Lace pattern.   The chart shows the method of design.   The size of the diamond can be increased or decreased by adding or subtracting 2 rows between the unit rows (*see* chart).

A Travelling Unit can be composed of any convenient number of stitches.   Fig. 68 shows a Travelling Rib of 3 and 3, another of 2 and 2, and a third of one travelling stitch.   The single stitch is a Cross Knit stitch and travels in every row, Knit and Purl.

TRAVELLING RIB (ON PURL BACK-GROUND).   *Fig. 87.*

See central panel of Jersey (*Fig.* 68).   Note the Chart begins in Row 3.

Cast On stitches divisible by 18 and 6 over for edge stitches, which are not shown on Chart.

Row 1:   P.9.   * K.6, P.12. *   Repeat * to *, ending K.6, P.9.
Row 2:   K.9.   * P.6, K.12. *   Repeat * to *, ending P.6, K.9.
Row 3:   P.9.   * Sl.3 Knit stitches on spare needle, drop to back. K.3 stitches.   K.3 off spare needle, P.12. *   Repeat * to *.   Purl last 9 stitches.
Rows 4, 6, and 8:   K.9.   * P.6, K.12. *   Repeat * to *, ending P.6, K.9.
Rows 5 and 7:   P.9.   * K.6, P.12. *   Repeat * to *, ending K.6, P.9.
Row 9:   P.6.   * Sl.3 Purl stitches on spare needle, drop to back. K.3, P.3 off spare needle.   Sl.3 Knit stitches on spare needle, drop to front.   P.3.   K.3 off spare needle. P.6. *   Repeat * to *.
Rows 10, 12, and 14:   K.6.   * P.3, K.6. *   Repeat * to *, ending P.3, K.6.
Rows 11 and 13:   P.6.   * K.3, P.6. *   Repeat * to *, ending K.3, P.6.
Row 15:   P.3.   * Sl.3 Purl stitches on spare needle, drop to back. K.3.   P.3 off spare needle.   P.6.   Sl.3 Knit stitches on spare needle, drop to front.   P.3.   K.3 off spare needle. *   Repeat * to *.   Purl last 3 stitches.
Rows 16, 18, and 20:   K.3, P.3.   * K.12, P.6. *   Repeat * to *, ending K.12, P.3, K.3.
Rows 17 and 19:   P.3, K.3.   * P.12, K.6. *   Repeat, * to *, ending P.12, K.3, P.3.

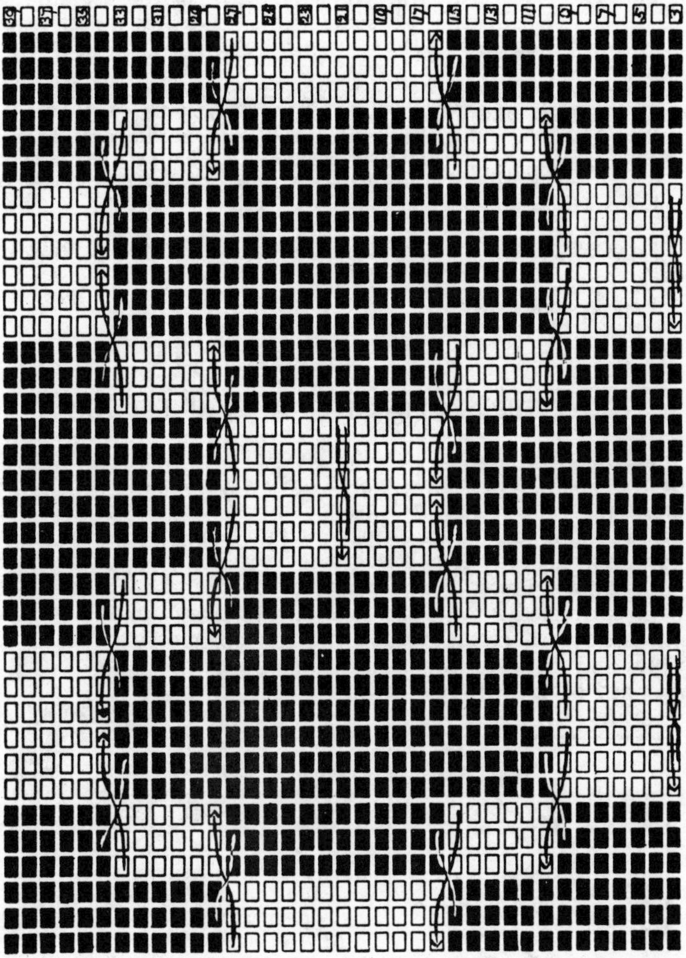

FIG. 87.—Travelling Rib on Purl Background. Chart.

Row 21: P.3, K.3. * P.12. Sl.3 Knit stitches on spare needle, drop to front. K.3. K.3 off spare needle. * Repeat * to *, ending P.12, K.3, P.3.

Rows 22, 24, and 26: K.3, P.3. * K.12, P.6. * Repeat * to *, ending K.12, P.3, K.3.

Rows 23 and 25: P.3, K.3. * P.12, K.6. * Repeat * to *, ending P.12, K.3, P.3.

Row 27:   P.3.   * Sl.3 Knit stitches on spare needle, drop to front. P.3.   K.3 off spare needle.   P.6.   Sl.3 Purl stitches on spare needle, drop to back.   K.3.   P.3 off spare needle. *   Repeat * to *, ending P.3.

Rows 28, 30, and 32: K.6.   * P.3, K.6. *   Repeat * to *.

Rows 29 and 31: P.6.   * K.3, P.6. *   Repeat * to *.

Row 33:   P.6.   * Sl.3 Knit stitches on spare needle, drop to front. P.3.   K.3 off spare needle.   Sl.3 Purl stitches on spare needle, drop to back.   K.3.   P.3 off spare needle. P.6. *

Rows 34, 36, and 38: K.9.   * P.6, K.12. *   Repeat * to *, ending P.6, K.9.

Rows 35 and 37: P.9.   * K.6, P.12. *   Repeat * to *, ending K.6, P.9.

Repeat from Row 3.

MOTIF 6.   MAKING A PLAITED RIB

Fig. 88.   A Plaited Rib must contain a number of stitches divisible by 3, and the plaiting process employs both Motifs, right and left, as described in Figs. 78 and 79, and indicated by the arrows in Fig. 88.   This diagram should be read from the bottom upwards.   The Plait is exaggerated so that the movement can be clearly followed.   The number of stitches chosen for the plait is divided into 3, and it is always the △ middle group of stitches which cross over on the △ top, crossing first to the right and then to the left, the spare needle being dropped back or front accordingly.

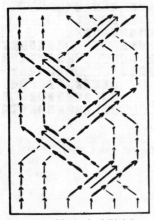

FIG. 88.—Method of Plaiting.

FIG. 89.—Decorative use of a Plaited Rib, as a vertical stripe on leggings.

Cast On 6 stitches plus 4 edge stitches and follow the plaiting process as given in Fig. 88.

Row 1: (1st Cross). P.2. (K.2, over 2 BACK) K.2, P.2.

Rows 2, 3, and 4: Stocking Stitch

Row 5: (2nd Cross). P.2, K.2. (K.2 over 2 FRONT), P.2.

Rows 6, 7, and 8: Stocking Stitch.

Row 9: (3rd Cross). As Row 1.

Rows 10, 11, and 12: Stocking Stitch.

Row 13: (4th Cross). As Row 5.

Rows 14, 15, and 16: Stocking Stitch. Repeat.

The same method is employed for larger Plaits of 9 or 12 stitches, but then, for better proportion, the crossing would be made every 6th or 8th row, respectively.

DESIGN

The Plait, just as a Cable Rib, must be bordered either side by Purl or other contrasting stitches, otherwise the plaited effect is lost (*see* Fig. 90). For more elaborate background *see* Old Scottish Stitch (Fig. 91). Plaits are generally introduced on garments for special effects (*see* Fig. 89). But they can, if desired, be used all over the fabric in the same way as Cable Rib, as follows :—

PLAITED RIB PATTERN (2 × 2 × 2). *Fig. 90.*

Cast On stitches divisible by 10 and 4 over.
Rows 1 and 3: * P.4, K.6. * Repeat, ending P.4.
Rows 2 and 4: K.4. * P.6, K.4. * Repeat * to *.
Row 5: * P.4, S.2 on spare needle and drop to back. K.2, K.2 on spare needle, K.2. * Repeat, ending P.4.
Rows 6 and 8: K.4. * P.6, K.4. * Repeat * to *.
Row 7: * P.4, K.6. * Repeat, ending P.4.
Row 9: * P.4, K.2, S.2 on spare needle, drop to front. K.2, K.2 on spare needle. * Repeat, ending P.4.
Row 10: K.4. * P.6, K.4. * Repeat * to *.

Repeat from Row 3.

FIG. 90.—Plaited Rib Pattern.

OLD SCOTTISH STITCH. *Fig. 91.*

An elaborate design combining the use of Plaited Rib and Faggot Stitch. Note by this old method the Motif covers two rows, as the stitches are slipped off and kept front to the end of row and then purled in next. **△** Note (S.2 *) and (S.4 *).

This pattern is taken from an early 17th-century Scottish bonnet. It can be knitted in strips as in photograph and used as an insertion on bedspreads or to form a frame (as on modern eiderdowns). The centre panel of spread would then be composed of a square. Also used for insertion strips on knitted table-covers. Suitable for elaborate centre front of jumper. Can be used as a repeat pattern by casting on a multiple of 28 stitches.

FIG. 91.—Old Scottish Stitch.

Cast On 28 stitches.

Row 1: P.2, K.2, O., K.2 tog., P.2, K.3, O., K.2 tog., K.4, O., K.2 tog., K.1, P.2, K.2, O., K.2 tog., P.2.

Row 2: K.2, P.2, O., P.2 tog., K.2, P.3, O., P.2 tog., P.4, O., P.2 tog., P.1, K.2, P.2, O., P.2 tog., K.2.

Rows 3 and 4: Same as Rows 1 and 2.

Row 5: P.2, Sl. 2 * (stitches on spare needle and keep in front to end of row), K.2, P.2, K.3, O., K.2 tog., K.4, O., K.2 tog., K.1, P.2, (S.2 *), K.2, P.2.

Row 6: K.2, P.2 * (these are the stitches off extra pin), P.2, K.2, P.3, O., P.2 tog., P.4, O., P.2 tog., P.1, K.2, (P.2 *), P.2, K2.

Repeat 1st and 2nd rows 5 more times—*i.e.*, 10 rows in all.

Rows 17 and 18: Same as Rows 5 and 6.

Rows 19 and 20: Same as Rows 1 and 2.

Row 21: P.2, K.2, O., K.2 tog., P.2, K.12, P.2, K.2, O., K.2 tog. P.2.

Row 22: K.2, P.2, O., P.2 tog., K.2, P.12, K.2, P.2, O., P.2 tog., K.2.

Row 23: P.2, K.2, O., K.2 tog., P.2, (S.4 *), (slip these 4 stitches off on extra needle as before and drop to front), K.8, P.2, K.2, O., K.2 tog., P.2.

Row 24: K.2, P.2, O., P.2 tog., K.2, P.4, (P.4 *), (these are the 4 stitches off extra needle), P.4, K.2, P.2, O., P.2 tog., K.2 .

Row 25: P.2, K.2, O., K.2 tog., P.2, K.12, P.2, K.2, O., K.2 tog. P.2.

Row 26: K.2, P.2, O., P.2 tog., K.2, P.12, K.2, P.2, O., P.2 tog. K.2.

Rows 27 and 28: Same as Rows 25 and 26.

Row 29: P.2, (S.2 *), K.2, P.2, K.8, (S.4 *), P.2, (S.2 *), K.2, P.2.

Row 30: K.2, (* P.2), P.2, K.2, P.4, (P.4 *), P.4, K.2, (P.2 *), P.2, K.2.

Rows 31 and 32: Same as Rows 25 and 26.

Rows 33, 34, 35 and 36: Same as Rows 23, 24, 25 and 26.

Row 37: P.2, K.2, O., K.2 tog., P.2, K.8, (S.4 *), P.2, K.2, O., K.2 tog., P.2.

Row 38: K.2, P.2, O., P.2 tog., K.2, P.4, (P.4 *), P.4, K.2, P.2, O., P.2 tog., K.2.

Row 39: P.2, (S.2 *), K.2, P.2, K.12, P.2, (* S.2), K.2, P.2.

Row 40: K.2, (P.2 *), P.2, K.2, P.12, K.2, (* P.2), P.2, K.2.

Row 41: P.2, K.2, O., K.2 tog., P.2, K.12, P.2, K.2, O., K.2 tog., P.2.

Row 42: K.2, P.2, O., P.2 tog., K.2, P.12, K.2, P.2, O., P.2 tog., K.2.

Rows 43, 44, 45, 46, 47 and 48: Same as Rows 23, 24, 25, 26, 27 and 28.

Row 49: P.2, K.2, O., K.2 tog., P.2, K.8., (S.4 *), P.2, K.2, O., K.2 tog., P.2.

Rows 50, 51, 52, 53 and 54: Same as Rows 38, 39, 40, 41 and 42.

Row 55: P.2, K.2, O., K.2 tog., P.2, K.12, P.2, K.2, O., K.2 tog., P.2.

Row 56: K.2, P.2, O., P.2 tog., K.2, P.12, K.2, P.2, O., P.2 tog., K.2.

Repeat from Row 1.

Fig. 92.—Plaited Motif in Ornament.

ORNAMENTAL USE OF PLAIT

In Fig. 92 a single plaited Motif is used as an ornament to cross the fabric of a jumper.

The middle " arm " of the plait continues upwards to the neck, the two side " arms " are " travelled " as in Fig. 87 to make a " V " to the shoulder. The yoke is Trellis Lace Pattern, with bias movement (Fig. 156).

The same single plaited Motif is on the sleeve tops. A Motif can be crossed and travelled as shown, or it can be crossed, twisted once again and then travelled.

A Cable Cross can be treated in the same way.

All Cross Motifs have great decorative possibilities for garments in addition to their use as all-over repeating units of design.

MOTIF 7.　HORIZONTAL DROP AND CROSS-OVER PATTERNS

The method consists of lengthening the crossed stitches either by the use of one larger needle, or by one or several Throws (*see* Fig. 117, for method).

INTERLACING CROSS STITCH. *Figs. 93A, B, and C.*

Also known as INDIAN CROSS STITCH.

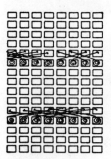

FIG. 93B.—Working Method.

FIG. 93A.—Chart.

To make a " Throw "
see Fig. 117.

FIG. 93C.—Interlacing Cross Stitch
or Indian Cross Stitch.

Cast On stitches divisible by 8.

Rows 1-3: Knit (Garter Stitch).

Row 4: K.1.　* Insert needle in next stitch and throw yarn 4 times round point of needle and K.1. *　Repeat on every stitch to the end of the row (*see* Fig. 93B).

Row 5: * S.1 and drop the 4 Throws made in previous row. * Repeat 7 more times.　There are 8 long slipped stitches now on right needle.　Stretch stitches upwards to make of equal length.　Now pass the left needle through the first 4 stitches and lift them over the second 4 stitches, as in Fig. 93C. Transfer all 8 stitches crossed in this way to left needle and knit them in this order.　Repeat on the next 8 stitches, and so on until row is completed.　Be careful not to twist stitches when crossing them.

Rows 6-9: Knit.

Row 10: Same as Row 4.

Row 11: Same as Row 5, only, to alternate the groups of crosses, begin by crossing only 4 long stitches, instead of 8.   Cross 2 over 2.   Then continue as in Row 5, crossing as in Fig. 93**C.**

Rows 12–15: Knit (Garter Stitch).

Repeat from Row 4.

Uses.   As an insertion, or in repeat for pram-covers, etc.   The insertion can be broadened or narrowed by increasing or decreasing the number of Throws, and varied by crossing different numbers to the unit.

GRECIAN PLAIT STITCH.   *Fig. 94.*

Use two needles, one small and one large, the large needle to be twice the size of the smaller.   Fabric reversible.

FIG. 94.—Grecian Plait Stitch.

Cast On an even number on large needle.
> **Row 1:** Small needle.   Knit.
> **Row 2:** Large needle.   Purl.
> **Row 3:** Lift 2nd stitch over 1st and knit it, and then knit the 1st
> stitch.   Lift 4th stitch over 3rd, knit it, and then
> knit the 3rd.   Repeat all along the row.
> **Row 4:** Large needle.   Purl.

Repeat rows 3 and 4.

THREADED CROSS STITCH.

Also known as DIAPER PATTERN and FLECKED STITCH.

One stitch is drawn through another on the same principle as in Fig.
93C.

Cast On stitches divisible by 4 and 2 over.
> **Row 1:** K.1.   * Insert needle purlwise through next stitch, and
> draw the stitch beyond this through it.   Knit this
> stitch and slip it off the needle.   Now knit the first
> stitch into the back and slip it off the needle.   K.2. *
> Repeat * to *, ending K.1.
> **Row 2:** Purl.
> **Row 3:** K.1.   * K.2, now draw and cross the next 2 stitches as in
> Row 1. *   Repeat * to * to last stitch, K.1.
> **Row 4:** Purl.

Repeat these 4 rows.

SLIP-STITCH MOTIFS AND PATTERNS

Designing Units—Slipped Stitches and Stranded Slip Stitches

Slip-Stitch Motifs are very simple, but they make the most effective patterns, and permit of a pretty play of yarn movements.

The method consists of slipping a stitch from the left to right needle without knitting it, while carrying the yarn either behind or before the stitch so slipped. In this way the Motif has two versions of ornament :—

1. Patterns designed with Slipped Stitches such as Heel Stitch (Fig. 96), etc. Here the yarn, being stranded behind the Slipped Stitch, does not show. The repeating Motif is then the Slipped Stitch only and may consist of one or two Units.

2. Patterns designed with the yarn stranding across the front of the Slipped Stitch, such as Figs. 105–108. These are STRANDED SLIPPED STITCHES, and in such patterns the repeating Motif of design is the Stranded yarn, and may consist of one or several Units.

EFFECT ON FABRIC.

When a stitch is slipped, it is lifted out of its own row and knitted on the next (*see* Fig. 96), where one row is coloured black to show what happens. This lifting of stitches from one row and knitting them in the next very naturally tends to △ thicken the fabric, as it reduces the natural depth of the stitches. The technical term for such is CLOSE FABRICS, and they make, indeed, close cosy wear, being popular for all sports clothes, gloves, socks, boys' knickers, etc., and for any purpose where extra thick and strong fabrics are needed.

DESIGN

The following Slip patterns have been divided into two groups so that the difference and the designing method can be clearly seen.

The Slipped-Stitch Motifs are used in vertical arrangement only, and when two different-coloured yarns are employed, these patterns become most intriguing.

The Stranded-Slip Motifs are used in horizontal arrangement, and the repeating Motif may consist of either one or several stranded stitches as shown.

The two symbols used in the charts are quite distinct, and show very clearly how easily these patterns are created. The designer will note that Slip and Cross Motifs blend very effectively; one example is given in Fig. 104.

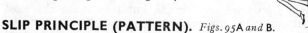

SLIP PRINCIPLE (PATTERN). *Figs. 95A and* B.

△△ When a stitch is slipped as a Pattern Principle, it must always be slipped PURLWISE. The reason is shown in Fig. 95 A, where the stitch which has been slipped purlwise now lies at the same angle as the previous stitch, which has been knitted. △ Both show the right side of the loop turned towards the knitter. In the next row, when this stitch will be purled (or knitted) it will be in alignment with the ordinary knit stitches. That is, an ordinary, but little longer knit stitch (*see* Fig. 96B). The directions read S.1, so the purlwise must be understood, when this stitch is used as a repeating motif, making pattern.

FIG. 95A.   FIG. 95B.

In Fig. 95B the stitch has been slipped knitwise. Here the left side of the loop is turned towards the knitter. In the next row △ this stitch, when knitted, will be crossed or twisted. Sometimes, for special pattern effects, this crossed stitch is required, and then the directions will specially state "Slip Knitwise". Unless this is stated always slip purlwise. (*See also* page 295 for Decreasing Slip Principle.) Abb. : S.1, P.W.

VERTICAL SLIP PATTERN

The Slipped stitches are arranged vertically as in Ribbing. The first pattern is one Slip Stitch alternating with one Knit Stitch. Notice how in Fig. 96 the Slipped Stitch is lifted out of its own row. This causes the fabric to thicken.

CLOSE STITCH

Cast On an odd number of stitches.
    Row I: * K.1, S.1. *   Repeat, ending K.1.
    Row 2: Knit.

Repeat these 2 rows.
USES. For driving- and sport-gloves. Particularly smart in cotton yarns.

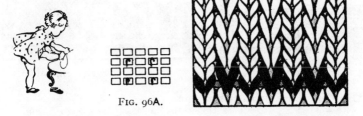

FIG. 96A.

FIG. 96B.—Heel Stitch.

HEEL STITCH. *Figs. 96A and B.*

Cast On an odd number of stitches.
    Row I: * K.1, S.1. *   Repeat, ending K.1.
    Row 2: All Purl.

Repeat these 2 rows.

USES. For strengthening the heels of stockings. Also as a thick jersey fabric, or for boys' knickers.

ELONGATED SLIP

The stitches are lengthened by throwing the yarn two or three times round the point of the needle △ after it has been inserted through the stitch. The directions read : K.1 or P.1 (2 throws) or (3 throws), as required.

△ *See* Figs. 117A and 117B for method of making a THROW, and note there the difference between a Throw and an Over.

This elongated stitch can be slipped purlwise over three or more consecutive rows before it is finally included as a stitch and knitted. The chart (Fig. 97A) shows this to be the same stitch by using one long slip symbol. The method is effective in one or two colours as shown in Fig. 99.

ELONGATED SLIP STITCH. *Figs. 97A and B.*

The Elongated Stitch is used as a repeating Motif on the half-drop principle. Edge stitches not showing.

FIG. 97A.   FIG. 97B.—Elongated Slip Stitch.

Cast On stitches divisible by 12 and 5 over.
    Row 1: P.2. * (P.1 (2 throws)), P.5. * Repeat * to *, ending (P.1 (2 throws)), P.2.
    Row 2: P.2. * S.1, dropping both throws, P.5. * Repeat * to *, ending S.1, P.2.
    Row 3: K.2. * S.1, K.5. * Repeat * to *, ending S.1, K.2.
    Row 4: P.2. * S.1, P.5. * Repeat * to *, ending S.1, P.2.
    Row 5: * P.5, including slipped stitch (P.1 (2 throws)). * Repeat, ending P.5.
    Row 6: P.5. * S.1, P.5. * Repeat * to *.
    Row 7: * K.5, S.1. * Repeat, ending K.5.
    Row 8: P.5. * S.1, P.5. * Repeat * to *.
Repeat these 8 rows.

ELONGATED CROSSED SLIP STITCH. *Figs. 98A and B.*

Same method of design as Fig. 97, only the stitches are slipped knitwise in 3rd row to cross them (*see* chart. Edge stitches not shown).

Cast On stitches divisible by 4 and 2 over.
    Row 1: K.2. * (K.1 (2 throws)), K.3. * Repeat * to *, ending (K.1 (2 throws)), K.2.
    Row 2: P.2. * S.1 (dropping both throws), P.3. * Repeat * to *, ending S.1, P.2

FIG. 98B.—Elongated Cross Slip Stitch. FIG. 98A.

Row 3: K.2. * S.1 (knitwise), K.3. * Repeat * to *, ending S.1, K.2.

Row 4: P.2. * S.1, P.3. * Repeat * to *, ending S.1, P.2.

Row 5: K.4. * (K.1 (2 throws)), K.3. * Repeat * to *, ending (K.1 (2 throws)), K.4.

Row 6: P.4. * S.1, P.3. * Repeat * to *, ending S.1, P.4.

Row 7: K.4. * S.1 (knitwise), K.3. * Repeat * to *, ending S.1, K.4.

Row 8: P.4. * S.1, P.3. * Repeat * to *, ending S1, P4.

Repeat these 8 rows.

TWO COLOURS

A second colour can be introduced and the Slipped stitches carried over 1 or more rows, and so produce an effect of checks or hexagons.

PIN CHECK. *Fig. 99.*

Use two different-coloured yarns of same ply.

Cast On an odd number of stitches.

Row I (light): Purl.

Row 2 (dark): P.1. * S.1, keeping yarn to front, P.1. * Repeat * to *.

Row 3 (dark): * P.1, yarn to back between needles, S.1, yarn forward. * Repeat, ending P.1.

Row 4 (light): Purl.

FIG. 99.—Pin Check.

Repeat these 4 rows.

To alternate the check, arrange the units as in Fig. 100. The chart indicates stitches and motifs, and not colours.

PIN CHECK (ALTERNATED). *Fig. 100.*

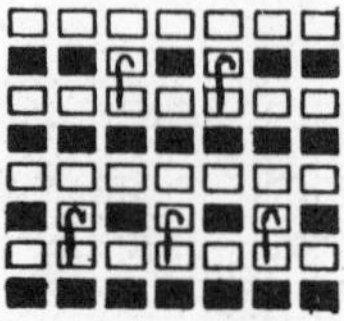

Use two different-coloured yarns of same ply.

Cast On odd number of stitches.
Rows I to 4: Same as Pin Check, Fig. 5.
Row 5 (light): Purl.
Row 6 (dark): P.2. * S.1, keeping yarn to front. P.1. * Repeat * to *, ending P.1.
Row 7 (dark): P.2. * Yarn to back between needles, S.1. Yarn forward, P.1. * Repeat * to *, ending P.1.
Row 8 (light): Purl.

Repeat these 8 rows.

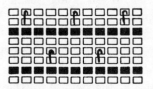

FIG. 100.—Pin Check (Alternated).

OVER CHECK. *Fig. 101.*

Use two different-coloured yarns of same ply.

Cast On stitches divisible by 4 and 3 over.

Row I (dark): Knit.
Row 2 (dark): Knit.
Row 3 (light): * K.3, S.1 (dark). * Repeat, ending K.3.
Row 4 (light): P.3 (light). * S.1 (dark), as before, P.3. * Repeat * to *.
Rows 5 and 6 (dark): Knit.
Row 7 (light): K.1. * S.1 (dark), K.3. * Repeat * to *, ending S.1, K.1.
Row 8 (light): P.1. * S.1 (dark), P.3. * Repeat * to *, ending S.1, K.1.

FIG. 101.—Over Check.

Repeat from Row 1.

HEXAGON PATTERN. *Figs. 102A and B.*

Also known as HONEYCOMB KNITTING.

The stitches are slipped in pairs over 4 rows, but as they are the same two stitches and not elongated, they contract the fabric into hexagonal shapes. Two different-coloured yarns of similar ply are used.

Cast On stitches divisible by 8 and 6 over.
Row I (dark): Knit.
Row 2 (dark): Knit.
Row 3 (light): K.2. * S.2 (dark purlwise), K.6 (light). * Repeat * to *, ending S.2, K.2.
Row 4 (light): P.2. * S.2 (dark (same 2 as in last row)), P.6 (light). * Repeat * to *, ending S.2 (dark), P.2.

Fig. 102B.—Hexagon Pattern.

Rows 5 and 7 (light): Same as Row 3.
Rows 6 and 8 (light): Same as Row 4.
Row 9 (dark): Knit, including all the slipped stitches.
Rows 10, 11, and 12: Knit, using dark yarn.
Row 13 (light): K.6. * S.2 (dark), K.6 (light). * Repeat * to *.
Row 14 (light): P.6 (light). * S.2 (dark), P.6 (light). * Repeat * to *.
Rows 15 and 17 (light): Same as Row 13.
Rows 16 and 18 (light): Same as Row 14.
Row 19 (dark): Knit, including all slipped stitches.
Rows 20 21, and 22 (dark): Knit.

Fig. 102A.

Repeat from Row 3 for length required.

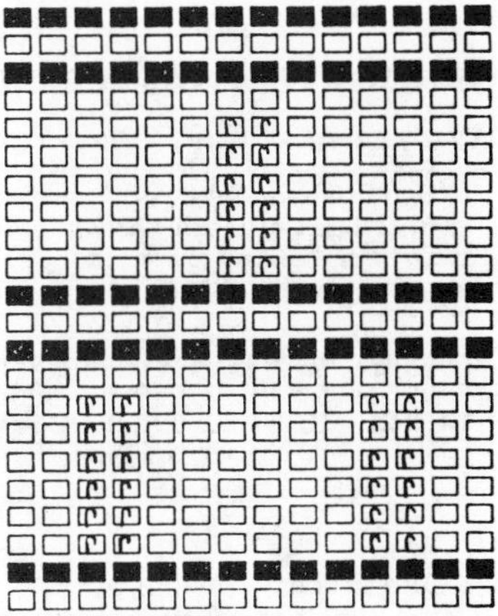

Cast off on Row 12 so that the end of the pattern corresponds with the beginning.

Uses. For cot and pram-covers, cushions, etc. Can also be knitted in one colour only.

CORRUGATED FABRIC

The stitches are slipped in groups which are vertically arranged, and the stranded yarns kept taut at the back, so that the surface appears Hooped or Corrugated. The fabric can be in one or in two colours and in Stocking Stitch or Garter Stitch. In Fig. 103 the two colours are arranged vertically.

CUSHION.

The cushion is knitted in Corrugated Garter Stitch. The depth of the fabric is here used as the width of the cushion, which measures $20\frac{1}{2} \times 14\frac{1}{2}$ ins. The colours are pale and dark grey. 4-ply wool, 8 oz. of each shade. Needles, size 10, or Standard, size 6. Cast on 180 stitches and knit as follows for depth of $19\frac{1}{2}$ ins. For directions for making the Knitted Fringe on same needles see page 158. For back of cushion knit in Moss Stitch, casting on 85 stitches, and knit using both wools together see Fig. 40B.

CORRUGATED GARTER STITCH. *Figs. 103A and B.*

Also known as CARTRIDGE-BELT PATTERN.

Use two different colours or tones of same ply—dark and light. Keep the yarn to back of fabric throughout when slipping the stitches.

Fabric can be knitted round or single. Directions given for single fabric.

FIG. 103A.

Cast On stitches divisible by 12.

(**Dark**) (back of fabric): Knit one complete row.

Row 1 (light) (front of fabric): K.3. * Slip purlwise 6 dark stitches, K.6 light stitches. * Repeat * to *, ending S.6 dark, K.3 light.

Row 2 (light): K.3 light. * Yarn forward, S.6 dark, same as before, yarn to back, K.6 light. * Repeat * to *, ending S.6 dark, K.3 light.

Row 3 (dark): S.2, K.1 light. * K.6 dark, S.6 light. * Repeat * to *, ending K.6 dark, K.1, S.2 light.

Row 4 (dark): S.2, K.1 light. * K.6 dark, yarn forward, S.6 light

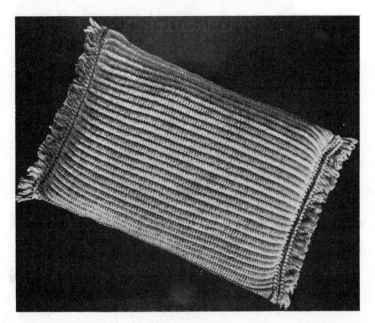

FIG. 103B.—Cushion in Corrugated Garter Stitch, finished with knitted Faggot Fringe.

same as before. * Repeat * to *, ending K.6 dark, K.1, S.2 light.

Repeat from Row 1 for the required length.

The slight difference made to the edge stitches in Rows 3 and 4 will prevent the edges curling and form a decorative border.

CORN-ON-THE-COB STITCH: *Figs. 104A and B.*

Also known as KNOTTED CLOSE STITCH.

The Slipped Stitch is taken over two rows. For a second Motif a Cross Knit Stitch is used on the third row (*see* chart).

Use two different-coloured yarns of the same ply. Looks most effective in 4-ply and thicker yarns. The colours are arranged vertically and referred to as light and dark.

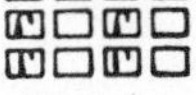

Cast On an even number of stitches.
    (**Light**) (back of fabric): Knit the complete row and then begin Pattern.

FIG. 104A.

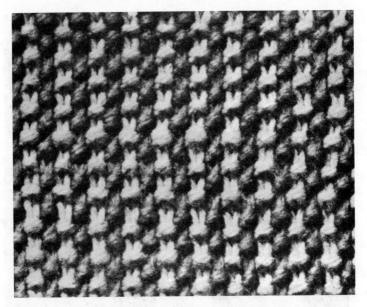

FIG. 104B.—Corn-on-the-Cob Stitch.

Row I (dark) (front of fabric): * K.1, S.1. * Repeat * to *.
Knit the last Stitch.

Row 2 (dark): * Yarn forward, S.1, yarn back, K.1. * Repeat
(*i.e.*, slip all light stitches and knit all dark, bringing yarn
forward and taking it back after each Slip Stitch).

Row 3 (light): * S.1, K.1 into back of stitch. * Repeat (*i.e.*, knit
all light stitches into back of stitch and slip all dark stitches),
keeping yarn to back throughout.

Row 4 (light): * K.1, yarn forward, S.1, yarn to back. * Repeat
(*i.e.*, knit light stitches and slip dark stitches. Yarn forward
and back as before).

Repeat from Row 1, knitting all dark stitches and slipping all
light stitches purlwise. Keep yarn to back throughout.

STRANDED SLIP STITCHES. PATTERN

The Stranded yarn is made to span across the front of the Slipped Stitch, and so becomes the repeating Motif. This Motif can have a Unit of one or several stitches, which can be arranged in groups, or to alternate, or to move diagonally.

An effect of weaving is obtained by alternating single units in both rows Knit and Purl as in Fig. 105.

△ Note the new symbol, which now has a line across the base to indicate that the strand is to show on the surface. Remember to read the charts correctly (*see* page 6).

WOVEN RIB. I AND I

The Motifs are arranged vertically.

Cast On an odd number of stitches.
> **Row I:** K.1. * Yarn forward, S.1, yarn to back, K.1. * Repeat * to *.
> **Row 2:** Purl.

Repeat these 2 rows.

WOVEN RIB. 2 AND 2

Cast On stitches divisible by 4 and 2 over.
> **Row I:** K.2. * Yarn forward, S.2, yarn back, K.2. * Repeat * to *. Keep the stranded yarn loose.
> **Row 2:** Purl.

Repeat these 2 rows.

WOVEN CHECK OR HOPSAC STITCH. *Figs. 105A and* B.

FIG. 105A.

FIG. 105B.—Hopsac Stitch.

An effect of weaving is given to the fabric by bringing the yarn forward between the needles before slipping the stitch and taking it to the back again after the stitch is slipped.   This can be done on Knit rows only or on both rows.   This Pattern should be knitted on △ large needles unless a thick close fabric is particularly required.

The motifs are alternated on both rows.

Cast On an odd number of stitches.

> **Row 1:** K.1.   * Yarn forward, S.1, yarn back, K.1. *   Repeat * to *.
>
> **Row 2:** P.2.   Yarn to back, S.1, yarn forward, P.1.

Repeat these 2 rows.

USES.   Close, warm fabric for gloves and sports wear.

HONEYCOMB SLIP STITCH.   *Figs. 106A and* B.

Round Fabric

For further illustration *see* Fig. 34, third sock top.

The Motifs are alternated on every second row.   Compare the charts, Figs. 106A and 107.   Can also be used in Flat Knitting, but then Rows 2 and 4 would be Purl.

Cast On an even number of stitches on each needle.

> **Round 1:** * P.1, S.1. *
> **Round 2:** Knit.
> **Round 3:** * S.1, P.1.*
> **Round 4:** Knit.

Repeat these 4 rounds.

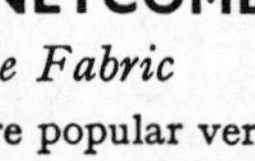

FIG. 106A.

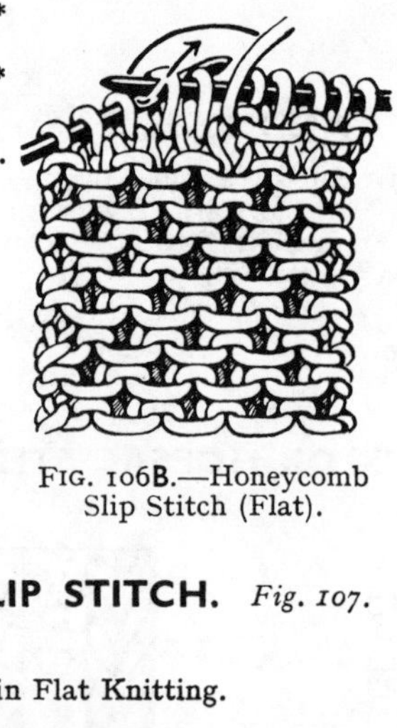

FIG. 106B.—Honeycomb Slip Stitch (Flat).

HONEYCOMB SLIP STITCH.   *Fig. 107.*

Single Fabric

More popular version in Flat Knitting.

Cast On an odd number of stitches.

> **Row 1** (front of fabric):   Knit.
> **Row 2:** K.1.   * S.1, K.1. *   Repeat * to *.
> **Row 3:** Knit.
> **Row 4:**   * S.1, K.1. *   Repeat, ending S.1.

Repeat these 4 rows.

FIG. 107.

HERRINGBONE SLIP STITCH. *Figs. 108A and* B.

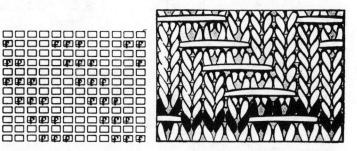

FIG. 108A.   FIG. 108B.—Herringbone Slip Stitch.

The stranded motif spans three stitches and moves diagonally.

Yarn forward between needles. Slip 3 stitches purlwise. Take yarn to back again and K.3. This is repeated all through the pattern and must be understood when S.3, K.3 is stated.

Cast On stitches divisible by 6.

Row I: * S.3, K.3. *   Repeat.
Row 2: Purl, and all even rows Purl.
Row 3: K.1.   * S.3, K.3. *   Repeat * to *, ending S.3, K.2.
Row 5: K.2.   * S.3, K.3. *   Repeat * to *, ending S.3, K.1.
Row 7: * K.3, S.3. *   Repeat.
Row 9: S.1   * K.3, S.3. *   Repeat * to *, ending K.3, S.2.
Row II: S.2.   * K.3, S.3. *   Repeat * to *, ending K.3, S.1.
Row 12: Purl.

Repeat these 12 rows.

SHADOW RIB DIAGONAL

The reverse side of Herringbone Slip Stitch as detailed above. This shows a Purl fabric with an illusive diagonal rib. Very smart for sports wear, cushions, etc.

BUTTERFLY SLIP STITCH. *Figs. 109A, B, and* C.

Method shows the stranded units arranged vertically to form separate repeating Butterfly Slip Motifs. The yarn is brought forward before slipping the stitches and taken back to continue knitting (*see* Fig. 109B). The Chart (Fig. 109A) shows the Motifs arranged to alternate. Edge stitches not shown.

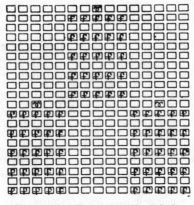

FIG. 109A.—Butterfly Slip Stitch. Chart.

Cast On stitches divisible by 10 and 4 over.

Rows 1, 3, 5, 7, and 9: K.2. * Yarn forward, S.5, yarn back, K.5. * Repeat * to *, ending yarn forward S.5, yarn back, K.2.

Rows 2, 4, 6, and 8: Purl.

Row 10: P.4. * On the next stitch, which is the middle of the 5 slipped stitches, insert the right needle upwards through the 5 loose strands and transfer them to the left needle. Now purl this stitch together with the 5 loose strands. Purl 9 more stitches. * Repeat * to *, ending P.4. (*see* Fig. 109C).

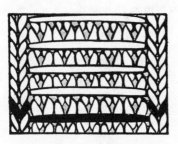

FIG. 109B.—Working method.

FIG. 109C.—Butterfly Slip Stitch.

Rows 11, 13, 15, 17, and 19: K.7. * S.5 (as before), K.5. * Repeat * to *, ending S.5, K.7.

Rows 12, 14, 16, and 18: Purl.

Row 20: P.9. * Purl and Butterfly the next stitch as in Row 10. P.9. * Repeat * to *.

Repeat these 20 rows.

LADDER AND HEMSTITCH MOTIFS AND PATTERNS

Designing Units—Dropped and Lengthened Stitches

A Ladder is made by dropping a stitch, which will leave an open space, as in Fig. 110. Long ladders in repeat make ornamental insertion-like Motifs, closely resembling Hemstitching. Shorter ladders are used as repeating spot Motifs (*see* Fig. 114).

Ladders are the first and simplest methods of imparting a lace-like or " open " effect to a knitted fabric, and can be given very elaborate expression.

A dropped stitch will only make a vertical ornament, so the nearest approach to "Hemstitching" running horizontally across the fabric must be made by lengthening the stitch, as in Fig. 117. This can be used as an ornamental horizontal insertion, or in repeat as an all-over open fabric. (Compare Figs. 112 and 123.)

Both methods, vertical and horizontal, are shown in the following designs, but since each has many special designing features, they are treated separately. Like the Slip Stitch, these Ladder Motifs are often blended with the Cross Motif (*see* Figs. 113 and 121).

CONTROLLING A DROPPED STITCH

△ Each Ladder, long or short, must be erected on a PLATFORM, which then becomes the buffer at which the stitch, when dropped, will stop. Without this, the Ladder would run as in a stocking, and so pass from a feature of design to an ugly mistake.

△ This Platform and the length of the Ladder form the repeating unit of design.

Care must be taken that the right "Ladder" stitch is dropped, and to avoid any mistake this can be arranged to contrast, such as a Purl Stitch on a Stocking Stitch Fabric (*see* Fig. 110), or a Knit Stitch on a Purl Fabric, or the centre stitch of a rib, as in Fig. 112.

A stitch, when dropped, will leave an open ladder space about three times the normal width of the stitch, and in closely spaced, long ladder patterns this will add considerably to the width of the fabric, so allowance must be calculated. For this reason a ladder can sometimes be used as a convenient means of enlarging the width of a garment.

MAKING A PLATFORM

Platform for a Single Ladder. ∆ *Make* 1. Raised (open). Abb. M.1 (R.o.). Raise the running thread between the stitches and knit an extra stitch (*see* Fig. 282).

Platform for a Double Ladder. At position for Ladder, cast off 2 stitches. On following row, knit up the loops of these 2 stitches and build the Ladder on this double buffer.

LONG-LADDER PATTERN. *Figs. 110*A *and* B.

Method of designing shown in Fig. 110A.

FIG. 110A.—Chart. Long-Ladder Pattern.

FIG. 110B.—Long-Ladder Pattern.

Cast On stitches divisible by 11 and 6 over.

Row 1: K.2. * M.1 (R.o.), K.2, M.1 (R.o.), K.9. * Repeat * to *, ending M.1 (R.o.), K.2, M.1 (R.o.), K.2.

Row 2: P.2, K.1 (this is the MADE stitch), P.2, K.1. * P.9, K.1, P.2, K.1. * Repeat * to *, ending P.2.

Row 3: K.2. * P.1, K.2, P.1, K.9. * Repeat * to *, ending P.1, K.2, P.1, K.2.

Repeat Rows 2 and 3 for the required length, and in casting off drop the Purl stitches off the needle and allow them to unravel to the original platform erected on the MADE stitch in Row 1.

USES. Long Ladders can be arranged on a Stocking Stitch ground as in Fig. 110A, but look more effective on a 4 and 4 or 6 and 6 Welt (*see* Fig. 22), as on these fabrics the vertical Ladders cross the horizontal Welts, and give an effect of checks. Experiment should be made.

DECORATIVE LADDER

When two or more stitches are dropped in pairs, as in Fig. 111, the Ladder needs further decoration as shown. Use matching yarn and count 4 bars up. Insert the needle downwards under 2 bars, and out over 2. Now twist the needle as directed by the arrows.

The stitches bordering the Ladder either side should be of similar character, as these then form an enclosure.

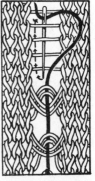

Wider borders of 2 or more Knit stitches can be used either side of the ladder, or more elaborate enclosures can be designed to take geometric shapes of half diamonds, chevrons, etc., when the Ladder is to occupy some important central position.

△ A double-width Ladder must have a Platform of two Cast-off stitches. On the next row knit-up the two loops, and build the ladder on these. When decorating include the loops of these 2 Cast-off stitches, to avoid a gap.

FIG. 111.—Decorative Ladder.

LONG-LADDER RIB. *Figs. 112A and B.*

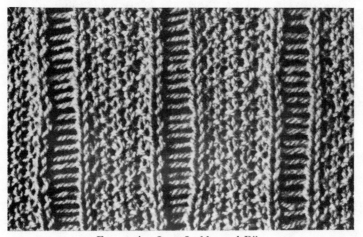

FIG. 112A.—Long Ladder and Rib.

The Ladder Motif is arranged between 2 Knit stitches which form a border and on a Moss-Stitch background.

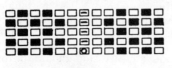

FIG. 112B.

Cast On stitches divisible by 7 and 5 over.

Row 1: * K.1, P.1, K.1, P.1, K.2, M.1 (R.o.), K.1. * Repeat, ending K.1, P.1, K.1, P.1, K.1.

Row 2: K.1, P.1, K.1, P.1, K.1. * P.3, K.1, P.1, K.1, P.1, K.1. * Repeat * to *.

Row 3: * K.1, P.1, K.1, P.1, K.4. * Repeat, ending K.1, P.1, K.1, P.1, K.1.

Repeat Rows 2 and 3 for required length.

In casting off drop all the MADE stitches (the centre stitch of every rib).

LONG-LADDER AND CABLE RIB. *Figs. 113A and B.*

FIG. 113A.

Designing Chart Fig. 113A.

This shows yet another and very favourite use of a Long-Ladder Motif, arranged either side of a Cable Pattern. The Platform stitch is repeated every 7th stitch in Row 1. The chart shows a simple method of designing such patterns. The crossed arrows indicate the position of the Cross-Over of the Cable Rib.

FIG. 113B.—Long-Ladder Motif dividing Cable Patterns.

SPOT-LADDER MOTIF PATTERN. *Figs. 114A, B, and C.*

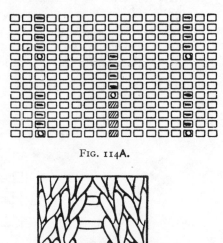

FIG. 114A.

FIG. 114B.—Working Method.   FIG. 114C.—Spot-Ladder Motif.

Shorter ladders can be arranged on the half-drop principle like Spot Motifs all over the fabric, as charted in Fig. 114A.

Each little ladder must start from its own platform on a MADE stitch (M.1 (R.O.), *see* Fig. 282), as shown by the BLACK stitch in Fig. 114B. This made stitch then becomes part of the fabric for 3 or more rows (or rounds). It is then dropped and reveals a little Ladder Motif erected over the original Platform stitch as in Fig. 114C. In charting these designs, note that the Ladder beginning on Row 5 is anticipated below by blank or lined spaces indicating no stitch. *See* Fig. 62.

Cast On stitches divisible by 10 and 4 over.
    Row 1: K.2. * M.1 (R.O.), K.10. * Repeat * to *, ending M.1 (R.O.), K.2.
    Row 2: Purl.
    Row 3: Knit.
    Row 4: Purl.

Row 5: K.2. * Drop 1, K.5, M.1 (R.o.), K.5. * Repeat * to *,
ending Drop 1, K.2.
Row 6: Purl.
Row 7: Knit.
Row 8: Purl.
Row 9: K.2. * M.1 (R.o.), K.5, Drop 1, K.5. * Repeat * to *,
ending M.1 (R.o.), K.2.

Repeat from Row 2 for required length.

BUTTERFLY DROP MOTIF.   *Figs. 115A, B, and C.*

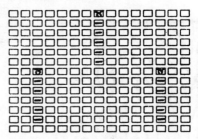

FIG. 115A.

FIG. 115B.—Working Method.

FIG. 115C.—Butterfly Drop Motif.

Butterfly Motifs (Fig. 115C) repeated on half-drop principle (*see* Fig. 115A)
all over the fabric.   △ No Platform stitch is necessary, as the basic stitch
is caught up and knitted (*see* Fig. 115B).

"To BUTTERFLY." Decide on length of ladder. In Fig. 115A this is six
rows down, leaving five strands. Insert needle in this stitch and unravel
to here (*see* Fig. 115 B).

To give the "Butterfly" effect, the five ladder-like strands are also
placed over the left needle, and the right needle inserted through the
stitch and the five strands, and all are knitted as one stitch (*see* Fig. 115C,
showing the completed "Butterfly"). The 7th row is coloured black so
that the journey of the yarn in this row can be clearly seen. The whole
action is referred to as "Butterfly".

Cast On stitches divisible by 10 and 5 over.
    Row 1: Knit.
    Row 2: Purl.
    Row 3: Knit.
    Row 4: Purl.
    Row 5: Knit.
    Row 6: Purl.
    Row 7: K.2. * Drop 1 for 5 rows and Butterfly, K.9. * Repeat * to *, ending Drop 1 and Butterfly, K.2.
    Rows 8 to 12: Stocking Stitch as before.
    Row 13: K.7. * Drop 1 and Butterfly, K.9. * Repeat * to *, ending Drop 1 and Butterfly, K.7.

Repeat from Row 2.

BUTTERFLY CLOQUÉ. *Fig. 116.*

Also known as COIN STITCH.

The same Butterfly Motif as in Figs. 115B and C is used, but spaced nearer together to give a blistered cloqué effect. This is accentuated by using two different colours, light and dark, or two tones of the same colour.

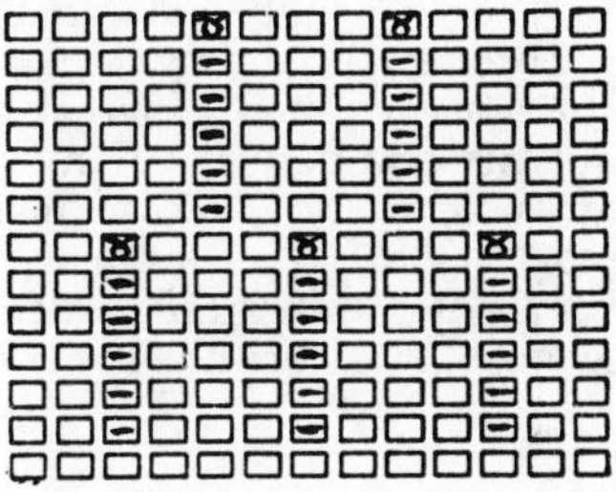

FIG. 116.

Cast On stitches divisible by 4 plus 5 edge stitches.
    Row 1 (dark): Knit.
    Row 2 (dark): Purl.
    Rows 3 to 6 (light): Stocking Stitch Fabric.
    Row 7 (dark): K.2. * Drop next stitch over 5 rows, picking up dark stitch of 2nd row and Butterfly, K.3. * Repeat * to *, ending Butterfly, K.2.
    Row 8 (dark): Purl.
    Rows 9 to 12 (light): Stocking Stitch.
    Row 13 (dark): K.4. * Butterfly, K.3. * Repeat * to *, ending K.1.
    Row 14 (dark): Purl.

Repeat from Row 3.

HORIZONTAL PATTERN

For horizontal " Hemstitched " Motifs and fabrics the stitches are increased in depth across the △ full width of the fabric. The effect can be obtained (1) Using a larger needle (Gauge Method), (2) throwing the yarn twice or more round the point of the needle and dropping the extra Throws in the next row (Elongated Method). Both methods enlarge the stitch and produce open rows across the fabric, and both can be worked from either the △ front or the back of the fabric. The patterns are designed in rows, so the number to cast-on depends on the width of fabric required.

GAUGE METHOD

The simplest method of enlarging a stitch is to use an occasional large needle, about twice the size or more. The needle then becomes the repeating unit, and can be used every other row, or every 4th or 6th row, according to pattern. The principle can be extended to 2 or even more different needle sizes, though there must be regularity and design. Many lace patterns permit of this treatment successfully, likewise many of the Crossed Patterns (*see* Fig. 94).

The varying of needle sizes is equivalent to changing the gauge of the " machine ". Hence the name Gauge Pattern.

GAUGE PATTERN

Use one small needle and one large needle twice the size of the small.

Cast On any number of stitches.
   Row 1: Small needle. Knit.
   Row 2: Large needle. Purl.

   Repeat Rows 1 and 2.

ELONGATED METHOD

The stitches are lengthened to any required depth in a Throw, and a row of extra long stitches can be afterwards decorated with Embroidery Stitches, Darning, Hemstitching, etc.

△ **MAKING A THROW.** *Figs. 117A and B.*

The stitches are lengthened by adding an extra Throw of the yarn taken over and round the needle △ after it has been inserted through the stitch. Normally it takes one Throw round the

FIG. 117A.—Row 1. Making a Throw.

FIG. 117B.—Row 2. Purl Stitch and Drop Throw.

needle to make a stitch; when another Throw is made, this makes it 2 Throws, or a Double Throw, as follows:

Insert needle knitwise into stitch and cast yarn twice round point of needle (*see* Fig. 117A) before knitting stitch. On next row purl stitch only and △ drop second Throw (*see* Fig. 117B). When row is completed, hold needle level and pull the fabric smartly to evenise length of all the stitches. A Throw can be made 2, 3, or 4 times round the point of the needle, according to depth of stitch required, but on the succeeding row, all the Throws are dropped (*see* Fig. 93).

△ Note the difference between a "Throw" and an "Over". A "Throw" is made △ after the needle is inserted into the stitch, but an "Over" is made △ before the needle is inserted into the stitch. (*see* Fig. 283). **Abb.** (K.1 (2 Throws)) or (K.1 (3 Throws)).

ELONGATED STOCKING STITCH. *Fig. 118.*

Cast On any number of stitches.
    Row 1: Knit, using " double Throw " on every stitch, as in Fig. 117A.
    Row 2: Purl, purling the stitch and dropping the second Throw (*see* Fig. 117B).

Repeat Rows 1 and 2.

FIG. 118.—Elongated Stocking Stitch.

Both sides of the fabric are decorative (*see* Fig. 119).
If a **very** " open " fabric is required, both rows can be elongated.

USES IN DESIGN

One row can be used as an insertion or repeated at wide intervals, or used singly as a row for any particular effect, such as a band of openwork across a garment at the yoke, etc.

DOUBLE ELONGATED STITCH (OPEN). *Fig. 119.*

This is knitted in the same way as Elongated Stitch, Figs. 117A and B, only THREE Throws are made instead of two.

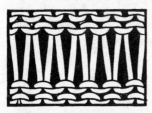

FIG. 119.—Double Elongated Stitch. Insertion.

Cast On any number of stitches.

Row 1: Knit. Insert the needle through the stitch and throw the yarn 3 times over the point and knit. Repeat this on each stitch.

Row 2: Purl, purling the stitch only, and dropping the second and third throws.

Repeat these 2 rows.

MAKING A FANCY CROSSED THROW. *Figs. 120A and B.*

This is a fascinating method of throwing the yarn in order to produce a firm, elongated Cross Stitch. Insert the needle knitwise

FIG. 120A.—Throwing the Yarn.

FIG. 120B.—Drawing through the Stitch.

into the stitch and throw the yarn under and over the right needle, and then under and over the left needle and under the right needle again, as in Fig. 120A. Slightly open the needles and draw through the loop, singly as shown in Fig. 120B, and slip it off the needle, together with the stitch and second throw.

The result in total is a row of deep Crossed stitches.

USES. A single row can be used as an Insertion, in imitation of hem-stitching (*see* Fig. 121), and on any suitable background shown in the Solid

Fabrics. When used as an Insertion on Fancy Fabrics, the preceding and succeeding rows should be of similar stitches, as in Figs. 123 and 124. Every row can be elongated, and so produce a fabric of Elongated Crossed Garter Stitch. This Fancy Throw can only be designed horizontally, and so achieves its best effect when begun on △ back rows, though it can be used in single rows on either side of the fabric.

FIG. 121.—Crossed Elongated Stitch.
Insertion.

ELONGATED CROSSED GARTER STITCH. *Fig. 122.*

Also known as CRESTED GARTER STITCH and VEIL STITCH.

KNITTED VEILS. Silk and fine wool veils and chignons are knitted using this stitch and large wooden needles, Size o.

FIG. 122.—Elongated Crossed
Garter Stitch.

Cast On any number of stitches. Begin on back of fabric.
Row 1: Insert the needle knitwise and throw the yarn as in Figs. 120A and B. Repeat on each stitch.
Row 2 and all succeeding rows the same.

At the end of each row, the stitches should be evenised by pulling the fabric smartly into shape all along the row. Hold the needle firmly while doing so,

CRESTED GARTER INSERTION STITCH. *Fig. 123.*

One row of stitches using Fancy Crossed Throw (Figs. 120**A** and **B**) on front rows is here used as a Hemstitch insertion on a fabric of Moss Stitch. The row before and after the insertion is Purl, so that it appears " enclosed ". Figs. 112 and 123 should be compared, as one shows the Vertical and the other the Horizontal use of the Designing Units.

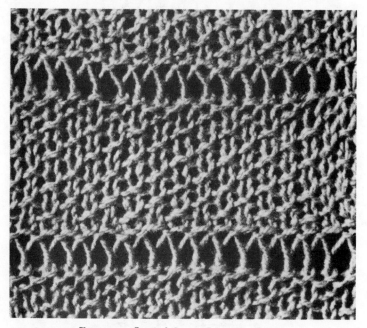

Fig. 123.—Crested Garter Insertion Stitch.

Cast On an uneven number of stitches.
    Rows 1 to 9: Moss Stitch.
    Row 10 (back of fabric): Knit.
    Row 11: Knit, using Fancy Crossed Throw as in Figs. 120**A** and **B**.
    Row 12: Knit.

Repeat these 12 rows, or increase the depth of Moss Stitch **Fabric** as required.

DOUBLE-CRESTED GARTER INSERTION STITCH.

Figs. 124A and B.

Two rows of stitches made with the Fancy Crossed Throw (Fig. 120), are used as an insertion between two different enclosures.   More elaborate enclosures consisting of Chevrons, etc., can also be designed.

FIG. 124A.

FIG. 124B.

First Design. *Fig. 124*A.

Cast On any number of stitches.
    Rows 1 to 7: Stocking Stitch.
    Row 8 (back of fabric): Knit, using Fancy Crossed Throw on all
            stitches.
    Row 9 : Knit, using Fancy Crossed Throw.
    Row 10: Knit.

Repeat from Row 1, or use as required.

Second Design. *Fig. 124*B.

The Insertion is enclosed between a Welt.

Cast On any number of stitches.
    Rows 1 to 9: Stocking Stitch.
    Row 10 (back of fabric): Knit.
    Row 11: Purl.
    Row 12 (back of fabric): Knit, using Fancy Crossed Throw on all
            stitches.
    Row 13: Knit, using Fancy Crossed Throw.
    Row 14: Knit.
    Row 15: Purl.
    Row 16: Knit.
    Rows 17 to 26: Stocking Stitch.

Repeat from Row 10, or use as required.

EYELET MOTIFS AND PATTERNS

Designing Units—Overs and Decreases

Each Knitted Eyelet or Hole is a small individual Motif repeated in much the same way as in Eyelet embroidery or *Broderie Anglaise*. It is the most ornamental Motif in knitting, and can be grouped in almost any geometric or floral shape (*see* Fig. 138). Each Eyelet is composed of two separate units :—

> 1. An Over.
> 2. A Decrease.

It is the Decrease which is the ornamental unit. In charting, each unit must occupy one square.

Eyelets can be Single, Double, Bold, Grand, and Reversed, so the technique of each is first described, and then shown in repeat designs.

SINGLE EYELETS

A Single Eyelet has one Over and one Decrease and so occupies 2 squares on the Chart. There are two different single Eyelets :—

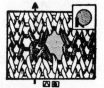

> 1. Chain Eyelet.
> 2. Open Eyelet.

CHAIN EYELET. *Fig. 125A and B.*

(O., K.2 tog.) Over, Knit 2 stitches together (*see* Overs, page 292).

The completed Eyelet is shown in Fig. 125. The first stitch of the Decrease falls **Δ** behind the second, which leaves the vertical chain of knitted stitches either side unbroken and relatively undisturbed (*see* arrow). This is a designing feature (*see* Fig. 128).

FIG. 125 A *and* B.— Chain Eyelet and Chart.

USES. Chain Eyelet is the simplest, and so the most popular Eyelet, and because of the unbroken chain it is the nearest approach to an embroidered Eyelet.

OPEN EYELET. *Fig. 126*A *and* **B.**

▲ ▲ The stitch is slipped knitwise, as it is part of a Decrease; *see* page 295 also Fig. 95 for comparison of Slip Stitch when used as a Pattern Principle.

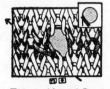

FIG. 126A *and* B.—
Open Eyelet and
Chart.

Over. Slip 1. Knit the next stitch and pass the slipped stitch over the knitted stitch (O., S.1, K.1, p.s.s.o.).

The completed Eyelet is shown in Fig. 126. The first stitch of the Decrease now falls ▲ over the second, and so breaks the vertical chain (*see* arrow), but draws the Eyelet more open.

USES. Open Eyelet is more individual, and so better as a single repeating motif (*see* Fig. 127).

SINGLE EYELETS IN DESIGN

For comparison of the two Eyelets *see* Fig. 127, and note the difference between the two Decreases when arranged in repeat on the fabric. They do not match. These two Eyelets should not be mixed indiscriminately on one fabric.

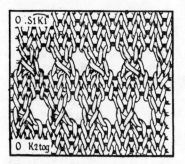

FIG. 127.—Comparison of Chain
and Open Eyelet.

Eyelets can be arranged horizontally, vertically, and diagonally, in the same way as any other motif. They can be grouped in geometric shapes, diamonds, etc., or used as repeating motifs, and lastly in free-hand designs, simple or elaborate, as inspired by designs prepared for *Broderie Anglaise*.

The objective in design is to retain the round open individuality of each Eyelet, so the first thing to ascertain is how close one Eyelet can approach the next without either losing its individuality.

Horizontally they can be grouped in rows as close together as possible, merely divided by the Decrease (*see* Fig. 128A).

Vertically each Eyelet must be divided by three rows (*see* Fig. 128A). If placed closer than this the Eyelet loses its individuality and becomes Faggot (*see* Fig. 147). When alternated and in diagonal pattern they appear nearer, but this is an illusion, as each Eyelet is still divided vertically by three stitches, grouped immediately beneath and above it (*see* Fig. 129B).

For close Diagonal grouping of Eyelets *see* Figs. 151 to 153, noting △ the shadowed part of each diagram. Any pair of these Diagonal lines, choosing the Eyelet or shadowed portion, can be arranged in the same Diagonal formations as in Fig. 149. Compare also Figs. 130 and 155.

YARNS AND NEEDLES

Needles and yarns should be kept proportionately fine, as large needles incline the Eyelet to become lank and degenerate into a loose HOLE. With a 3-ply wool use needles No. 12 (Standard Size 3).

BROKEN KEY PATTERN. *Figs. 128*A *and* B.

Showing vertical and horizontal arrangement of Chain Eyelet in the closest possible approach. Compare with Fig. 127.

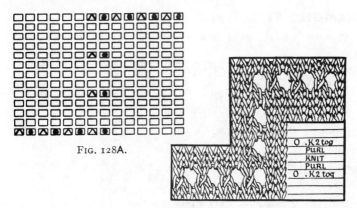

FIG. 128A.

FIG. 128B.—Broken Key Pattern.

Cast On stitches divisible by 14 and 4 over.

> **Row 1:** K.2. * K.6, (O., K.2 tog.) 4 times. * Repeat * to *, ending K.2.
>
> **Row 2:** Purl. (Purl all the overs.)
>
> **Row 3:** Knit.
>
> **Row 4:** Purl.
>
> **Row 5:** K.2. * K.6, O., K.2 tog., K.6. * Repeat * to *, ending K.2.

Rows 6, 7, and 8: Same as Rows 2, 3, and 4.
Row 9: Same as Row 5.
Rows 10, 11, and 12: Same as Rows 2, 3, and 4.
Row 13: K.2. * (O., K.2 tog.) 4 times, K.6. * Repeat * to *, ending K.2.
Rows 14, 15, and 16: Same as Rows 2, 3, and 4.

Repeat from Row 1.

EYELET RIB.

Vertical arrangement of Chain Eyelets alternated on Ribbed Fabric (3 and 2).

Cast On stitches divisible by 10 and 2 over.
Row 1: P.2.   * K.1, O., K.2 tog., P.2, K.3, P.2. * Repeat * to *.
Row 2: * K.2, P.3. * Repeat, ending K.2.
Row 3: P.2. * K.3, P.2, K.1, O., K.2 tog., P.2. * Repeat * to *.
Row 4: * K.2, P.3.* Repeat, ending K.2.

Repeat from Row 1.

DIAMOND EYELET PATTERN. *Figs. 129A and* B.

Showing diagonal lines of Chain Eyelet in diamond design.

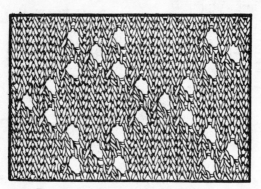

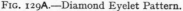

Fig. 129A.—Diamond Eyelet Pattern.

Cast On stitches divisible by 12 and 6 over.
Row 1: K.2.   * O., K.2 tog., K.10. * Repeat * to *, ending O., K.2 tog., K.2.
Row 2: Purl.
Row 3: K.4.   * O., K.2 tog., K.6, O., K.2 tog., K.2. * Repeat * to *, ending K.2.
Row 4: Purl.

Row 5: K.6. * O., K.2 tog.,
             K.2, O., K.2 tog.,
             K.6. * Repeat *
             to *.
Row 6: Purl.
Row 7: K.8. * O., K.2 tog.,
             K.10. * Repeat
             * to *, ending O.,
             K.2 tog., K.8.
Row 8: Purl.
Row 9: Same as Row 5.
Row 10: Purl.
Row 11: Same as Row 3.
Row 12: Purl.

FIG. 129B.—Chart.

Repeat these 12 rows.

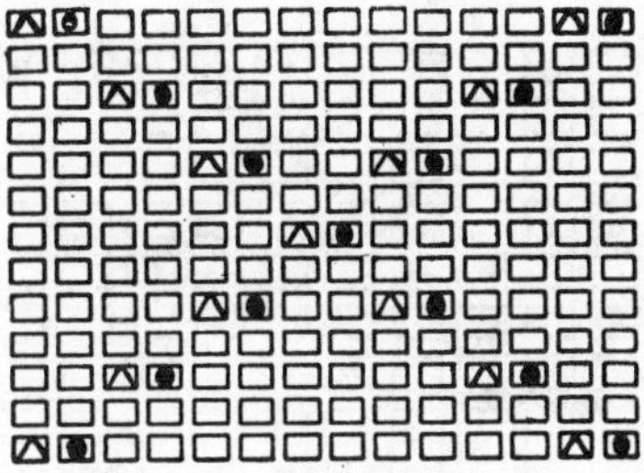

SPOT EYELET PATTERN.

Also known as BRODERIE ANGLAISE FABRIC.

Open Eyelet used as a repeating motif.
For principle of designing Spot pattern *see* Fig. 57.

Cast On stitches divisible by 12 and 6 over.
Row 1: K.2. * O., S.1, K.1, p.s.s.o., K.10. * Repeat * to *,
            ending O., S.1, K.1, p.s.s.o., K.2.
Row 2: Purl.
Row 3: Knit.
Row 4: Purl.
Row 5: K.8. * O., S.1, K.1, p.s.s.o., K.10. * Repeat * to *,
            ending O., S.1, K.1, p.s.s.o., K.8.
Row 6: Purl.
Row 7: Knit.
Row 8: Purl.

Repeat these 8 rows.

DIAGONAL DIAMOND EYELET PATTERN (CENTRED). *Figs. 130*A *and* B.

The pattern is derived by using the Shadowed Eyelet parts of the diagonal lines shown in Figs. 151A and B, and this Chart and Pattern should be compared with Figs. 155A and B, and the difference noted. In Fig. 130 the open spaces are spanned by the Decrease, making the Eyelet, and in consequence are thicker than those in Fig. 155, where they are spanned by the Over, making the Faggot Stitch.

The Chart shows the number of spaces between the designing units in Row 9, widest part of the diamond, to be 6, an even number. (The Picot Eyelet in the centre is merely ornamental.) In Fig. 155 the number is 5, uneven, because the doubling unit at the top of this diamond is the Decrease and can be made on 3 stitches, and so need occupy only 3 spaces on the

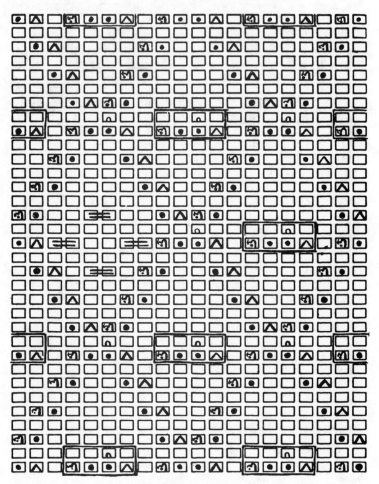

FIG. 130A.—Chart.

Chart.   The Double Over at the top of the diamond in Fig. 130 must occupy 4 spaces.   So any Diagonal Diamond Eyelet must always be founded on an even number of spaces.

The centre of the diamond can be decorated as desired.   Here a Picot Eyelet, Fig. 132, is used, but the large diamond to the left of the chart suggests how Clustering Tie Stitch, Fig. 228, could be used with good results.

FIG. 130B.—Diagonal Diamond Eyelet Pattern (Centred).

The ladder-like effect shown at the top of the Pattern is derived by repeating *ad lib* Rows 9 and 10. The chart shows that Rows 1 and 9 are the chief pattern lines of this design, and experiment will reveal that great variety of effect and design can always be obtained Δ by repeating the chief pattern lines twice or several times as required. This applies to all patterns. It is a technical way of deriving and varying pattern, and experiment with some of the Lace and Solid patterns will often yield beautiful and even unexpected effects. Knitting, to the designer and the knitter, is never dull, there is always a surprise like this round the corner!

Cast On stitches divisible by 10, plus 4 for edge.

Row 1: K.2, O., S.1, K.1, p.s.s.o. * K.1, K.2 tog., O.2, S.1, K.1,
      p.s.s.o. * Repeat * to *, ending K.1, K.2 tog., O., K.2
      on last 5 stitches.

Row 2: Purl, and all even rows Purl.

Row 3: K.2. * K.2 tog., O., K.6, O., S.1, K.1, p.s.s.o. * Repeat
      * to * ending K.2.

Row 5: K.3. * K.2 tog., O., K.4, O., S.1, K.1, p.s.s.o., K.2. *
      Repeat * to *, ending K.3 instead of 2.

Row 7: K.4. * K.2 tog., O., K.2, O., S.1, K.1, p.s.s.o., K.4. *
      Repeat * to *.

Row 9: K.2, O., S.1, K.1, p.s.s.o. * K.1, K.2 tog., O.2, S.1, K.1,
      p.s.s.o. * Repeat * to *, ending K.1, K.2 tog., O.,
      K.2 on last 5 stitches.

Row 11: K.5. * O., S.1, K.1, p.s.s.o., K.2 tog., O., K.6. *
      Repeat * to *, ending K.5 instead of 6.

Row 13: K.4. * O., S.1, K.1, p.s.s.o., K.2, K.2 tog., O., K.4. *
      Repeat * to *.

Row 15: K.3. * O., S.1, K.1, p.s.s.o., K.4, K.2 tog., O., K.2. *
      Repeat * to *, ending K.3 instead of K.2.

Row 16: Purl.

Repeat these 16 Rows.

DOUBLE EYELETS

The Motif has now 4 designing units so must occupy four squares on the Chart.

To make a Double Eyelet the Over is preceded and succeeded by a Decrease. The Over can be Single or Double, but in the following row, △ whether it be Single or Double, it must be first purled and then knitted, in order to restore the correct number of stitches to the needle.

The decorative value of this Eyelet depends on the correct order or pairing of the decreasing units, the beauty of which can be seen in Fig. 134A.

There are two Double Eyelet Motifs :—

    1. Embroidery Eyelet.
    2. Picot Eyelet.

EMBROIDERY EYELET. *Fig. 131.*

FIG. 131.

The Chart shows that this Eyelet also has a unit of four squares, as the single Over is converted into two stitches in the next row to make good the number swallowed up by the 2 Decreases. Note the blank space left because of the single Over for this purpose. This makes a large clear round Eyelet.

Row 1: K.2 tog., O., S.1, K.1, p.s.s.o.

(Note the Over is single, and so has no picot, but the Decrease is double and paired, as before.)

Row 2: Purl the stitches, Δ and purl and knit into the Over.

PICOT EYELET. *Figs. 132A and B.*

The chart (Fig. 132A) shows that this Eyelet has a unit of four squares, and in design the full unit must be used to express each eyelet (*see* Fig. 134B). This makes a heart-shaped eyelet with a Picot centre.

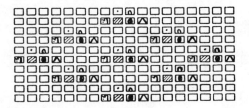

Fig. 132A.   Fig. 132B.—Picot Eyelet.

Row 1: K.2 tog., O.2, S.1, K.1, p.s.s.o.
Both the Over and the Decrease are double. The decreases shown in Figs. 125 and 126 (Chain and Open Eyelet) are used as a pair, one either side of the eyelet. The Double Over forms the picot in the middle.

Row 2: Purl all stitches and Purl the first Over and Knit the second.

EMBROIDERY EYELET DIAMOND PATTERN. *Figs. 133A and B.*

A simple repeating motif employing the use of Embroidery Eyelet Pattern charted to shown Diamond Motif only from Row 3 and edge stitches not shown.

Cast On stitches divisible by 21 and 3 over.
Row 1: Knit.

Fig. 133A.

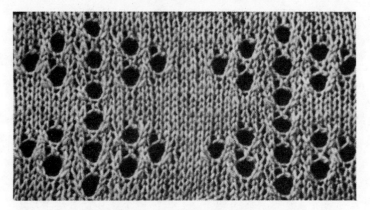

FIG. 133B.—Embroidery Eyelet Diamond Pattern.

Row 2: Purl.
Row 3: K.10. * K.2 tog., O., S.1 (k.w.), K.1, p.s.s.o., K.17. *
Repeat * to * ending K.10, instead of 17.
Row 4: Purl. Purl and Knit into each Over.
Row 5: K.6. * K.2 tog., O., S.1, K.1, p.s.s.o., K.4, K.2 tog., O.,
S.1, K.1, p.s.s.o., K.9. *   Repeat * to * ending K.6,
instead of 9.
Row 6: Purl. Purl and Knit into each Over.
Row 7: K.3. * K.2 tog., O., S.1, K.1, p.s.s.o., K.3. *   Repeat
* to *.
Row 8: Purl. Purl and Knit into all the Overs.
Row 9: Same as Row 5.
Row 10: Purl. Purl and Knit into each Over.
Row 11: Same as Row 3.
Row 12: Purl. Purl and Knit into each Over.

Repeat from Row 1.

PICOT EYELET DIAMOND PATTERN. *Figs. 134A and B.*

A design in Picot Eyelet. This motif when arranged Fan Shape is
sometimes known as PEACOCK'S TAIL PATTERN. The success of this pattern
depends entirely on the correct Pairing of the Decreasing Units. *See*
Fig. 297. Edge Stitches are not shown in Chart.
△ **Abb.:** (K.2 tog., O.2, Sl.1, K.1, p.s.s.o.) twice; repeat bracket twice
or as many times as the number states.

Cast On stitches divisible by 28 and 12 over.
Row 1: Knit.
Row 2: Purl.

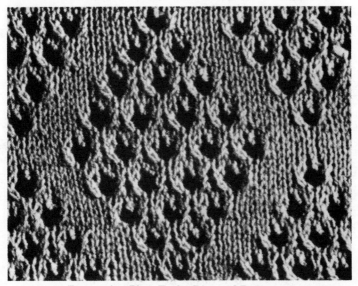

FIG. 134A.—Picot Eyelet Diamond Pattern.

Row 3: K.2. * (K.2 tog., O.2, Sl.1, K.1, p.s.s.o.) three times, K.4, K.2 tog., O.2, Sl.1, K.1, p.s.s.o., K.4, K.2 tog., O.2, Sl.1, K.1, p.s.s.o. * Repeat * to *, ending (K.2 tog., O.2, Sl.1, K.1, p.s.s.o.) twice, K.2.

Row 4: Purl. Purl the first Over and Knit the second. Purl the single Over once.

Row 5: Knit.

Row 6: Purl.

Row 7: K.2, O., Sl.1, K.1, p.s.s.o. * (K.2 tog., O.2, Sl.1, K.1, p.s.s.o.) twice, K.4, (K.2 tog., O.2, Sl.1, K.1, ps.s.o.) twice, K.4, K.2 tog., O.2, Sl.1, K.1, p.s.s.o. * Repeat * to *, ending K.2 tog., O.2, Sl.1, K.1, p.s.s.o., K.2 tog., O., K.2, on last 8 stitches.

Rows 8, 9, and 10: Same as Rows 4, 5, and 6.

Row 11: K.2. * (K.2 tog., O.2, Sl.1, K.1, p.s.s.o.) twice, K.4, (K.2 tog., O.2, Sl.1, K.1, p.s.s.o.) three times, K.4. * Repeat * to *, ending (K.2 tog., O.2, Sl.1, K.1, p.s.s.o.) twice, K.2.

Rows 12, 13, and 14: Same as Rows 4, 5, and 6.

Row 15: K.4. * K.2 tog., O.2, Sl.1, K.1, p.s.s.o., K.4, (K.2 tog., O.2, Sl.1, K.1, p.s.s.o.) four times, K.4. * Repeat * to *, ending K.2 tog., O.2, Sl.1, K.1, p.s.s.o., K.4.

Rows 16, 17, and 18: Same as Rows 4, 5, and 6.

Row 19: K.2.   * K.8, (K.2 tog., O.2, Sl.1, K.1, p.s.s.o.) five times. *
Repeat * to *, ending K.10.
Rows 20, 21, and 22: Same as Rows 4, 5, and 6.
Row 23: Same as Row 15.
Rows 24, 25, and 26: Same as Rows 4, 5, and 6.
Row 27: Same as Row 11.

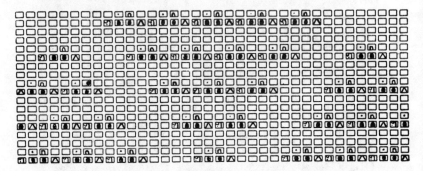

FIG. 134B.

Rows 28, 29, and 30: Same as Rows 4, 5, and 6.
Row 31: Same as Row 7.
Rows 32, 33, and 34: Same as Rows 4, 5, and 6.
Row 35: Same as Row 3.
Rows 36, 37, and 38: Same as Rows 4, 5, and 6.
Row 39: K.2, O., S.1, K.1, p.s.s.o.   * (K.2 tog., O.2, Sl.1, K.1,
p.s.s.o.) three times, K.8, (K.2 tog., O.2, Sl.1, K.1,
p.s.s.o.) twice. *   Repeat * to *, ending K.2 tog., O.2,
Sl.1, K.1, p.s.s.o., K.2 tog., O., K.2.
Row 40: Same as Row 4.

Repeat from Row 1.

CAT'S EYE PATTERN. *Fig. 135.*

Simple Shetland lace pattern, using Double Eyelet with unpaired
decreases.   The Double Over is made in Row 1, while the two decreasing
units are carried over to Row 2.   Makes a large eyelet and no picot.   For
further illustration of this pattern, *see* Fig. 159.   Fabric reversible.

Cast On stitches divisible by 4, plus 4 edge stitches.
Row 1: K.2.   * K.2, O.2, K.2. *   Repeat * to *, ending K.2.
Row 2: P.2.   * P.2 tog., P.1, K.1 (into Overs), P.2 tog. *   Repeat
* to *, ending P.2.

Row 3: K.2, O. * K.4, O.2. * Repeat * to *, ending K.4, O., K.2.

Row 4: P.2. Purl the Over. * P.2 tog., P.2 tog., P.1, K.1 into Overs. * Repeat * to *, ending Purl the Over. P.2.

Repeat these 4 rows.

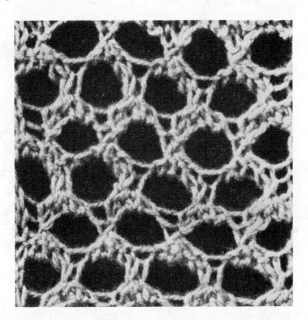

FIG. 135.—Cat's Eye.

EYELET BEADING.

Cast On 6 stitches.

Row 1: S.1 (edge stitch), S.1, K.1, p.s.s.o., O.2, K.2 tog., K.1.

Row 2: S.1, K.2, P.1, K.2.

Rows 3 and 4: Knit.

Repeat from Row 1 or use Rows 1 and 2 as insertion, as required.

BOLD EYELETS

Each Eyelet needs 4 rows before it is completed, and is extra large and bold. The repeating Motif in chart form is shown in Fig. 136A. (*See also* Fig. 138A.) △ Remember to read chart correctly (*see* page 5).

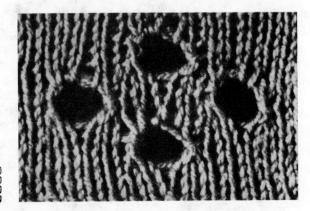

FIG. 136A.   FIG. 136B.—Bold Embroidery Eyelet.

BOLD EMBROIDERY EYELET. *Figs. 136A and B.*

In Design, both Eyelets, Bold or Twin, can be grouped in the same way as all other Eyelets, only producing bolder effects. Either can be used for Lace and Lace Edgings, and are particularly successful for special effects such as the centre of a flower as in Fig. 138.

Experiment on ten stitches to see method of making Eyelet only.

Row 1: K.3, K.2 tog., O.2, S.1, K.1, p.s.s.o., K.3.
Row 2: P.3, P.2 tog. (stitch and 1st Over), K.2 tog. (2nd Over and stitch), P.3.
Row 3: K.4, or Knit to eyelet, and here O.2, and finish row.
Row 4: P.3, P.2 tog. (stitch and 1st Over, △ including strand below), K.1, P.1, into 2nd Over and △ strand below. Finish row.

Be careful to include the strand below in 4th row, otherwise the eyelet is not " Bold " but " Twin ".

TWIN EMBROIDERY EYELET. *Fig. 137.*

This Eyelet is knitted as for Bold Embroidery Eyelet, with a difference in the 4th row, Δ as the strand below is omitted in making the decrease.

Rows 1, 2, and 3: Same as for Bold Embroidery Eyelet.

Row 4: P.2 tog. (stitch and 1st Over), K.1, P.1, into 2nd Over.

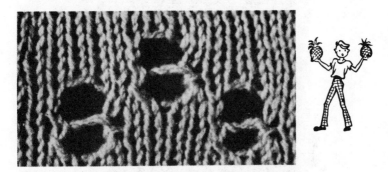

FIG. 137.—Twin Embroidery Eyelet.

BRODERIE ANGLAISE MOTIF. *Figs. 138A and B.*

UNITS : Bold Embroidery Eyelet and Chain Eyelet.

The Bold Embroidery Eyelet commences in Row 27 (*see* Chart).

These directions are given for a single Motif, but can be used as an all-over pattern by casting on stitches divisible by 16, plus edge stitches. Rows 35–38 are optional and not on Chart, but they improve the shape of Flower Motif.

Cast On 16 stitches.

Row 1: Knit.

Row 2: Purl.

Row 3: K.6, O., S.1, K.1, p.s.s.o., K.2, O., S.1, K.1, p.s.s.o., K.4.

Row 4: Purl. Purl Overs.

Row 5: K.8, O., S.1, K.1, p.s.s.o., K.6.

Rows 6 and 8: Purl.

Row 7: K.6, O., S.1, K.1, p.s.s.o., K.8.

Row 9: K.4, O., K.1, S.1, p.s.s.o., K.10.

Row 10: Purl.

Row 11: (K.2, O., S.1, K.1, p.s.s.o.) 3 times, K.4.

Row 12: Purl.

Row 13: K.8, O., S.1, K.1, p.s.s.o., K.6.

Row 14: Purl.

Row 15: K.10, O., S.1, K.1, p.s.s.o., K.4.

Row 16: Purl.

FIG. 138A.—Broderie Anglaise Motif Chart.

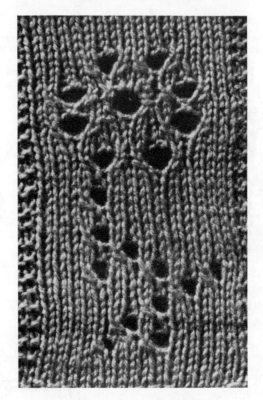

FIG. 138B.—Broderie Anglaise Motif.

Row 17: Knit.
Row 18: Purl.
Row 19: K.10, O., S.1, K.1, p.s.s.o., K.4.
Row 20: Purl.
Row 21: Knit.
Row 22: Purl.
Row 23: K.4 (K.2 tog., O.2, S.1, K.1, p.s.s.o.) twice, K.4.
Row 24: Purl.   Purl the 1st Over and Knit the 2nd.
Row 25: Knit.
Row 26: Purl.
Row 27: K.2, K.2 tog., O.2, S.1, K.1, p.s.s.o., K.4, K.2 tog., O.2,
          S.1, K.1, p.s.s.o., K.2.
Row 28: Purl, as Row 24.
Row 29: K.6, K.2 tog., O.2, S.1, K.1, p.s.s.o., K.6.

Row 30: P.6, P.2 tog. (stitch and 1st Over), K.2 tog. (2nd Over and stitch), P.6.

Row 31: K.2, K.2 tog., O.2, S.1, K.1, p.s.s.o., K.1, O.2, K.1, K.2 tog., O.2, S.1, K.1, p.s.s.o., K.2.

Row 32: P.6, P.2 tog. (stitch and Over, including strand below), P.1, K.1 into Over and strand, P.7.

Row 33: Knit.

Row 34: Purl.

Row 35: Same as Row 27.

Rows 36, 37, 38: Same as Rows 24, 25, 26.

Row 39: K.4 (K.2 tog., O.2, S.1, K.1, p.s.s.o.) twice, K.4.

Row 40: Purl, same as Row 24.

GRAND EYELET

A double or treble Over can be used and three, four, or five stitches made into this one Over. A classic example is Fig. 140, Diadem Eyelet Pattern, and a simple example is Fig. 139.

REVERSIBLE GRAND EYELET LACE.

Fig. 139. (*See* page 130).

Both sides of the fabric are alike.

Knit the 3rd row loosely, and use well-pointed and strong needles. If preferred, a larger needle (four sizes) can be used for Row 3. For further illustration of this pattern, *see* Fig. 159.

Cast On stitches divisible by 4, plus 4 edge stitches.

Row 1: P.2. * O., P.4 tog. * Repeat * to *, ending P.2.

Row 2: K.2. * K.1, (K.1, P.1, K.1) into Over. * Repeat * to *, ending K.2.

Row 3: Knit.

Repeat these 3 rows.

GRAND EYELET EDGING.

Cast on and knit 3 rows only of Grand Eyelet Lace (Fig. 139).

From here continue garment or article as required. These 3 rows will make an effective picot edging to cuffs, collars, ties, etc.

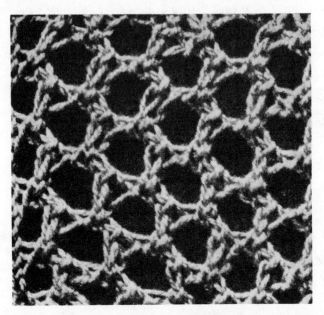

FIG. 139.—Reversible Grand Eyelet Lace.

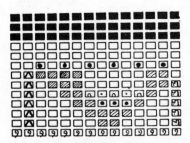

FIG. 140A.

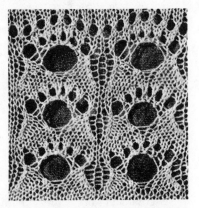

FIG. 140B.—Lace Diadem Eyelet.

LACE DIADEM EYELET PATTERN. *Figs. 140A and* B.

Also known in the Shetlands as THE CROWN OF GLORY PATTERN, and as CAT'S PAW !

This beautiful pattern consists of one Grand Eyelet with a crescent of six eyelets above it, the whole constituting one repeating motif only, and built on the Lace principle. The units are divided. The Decreases are arranged vertically either side, and in every row, front and back, which necessitates the use of the Purl Reverse (P.R.) in pairing. *See* Fig. 293. The Grand Eyelet is clustered in on Row 3, but the full quota of stitches is not made good until Row 7, and consolidated in Row 8. So it is built on the minus principle. Note the lined spaces on chart, indicating no stitch.

The Motif takes 13 stitches and 8 rows to complete, and here is shown in vertical repeat, plus one knit stitch which is used to divide the repeat. This stitch is strained open to a vase-like shape because of the minus character of the design. Horizontally the motif is divided by a Welt, as also shown in chart.

The first 8 rows of pattern therefore describe the Diadem Motif only, plus 1 K. St (14th space in chart), so the designer can arrange the motif in any formation required, the favourite Shetland method being the Half Drop Spot, *see* Figs. 56 and 57, when it is then known as Cat's Paw.

Cast On 14 stitches and 5 over.

Row 1: K.3. * S.1, K.1, p.s.s.o., K.9, K.2 tog., K.1. * Repeat * to *, ending K.2.

Row 2: P.2. * P.1, P.2 tog., P.7, P.R. * Repeat * to *, ending P.3.

Row 3: K.3. * S.1, K.1, p.s.s.o., K.2, O.3, K.3, K.2 tog., K.1. * Repeat * to *, ending K.2.

Row 4: P.2. * P.1, P.2 tog., P.2, (K.1, P.1, K.1, P.1, K.1), making 5 into Over, P.1, P.R. * Repeat * to *, ending P.3.

Row 5: K.3. * S.1, K.1, p.s.s.o., K.6, K.2 tog., K.1. * Repeat * to *, ending K.2.

Row 6: P.2. * P.1, P.2 tog., P.6. * Repeat * to *, ending P.3.

Row 7: K.3. * K.1, (O., K.1) 6 times, K.1. * Repeat * to *, ending K.2.

Row 8: Purl.

Row 9: Knit.

Row 10: Knit.

Row 11: Purl.

Row 12: Knit.

Repeat from Row 1.

NOTE.—To end or divide the pattern with a row of Eyelets, as in Fig. 140B, work Rows 11 and 12 as follows:—

Row 11: K.2. * (K.2 tog., O.) 7 times. * Repeat * to *, ending row with K.3

Row 12: Purl.

REVERSE PURL EYELET

This Eyelet is single and preferably designed in horizontal rows, and for bold effect on Purl Fabric, or between Purl Rows. A special method of throwing the yarn is necessary (*see* Over (Reversed), Fig. 289). The units occupy 2 squares in the Chart.

RIBBON EYELET. *Figs. 141A and B.*

Also known as GOFFER STITCH.

FIG. 141A.

FIG. 141B.—Ribbon Eyelet or Goffer Stitch.

O. (Revd.), P.2 tog.   Use Over (Reversed) as in Fig. 289.   The Stocking Stitch Fabric between the rows of Eyelets can be made to any depth required.   For further illustration of this Eyelet *see* Figs. 142 and 143.

Cast On an even number of stitches.
    Row I: Knit.
    Row 2: Knit.
    Row 3: P.1.   * O. (Revd.), P.2 tog. *   Repeat * to *, ending P.1.
    Row 4: Knit, knitting the Overs through the back.
    Row 5: Knit.
    Row 6: Purl.
    Row 7: Knit.
    Row 8: Knit.
    Row 9: P.2.   * O. (Revd.), P.2 tog. *   Repeat * to *.
    Row 10: Knit, knitting the Overs through the back.
    Row 11: Knit.
    Row 12: Purl.
Repeat from Row 1.

DIMPLE EYELET. *Fig. 142.*

Using Over (Reversed) as in Fig. 289.

Cast On an even number of stitches.
 Row 1: Knit.
 Row 2: Purl.
 Row 3: P.1. * O. (Revd.), P.2 tog. * Repeat * to *, ending P.1.
 Row 4: Purl, purling the Overs through the back.

FIG. 142.—Dimple Eyelet.

 Row 5: Knit.
 Row 6: Purl.
 Row 7: P.2. * O. (Revd.), P.2 tog. * Repeat * to *.
 Row 8: Purl, purling the Overs through the back.

Repeat from Row 1.

REVERSE EYELET CHECK. *Figs. 143A and B.*

The rows of Reversed Eyelets are broken by blocks of Stocking Stitch Fabric. Many fascinating designs can be arranged on this principle, as this Eyelet is always effective on a Purl ground of any shape. Here it is a small cube, but it could be diamond or any other shape.

NOTE.—In Rows 4 and 10 the Over (Reversed) is knitted through the back of the Over.

Cast On stitches divisible by 8, plus 3 edge stitches.
 Row 1: K.2. * P.3, K.5. * Repeat * to *, ending K.1.

FIG. 143B.—Reverse Eyelet Check.

Row 2: P.1.   * P.5, K.3. *   Repeat * to *, ending P.2.
Row 3: K.2.   * P.1, O. (Revd.), P.2 tog., K.5. *   Repeat * to *, ending K.1.
Row 4: P.1.   * P.5, K.3. *   Repeat * to *, ending P.2.
Row 5: K.2.   * P.3, K.5. *   Repeat * to *, ending K.1.
Row 6: Purl.
Row 7: K.1.   * K.5, P.3 *   Repeat * to *, ending K.2.
Row 8: P.2.   * K.3, P.5. *   Repeat * to *, ending P.1.
Row 9: K.1.   * K.5, P.1, O. (Revd.), P.2 tog. *   Repeat * to *, ending K.2.
Row 10: P.2.   * K.3, P.5. *   Repeat * to *, ending P.1.
Row 11: K.1.   * K.5, P.3. *   Repeat * to *, ending K.2.
Row 12: Purl.

Repeat these 12 rows.

FIG. 143A.

FAGGOT STITCH AND LACE FAGGOT STITCH MOTIFS

Designing Units—Overs and Decreases.

The name Faggot Stitch immediately suggests the dainty embroidery used for fancy seaming on dresses, lingerie, etc., and Faggot Stitch in knitting has much the same object (*see* Fig. 144), but with this difference—the knitted fabric is not cut and decoratively rejoined, but stitch and fabric are made at the same time, so the position of the Faggot Stitch lines must be planned out beforehand.

FIG. 144.—Decorative use of Faggot Stitch.

Faggot Stitch numbers amongst our oldest patterns, and was extensively used by the Master Knitters of the fifteenth and sixteenth centuries. The silk knitted knee-breeches of the early sixteenth century shown in Fig. 146 are an excellent example. Here the knitter has also imitated the then fashionable ribbon-like sections as worn on sleeves and breeches. Needless to say, these are not cut; each narrow section is knitted a certain number of rows, and when all are the same length they are united as a row by knitting straight across. The photo shows the back of the breeches, but the front is made in the same way, each little section being appropriately decorated with chevrons in Faggot Stitch.

THE FAGGOT STITCH MOTIF

The Faggot Stitch Motif consists of two separate units and these occupy two separate squares in the Chart :—

1. An Over.
2. A Decrease.

It is the △ OVER which makes the Faggot effect (*see* Fig. 145).

FIG. 145.—Making a Faggot Motif.

135

Historical Museum, Dresden.

Fig. 146.—Silk Knitted Breeches, old gold colour, early sixteenth century (back view), showing several Faggot Stitch patterns, also pockets and simulated strappings which are continued on the front.

There are two types : (1) Faggot Stitch Motif; (2) Lace Faggot Stitch Motif.

△ In Faggot Stitch Motif the Faggot has two strands, as the units are used on front rows only, and all back or even rows are Purl. In this way each Over is made on one row and purled in the next, and this makes the second strand (*see* Fig. 147).

These are Warp Motifs, and so can only be arrayed in vertical or diagonal lines.

△ In Lace Faggot Motif Stitch the units are used on △ every row, so the Over is not purled on the succeeding row, and thus appears as a single strand (*see* Fig. 169). These are **Welt Motifs,** and so can be arranged horizontally.

DESIGNING FAGGOT STITCH PATTERN

The Faggot Stitch Motif is composed of the same units as Eyelets, so it is only the order of arrangement that makes distinctive design.

The units can be arranged to make vertical or diagonal lines, as shown in Figs. 148 and 155, also Fig. 144, but not horizontal lines, because in this order the Over which makes the Faggot Stitch gets lost, and the Motif becomes an Eyelet (*see* in Fig. 147). Compare Figs. 147A and **B** and Figs. 128A and **B**, as these show the limitations of both Motifs, Faggot Stitch and Eyelet, and

FIG. 147A.

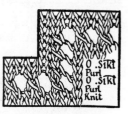

FIG. 147B.—Comparing Faggot Stitch and Eyelet.

since both employ the same units, this subtle difference should be noted.   In making a Faggot Stitch Motif the Over can precede the Decrease (O., K.2 tog.) or (O., S.1, K.1, p.s.s.o.)—or it can succeed the Decrease (K.2 tog., O.) △

△ There is, of course, a difference, because in knitting two stitches together the fabric is reduced or thickened at that particular spot by two stitches instead of one.   In long vertical repeats this will cause bias.   If the Over △ precedes the Decrease (O., K.2 tog.) the bias is to the right (*see* Fig. 156); if the Over △ succeeds the Decrease (K.2 tog., O.) the bias is to the left.

This natural bias is put to very clever use, as shown later.

When vertical lines are required in △ pattern they should be short, as in Fig. 148 because of this bias.   Long vertical lines can be used singly as insertions on garments (*see* Fig. 144).   Here the Decrease used to form the Faggot on the right of the garment should be reversed for those on the left, changing O., S.1, K.1, p.s.s.o. to K.2 tog., O.   This will correct bias and also give balance in design.

In diagonal arrangement the position of the Decrease (before or after the Over) varies, according to the diagonal, right or left. This is specially treated (Figs. 151–153).

The Charts in all cases show how the Motifs repeat in design.

LITTLE WINDOWS. *Figs. 148A and* B.

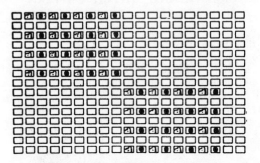

FIG. 148A.

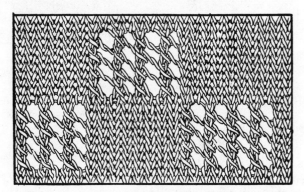

FIG. 148B.—Little Windows.

The " Little Windows " are oblong, but the same short lines can be grouped in other formations—diamonds, pyramids, or step patterns, etc. The Motif is repeated on front rows only (*see* Fig. 148A).

Cast On stitches divisible by 16 and 3 over.
    Row 1: K.2. * (O., S.1, K.1, p.s.s.o.) four times, K.8. *   Repeat
      * to *, ending K.1 on last stitch.
    Row 2 and all even rows: Purl.
    Rows 3, 5, and 7: Same as Row 1.
    Row 9: K.2. * K.8, (O., S.1, K.1, p.s.s.o.) four times. *   Repeat
      * to *, ending K.1.
    Rows 11, 13, and 15: Same as Row 9.
    Row 16: Purl.

Repeat these 16 rows.

DESIGNING DIAGONAL FAGGOT STITCH INSERTIONS

There are two diagonal lines to consider : one running to the right, and one to the left.

These lines can be long and sweep across the fabric right and left to form a lattice, as in Fig. 155A, or they can be short and grouped, as in Fig. 149 (A) Zig-zag lines; (B) Chevrons; (C) Diamonds (*see* Fig. 159 for these lines in pattern).

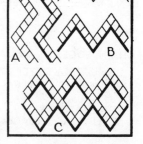

FIG. 149.—Designs in Right and Left Diagonals.

The Faggot Stitch Motif can be arranged to take all these shapes, but in moving diagonally the decreasing unit forms a decorative line or edge, as shown in Figs. 151–153, and must be arranged to pair. Also, the order of the two units must be varied, according to the diagonal, right or left, so as to keep the Over clearly defined as a Faggot Stitch. If this is not done, the units form diagonal lines of Eyelets as shown by the shadowed parts of Figs. 151–153.

△ In forming a right diagonal, the Decrease precedes the Over (*e.g.*, K.2 tog., O.).

△ In forming a left diagonal the Decrease succeeds the Over (*e.g.*, O., S.1, K.1, p.s.s.o.).

There are three different Decreases used in Diagonal Faggot : (1) K.2 tog.; (2) S.1, K.1, p.s.s.o.; (3) K.2 tog. B. (*see* page 303). Each produces a different decorative edge : (1) Chain; (2) Soft; (3) Crossed. This necessitates six diagrams to show each edge correctly made on a left and right diagonal, and the △△ two edges which pair correctly left and right should be used together in forming chevrons, diamonds, etc., as in Figs. 146, 149, and 158.

These valuable diagrams should always be consulted when diagonal lines of Faggot Stitch or Eyelets are required. Compare Figs. 130 and 155.

PRACTICAL EXPERIMENT

The chart Fig. 150 shows Fig. 151B only. Knit this as follows and note the mistake.

Cast On 7 stitches ; all even rows are purled.
   Row 1: K.1, K.2 tog., O., K.4.
   Row 3: K.2, K.2 tog., O., K.3.

FIG. 150.

Row 5: K.3, K.2 tog., O., K.2.
Row 7: K.4, K.2 tog., O., K.1.
Row 9: K.3, K.2 tog., O., K.2.
Row 11: K.2, K.2 tog., O., K.3.
Row 13: K.1, K.2 tog., O., K.4.

Afterwards knit the light parts only of both Figs. 151A and B, and see the difference—*i.e.*, the decreasing unit for Rows 1 to 7 will be "O., S.1, K.1, p.s.s.o.", and on Rows 9 to 13, "K.2 tog., O." Figs. 152 and 153 can be tried out on the same seven stitches, using the different Decreases as indicated on the white parts of the diagrams only.

CHAIN EDGE. *Figs. 151*A *and* B.

How to obtain a right and left diagonal line of Faggot stitches bordered with a hard chain edge (*see* light parts of diagrams).

LEFT DIAGONAL. O., S.1, K.1, p.s.s.o. The Decrease succeeds the Over, and encroaches one stitch to the left in each Knit row.

FIG. 151A.—Chain Edge, Left.

FIG. 151B.—Chain Edge, Right.

FIG. 152A.—Soft Edge, Broken Left.

RESULT. Faggot stitches bordered on left with hard chain edge (bottom half). This same order of units on a right diagonal produces Eyelets, and not Faggot Stitch, and so can only be used for Eyelet patterns.

RIGHT DIAGONAL. K.2 tog., O. Here the Decrease precedes the Over and moves one stitch to the right on each Knit row, as in Fig. 150.

RESULT. Faggot stitches bordered on the right with a hard chain edge (top half).

(The shadowed part shows that this same order of units on a left diagonal produce Eyelets, so cannot be used in Faggot patterns. This also applies to Figs. 152 and 153.)

△ These two light portions form a pair and should be used left and right when forming long lines as in Fig. 155, or short lines as in Fig. 146.

SOFT BROKEN EDGE. *Figs. 152A and B.*

LEFT DIAGONAL. O., K.2 tog. The Decrease succeeds the Over.

RESULT. Faggot stitches bordered on left with a soft broken edge (bottom half).

| FIG. 152B.—Soft Edge, Broken Right. | FIG. 153A.—Crossed Broken Edge, Left. | FIG. 153B.—Crossed Broken Edge, Right. |

RIGHT DIAGONAL. S.1, K.1, p.s.s.o., O. The Decrease precedes the Over.

RESULT. Faggot stitches bordered on right with a soft broken edge (top).

(Below, Eyelets as before.)

△ These two Right and Left diagonals form a second and alternative pair.

CROSSED BROKEN EDGE. *Figs. 153A and B.*

LEFT DIAGONAL. O., K.2 tog. B. The Decrease succeeds the Over.

RESULT. Faggot stitches bordered on left with edge of Crossed stitches.

RIGHT DIAGONAL.   K.2 tog. . B., O.   The Decrease precedes
the Over.

RESULT.   Faggot stitches bordered on right with edge of Crossed
stitches.
Δ These two lines offer a third choice.

QUEEN BESS'S STOCKINGS

Fig. 154 shows a pair of silk stockings worn by Queen Elizabeth,
an excellent example of Tudor knitting.   The pattern is composed
of diamonds in Faggot Stitch, each diamond being a separate
and complete motif, and not linked as in Fig. 153.   The design can
accordingly be planned by selecting a pair of diagonal lines as in
Figs. 151–153 and grouping them in diamond formation.

By courtesy of Lord Salisbury.

FIG. 154.—Silk Stockings, early sixteenth century, worn by Queen
Elizabeth.   Fabric in Diamond Faggot Stitch.

FAGGOT DIAMOND PATTERN.   *Figs. 155A and* B.

Showing how to use these diagonal lines in pattern.
The Decreases used are those shown in Figs. 151A and **B**, Chain Edge.
The chart (Fig. 155A) shows the methods of designing an all-over Diamond
Faggot.   The diagonal lines sweep left and right across the chart, and
where they cross a Double Decrease can be used instead of two Single

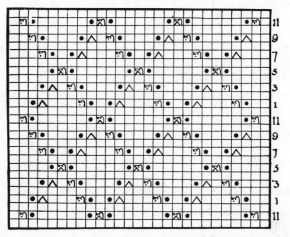

FIG. 155A.—Chart, Faggot Diamond Pattern.

Decreases. This make the point of the diamond sharper, but makes it necessary that the widest part of the Diamond should always be an odd number in width. *See* Chart, where the number is 5. Also compare with Figs. 130A and B.

Cast On stitches divisible by 8 and 3 over.
    Row 1: K.2. * O., S.1, K.1, p.s.s.o., K.3, K.2 tog., O., K.1. *
         Repeat * to *, ending K.1.
Row 2 and all even rows: Purl.

FIG. 155B.—Faggot Diamond Pattern.

Row 3: K.3. * O., S.1, K.1, p.s.s.o., K.1, K.2 tog., O., K.3. * Repeat * to *.

Row 5: K.4. * O., S.1, K.2 tog., p.s.s.o., O., K.5. * Repeat * to *, ending K.4 instead of 5.

Row 7: K.3. * K.2 tog., O., K.1, O., S.1, K.1, p.s.s.o., K.3. * Repeat * to *.

Row 9: K.2. * K.2 tog., O., K.3, O., S.1, K.1, p.s.s.o., K.1. * Repeat * to *, ending K.1.

Row 11: K.1, S.1, K.1, p.s.s.o., O.   * K.5, O., S.1, K.2. tog., p.s.s.o., O. * Repeat * to *, ending K.5, O., S.1, K.1, p.s.s.o., K.1.

Repeat these 11 rows.

TRELLIS FAGGOT PATTERN. *Figs. 156A and* B.

Also known as TRELLIS GROUND LACE.

An all-over mesh of Faggot stitches, to be used as a ground or finish to lace. Either method of forming Faggot Stitch can be used, but the position of the Over, before or after the Decrease, changes the angle of bias. △ On a chart this is not suspected, as the pattern on paper appears vertical (*see* Fig. 156A).

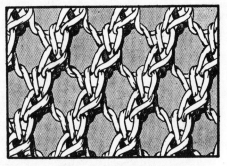

FIG. 156A.   FIG. 156B.—Trellis Faggot Pattern.

Right Bias. *Figs. 156A and* B.

The Over precedes the Decrease.

Cast On an odd number of stitches.
Row 1: K.1. * O., K.2 tog. * Repeat * to *
Row 2: Purl.

Repeat these 2 rows.

Left Bias.

The designing units are reversed, the Over succeeding the Decrease, so the bias is now in the opposite direction.

Cast On an odd number of stitches.
  Row I: * S.1, K.1, p.s.s.o., O. *   Repeat, ending K.1.
  Row 2: Purl.

Repeat these 2 rows.

VERTICAL TRELLIS FAGGOT.

The designing units of the two preceding examples are alternated on every other row, and so a better vertical effect is obtained.

Cast On an odd number of stitches.
  Row I: K.1.   * O., K.2 tog. *   Repeat * to *.
  Row 2: Purl.
  Row 3: * S.1, K.1, p.s.s.o., O. *   Repeat, ending
            K.1.
  Row 4: Purl.

Repeat these 4 rows.

ZIG-ZAG TRELLIS FAGGOT.

For method of charting, *see* Fig. 157A, omitting rib.

Cast On an even number of stitches.
  Rows I, 3, and 5: K.1.   * O., K.2 tog. *   Repeat * to *, ending
            K.1.
  Row 2 and all even rows: Purl.
  Rows 7, 9, and II: K.1.   * S.1, K.1, p.s.s.o., O. *   Repeat * to *,
            ending K.1.
  Row 12: Purl.

Repeat these 12 rows.

ZIG-ZAG TRELLIS FAGGOT AND RIB FANTASTIC.
Figs. 157A and B.

Also known as RIBBING FANTASTIC.

A rib of 3 stitches is introduced at intervals between Zig-zag Trellis Lace, and this, instead of being vertical, as the chart suggests, will follow a zig-zag course, in common with the bias of the Faggot Motif.   △ For the opposite of this, *see* Welting Fantastic, Fig. 178.

Rib can be made of any width, and the zig-zags of greater depth by increasing the number of rows from 12 to as many as required before changing the bias order of units.

The chart shows method of designing, only one-third of the number of rows being charted to save space (*see also* Fig. 158A).

Cast On stitches divisible by 19, plus 4 edge stitches.
Rows 1–11 (odd numbers): K.2. * (O., K.2 tog.) 4 times, K.3. *
Repeat * to *, ending (O., K.2 tog.) 4 times, K.2.

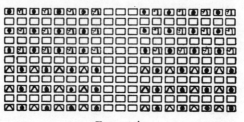

FIG. 157A.

Row 2 and all even rows: Purl.
Rows 13–23: K.2. * (S.1, K.1, p.s.s.o., O.) 4 times, K.3. * Re-
peat * to *, ending (S.1, K.1, p.s.s.o., O.) 4 times, K.2.
Row 24: Purl.

Repeat these 24 rows.

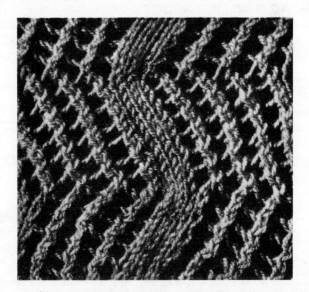

FIG. 157B.—Zig-zag Trellis and Rib Fantastic.

DESIGNING A FAGGOT STITCH BORDER

TRELLIS FAGGOT BORDER.—Figs. 158A and **B** show a practical use made of the Right and Left bias of Faggot Stitch, as explained in Fig. 156, which permits of a triangular shape being introduced quite naturally within the Faggot borders.

On the right of the Border is a vertical Faggot Stitch Insertion, on the left the Faggot takes first a Left bias (S.1, K.1, p.s.s.o., O.) as far as the point, and from here a Right bias (O., K.2 tog.).

The triangular portion between is built up on to this space, using a visible Increase (Over), which thus becomes an extra half Faggot Motif, *i.e.*, O. instead of O., K.2 tog., and so an additional Faggot decoration.

△ This Building Increase is no longer necessary after Row 13, as the triangle begins to decrease, but to maintain a symmetrical border the Faggot Stitch made by the Over must be retained, so it is converted into a full Faggot Stitch Motif, O., K.2 tog., and the triangle is diminished in shape by an extra Decrease (S.1, K.1, p.s.s.o., O.). The designing principle can be clearly seen by studying the chart (Fig. 158A) together with the written directions.

The triangle is completed at Row 27, and will be rebuilt again within the following point. The same Motif can be repeated, or another triangular Motif of different design introduced, and the two arranged to alternate (*see also* Fig. 159).

Figs. 158A and B, should be kept as an example of design for all Borders, △ as all the Decreases have been carefully paired and the Border scientifically planned. The points of the Border can be made to greater depth, and so enclose a still larger triangle by increasing the number of rows before and after the point. The principle of design will remain unaltered.

PICOT EDGE.—Lace edgings of this type are often finished with little Picot points. These are Edge Overs (Fig. 286), made before beginning the return row, *i.e.*, the row knitted with the back of the Lace facing the knitter. If long picots are desired, then O.2 is made before beginning the row. △ On the next row this Over is dropped, and not knitted, otherwise it would become an Increase instead of an ornament.

TRELLIS FAGGOT BORDER. *Figs. 158A and* B.

The square brackets enclose stitches forming the solid triangular shape in the middle. △ Before and after these are the Faggot stitches, forming the Border on the right and the Edge on the left. Compare with chart.

The first six stitches form the border. These are detailed in full in Row 1, and afterwards called " Border ". The edge is dealt with in the same way. Note the change of decrease at Row 15, which continues to Row 25.

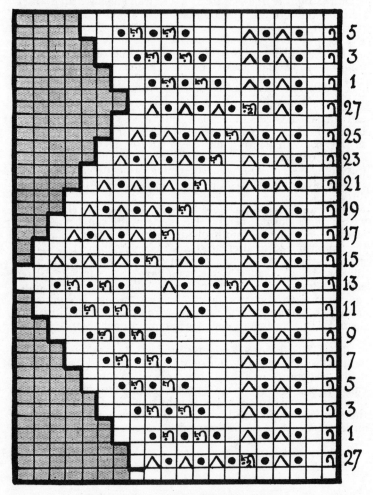

FIG. 158A.—Trellis Faggot Border Chart.

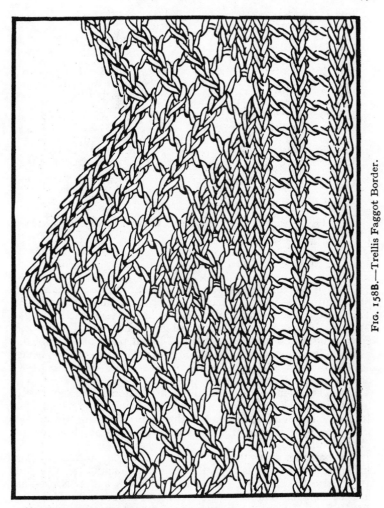

FIG. 158B.—Trellis Faggot Border.

Cast On 13 stitches.

All even rows are Purl.

Slip the first stitch purlwise in all Knit rows.

Row 1: BORDER: S.1, K.1, O., K.2 tog., O., K.2 tog., TRI-ANGLE [K.1, O.], EDGE (S.1, K.1, p.s.s.o., O.) twice, K.2.

Row 3: Border as in Row 1. [K.2, O.] Edge as in Row 1.

Row 5: Border. [K.3, O.] Edge.

Row 7: Border.   [K.4, O.]   Edge.
Row 9: Border.   [K.5, O.]   Edge.
Row 11: Border.   [K.2, O., K.2 tog., K.2, O.]   Edge.
Row 13: Border.   [S.1, K.1, p.s.s.o., O., K.1, O., K.2 tog., K.2, O.]   Edge.
Row 15: Border.   [K.2, O., K.2 tog., K.1, S.1, K.1, p.s.s.o., O., K.2 tog.]   Edge (O., K.2 tog.) twice, K.1.
Row 17: Border.   [K.4, S.1, K.1, p.s.s.o., O., K.2 tog.]   Edge as in Row 15 and from here onwards.
Row 19: Border.   [K.3, S.1, K.1, p.s.s.o., O., K.2 tog.]   Edge.
Row 21: Border.   [K.2, S.1, K.1, p.s.s.o., O., K.2 tog.]   Edge.
Row 23: Border.   [K.1, S.1, K.1, p.s.s.o., O., K.2 tog.]   Edge.
Row 25: Border.   [S.1, K.1, p.s.s.o., O., K.2 tog.]   Edge.
Row 27: S.1, K.1, O., K.2 tog., O., S.2, K.1, p.2s.s.o., O., K.2 tog. Edge.
Row 28: Purl.

Repeat from Row 1.

△ NOTE in Row 27 Double Central Chain Decrease is used (*see* Fig. 296).

LACE SAMPLER

Fig. 159 is a unique sampler of triangular shapes, collected for fitting into lace edgings such as described in Figs. 158A and **B**. The knitter, in making the collection, has divided each triangle by a double zig-zag of Faggot Stitch, which runs through the entire length and unifies the many different patterns assembled.

The edge consists of Faggot Stitch points, but these, being added to a straight edge, and not a triangle, as in Fig. 158, appear quite different, and for this reason.

The formation of all the different patterns can be easily followed, and should afford a simple exercise in original design. In studying the lace, remember that the points are always on the left. One length of lace faces in the wrong direction (a photographic licence).

The patterns show the Zig-zag line, Chevrons and Diamonds in Faggot Stitch, explained in Figs. 146–149 and Figs. 151 and 153. Also the small lace Motif in Figs. 158A and **B** is used as a Spot design. The other patterns are Cat's Eye and Grand Eyelet Lace. Eyelets are also used as Spot effects on different backgrounds.

Stadt Kunstgewerke Museum, Leipzig

FIG. 159.—Sampler of Triangular Motifs in different Faggot
Stitch Patterns.

DESIGNING LACE FAGGOT STITCH

Also known as GARTER LACE GROUNDS.

In all the previous Faggot Stitch patterns the designing units have been used on front rows only (*i.e.*, every other row), but in the more elaborate Lace Faggot Stitch the units are used on both rows, front and back, and also permit of horizontal arrangements and so of horizontal insertions and all-over " Ground " fabrics.

The Motif is still composed of an Over and a Decrease, but the Over can now be single or double, and the Decrease Knit or Purl. Experiment should be made with all the different Decreases shown on pages 295 to 299, as each will produce a different effect, and in an all-over repeat a different Lace Ground.

These " grounds " stand in the same relation to Lace Fabrics as Knit or Stocking Stitch Fabric stands to all previous designs. They are lace backgrounds, and carry solid Motif patterns (*see* Figs. 169 and 194), but they can be, and often are, used as all-over garment fabrics, since they make very attractive mesh Laces (*see* Fig. 168). They have a crisp quality and better width than Trellis Faggot Pattern, Fig. 156, as the units, being in both rows, have little or no bias.

FIGS. 160–168.

This collection shows both Faggot Stitch and Lace Faggot Stitch Motifs arranged as vertical insertions, bordered with edge stitches. To make a wide fabric, the whole of the directions, including edge stitches, can be used as a repeat. This will make an insertion-like fabric, or the Motif only can be repeated, thus making a lace mesh. The chart beneath each drawing shows the △ Motif only, without edge stitches. These Lace Fabrics look prettier knitted on fine needles.

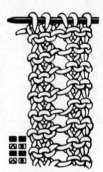

FIG. 160A and B.—
Purl Beading.

PURL BEADING.   *Fig. 160A and* B.

Showing Faggot Motif on Garter background.

Cast On 5 stitches.
   Row I: S.1, P..w, K.1, O., K. .og., K.1.
   Row 2: S.1, P.w., K.4.

Repeat these 2 rows.

WIDE FAGGOT BEADING. *Fig. 161.*

Using a double Over, dropping it in next row.

Cast On 5 stitches.
    Row 1: S.1, P.w., K.1, O.2, K.2 tog., S.1.
    Row 2: Purl. (Purl one Over and drop the
        second.)

Repeat these 2 rows.

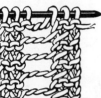

FIG. 161.

DOUBLE LADDER BEADING.
    Fig. 162 A and **B.**

The Over is double, and one is knitted
and the second purled. Edges in Garter
Stitch.

Cast On 6 stitches.
    Row 1: K.1, K.2 tog., O.2, K.2 tog.,
        K.1.
    Row 2: K.3, P.1 (the second Over),
        K.2.

Repeat these 2 rows.

Alternative: The same Beading, but
    using paired Decreases would be
    as follows:—

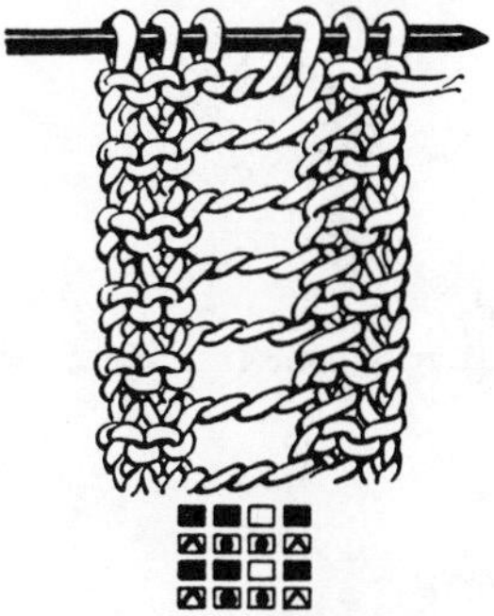

FIG. 162A and B.—Double
Ladder Beading.

Cast On 6 stitches.
    Row 1: K.1, K.2, O.2, S.1, K.1, p.s.s.o., K.1.
    Row 2: K.3, P.1 (the second Over), K.2.

Repeat these 2 rows.

LADDER BEADING

The ladder is similar to Fig. 162, but the edges are in Stocking Stitch.

Cast On 6 stitches.
    Row 1: K.1, S.1, K.1, p.s.s.o., O.2, K.2 tog., K.1.
    Row 2: P.3, K.1 (the second Over), P.2.
Repeat these 2 rows.

LACE LADDER INSERTION

Only one strand forms the ladder, instead
of a twisted strand, as in Fig. 162.

Cast On 6 stitches.
    Row 1: K 1, S.1, K.1, p.s.s.o., O.2, K.2 tog., K.1.
    Row 2: P. P.2 tog., O.2, P.1 (this is the second Over), return to
        left needle, take next stitch over, return to right needle, P.1.

Repeat these 2 rows.

LACE HERRINGBONE INSERTION. *Fig. 163A and B.*

Cast On 6 stitches.
    Row 1: S.1 (purlwise), (K.2 tog., O., K.2), S.1 (purlwise).
    Row 2: P.1, (K.2 tog., O., K.2), P.1.

Repeat these 2 rows.

To increase width repeat as between brackets, casting on 4 extra for each repeat.

USES. Often used for knitting string belts, using single or double Macramé string.

FIG. 163A and B.—Lace Herringbone Insertion.

LACE HERRINGBONE INSERTION REVERSED. *Fig. 164A and B.*

Cast On 6 stitches.
    Row 1: S.1, K.2, O., K.2 tog., K.1.

Repeat on all rows.

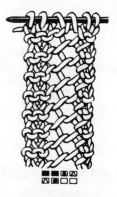

FIG. 164A and B.—Lace Herringbone Insertion Reversed.

FIG. 165A and B.—Double Herringbone Lace Faggot Insertion.

DOUBLE HERRINGBONE LACE FAGGOT. *Fig. 165A and B.*

Cast On 7 stitches.
    Row 1: S1, K.1, O., K.2 tog., O., K.2 tog., K.1.

All rows are the same.

LACE FEATHER FAGGOT INSER-
TION. *Fig. 166A and B.*

Cast On 4 stitches.
    Row 1: K.1, O., P.2 tog., K.1.

Repeat on every row.

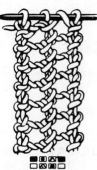

FIG. 166A and B.—Lace Feather Faggot Insertion.

VANDYKE FAGGOT. *Fig. 167.*

For extra repeats add 3 more stitches and repeat between the brackets.

Cast On 5 stitches.
    Row 1: S.1 (purlwise), (K.1, O.2, K.2 tog.), S.1 (purlwise).
    Row 2: Purl. Drop the second Over.
    Row 3: S.1 (purlwise), (K.2 tog., O.2, K.1), S.1 (purlwise).
    Row 4: Purl. Drop the second Over.

Repeat these 4 rows.

FIG. 167.

PURSE STITCH. *Fig. 168A and B.*

Also known as LACE FAGGOT STITCH GROUND.

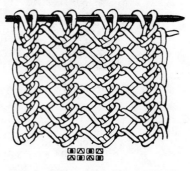

FIG. 168A and B.—Purse Stitch.

So called because it was used for knitting fine silk purses, such as Stocking and Miser purses, either with or without beads. It is also known as " Weft " of " Faggoting ", and looks exceedingly pretty knitted in cotton yarns for garments, gloves, etc. Two rows across a fabric will give a horizontal insertion.

Cast On an even number of stitches.
> **Row I:** Yarn forward, Over, P.2 tog.   * O., P.2 tog. *   Repeat * to *

Repeat on every row.

ZIG-ZAG LACE FAGGOT STITCH AND HORSESHOE PATTERN. *Figs. 169*A *and* B.

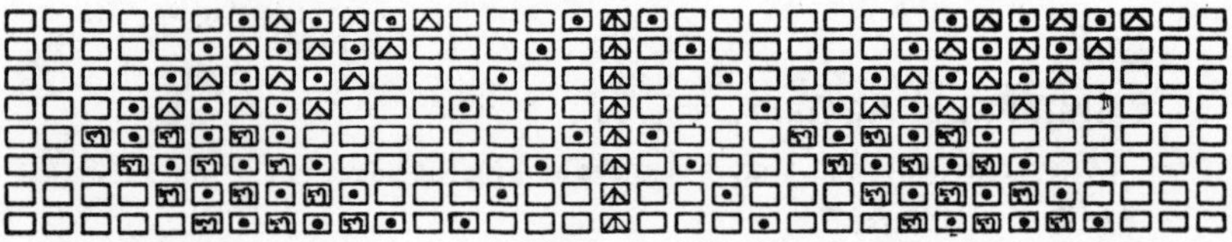

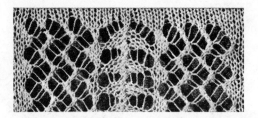

FIG. 169A.

For Horseshoe Pattern *see* Fig. 183. This is here inserted on a Lace Faggot background. The small " V "-shape points are built up in the same way as the triangle in the lace edging (Fig. 158). Compare chart with Fig. 157B to see the difference between Lace Faggot and Faggot. P.R. = Purl Reverse, *see* Fig. 293. Edge Stitches are shown on chart.

FIG. 169B.—Zig-zag Lace Faggot and Horseshoe.

Cast On stitches divisible by 19, plus 10 to end, and 4 edge stitches.
> **Row I:** K.2. * K.1, (O., S.1, K.1, p.s.s.o.) 3 times, K.3, O., K.3, K.3 tog., K.3, O. * Repeat * to *, ending K.1, (O., S.1, K.1, p.s.s.o.) 3 times, K.5.

Row 2: P.4, (P.R., O.) 3 times, P.2. * P.1, O., P.2, P.3 tog., P.2, O., P.3, (P.R., O.) 3 times, P.2. * Repeat * to *, ending P.2.

Row 3: K.2. * K.3, (O., S.1, K.1, p.s.s.o.) 3 times, K.3, O., K.1, K.3 tog., K.1, O., K.2. * Repeat * to *, ending K.3, (O., S.1, K.1, p.s.s.o.) 3 times, K.3.

Row 4: P.2, (P.R., O.) 3 times, P.4. * P.3, O., P.3 tog., O., P.3, (P.R., O.) 3 times, P.4. * Repeat * to *, ending P.2.

Row 5: K.2. * K.3, (K.2 tog., O.) 3 times, K.1, O., K.3, K.3 tog., K.3, O. * Repeat * to *, ending K.3, (K.2 tog., O.) 3 times, K.3.

Row 6: P.4, (O., P.2 tog.) 3 times, P.2. * P.1, O., P.2, P.3 tog., P.2, O., P.3, (O., P.2 tog.) 3 times, P.2. * Repeat * to *, ending P.2.

Row 7: K.2. * K.1, (K.2 tog., O.) 3 times, K.5, O., K.1, K.3 tog., K.1, O., K.2. * Repeat * to *, ending K.1, (K.2 tog., O.) 3 times, K.5.

Row 8: P.6, (O., P.2 tog.) 3 times. * P.3, O., P.3 tog., O., P.7, (O., P.2 tog.) 3 times. * Repeat * to *, ending P.2.

Repeat these 8 rows.

LACE FAGGOT CHAIN. *Fig. 170.*

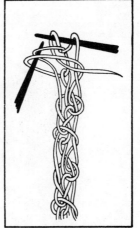

A knitted chain to be used for threading can be made as follows :—

The Over is made as before a Purl Selvedge Stitch. *See* Fig. 286.

Cast On 2 stitches.

Row 1: Yarn at back of needle. Insert needle purlwise through the 2 stitches and purl them together. (* O., P.2 tog. *)

Repeat for length required.

FIG. 170.—Lace Faggot Chain.

LACE FAGGOT FRINGE.   *See Figs. 40B and 103B.*

The cushions Figs. 40 and 103 are finished with a knitted fringe made as follows :—

Take four separate balls of yarn, two of light colour and two of dark colour.   △ The four yarns are held together and knitted four-fold.   Knit two lengths sufficient for short sides of cushion.   Cast off with care.

Cast On stitches divisible by 3.   (For the cushion fringe cast on 6 only.)
Row 1: * K.1, O., K.2 tog. *   Repeat.
Row 2 and each succeeding row: the same.

Repeat for length required, then cast off in the following special way.

△ Cast off 3 stitches only and draw through yarn and finish. Drop the remaining 3 stitches and unravel all 3 to the base of the strip, these will then form a looped fringe as shown in Figs. 40 and 103.   When making wider fringes the number cast off must be proportionate.

BIAS FABRICS

Designing Units—Made Stitches and Decreases.

Sports, School, or Regimental colours usually run diagonally across the fabric, or take some chevron shape, and these can be reproduced in knitting by the use of Bias Fabrics or Diagonal Knitting, as it is sometimes called. What is meant by bias is shown in Fig. 171, where the stitches forming the fabric run diagonally across the width, instead of vertically, and so rows of colour introduced at intervals will also run diagonally across the fabric.

There are two different bias angles, one running to the right (Fig. 171A), and the other running to the left (Fig. 171B).

DESIGN

Bias is given to a knitted fabric by using similar units to those employed for creating Eyelet and Faggot designs, *i.e.*, an Increase and a Decrease, but with this difference : they are not adjacent, but always divided. Also, the Increase chosen is preferably the MADE stitch and not the ornamental OVER, as in making Bias the units are not intended to be seen as ornament, they are there for the purpose of making Bias only. There are three rules to remember :—

    1. Both units are necessary to make one Bias Motif.
    2. The units are always separated by few or several stitches.
    3. The units are always vertically each above its own kind.

△ It is this separation of the units which causes the stitches lying between them to run diagonally and always towards the vertical line of Decreases, because here the stitches are being decreased or swallowed up, while from the other line of vertical units the stitches are being increased or made good again. It is the law of " Give and Take ", and what is taken must always be repaid.

Give and Take

BIAS OR DIAGONAL KNITTING.
    Fig. 171A to D.

Fig. 171A and B show how to make a Bias fabric of any △ width.

If a Right Bias is required, the Decrease is made at △ the beginning of each front row, and the Increase at the end of each front row (*see* Chart, Fig. 171C).

If a Left Bias is required, then the units are reversed, △ the Increase being made at the beginning and the Decrease at the end of all front rows.

On both fabrics the base line runs at a tilt, but at different angles, the △ deepest point being always beneath the Decrease.

△ The fabric between the two Bias units need not be Stocking Stitch. Every fabric will run diagonally when treated in this manner. For single fabrics, such as scarves, etc., Purl fabrics are preferable (*see* page 3), and Garter Stitch or Moss Stitch, both reversible fabrics, are the favourite choice.

Any type of Increase or Decrease arranged vertically in this manner will form Bias, but for Sports wear the Lace or Open Increase (Over) is not so appropriate, and the Solid or Invisible Increase, which better matches the Decrease and leaves no " lace " space, is used.

There are three different solid or invisible Increases, and all are used :—

> 1. M.I. Bar. Abbreviation : M.I. B.
> 2. M.I. Lifted. Abbreviation : M.I. L. or M.I. L.a.
> 3. M.I. Raised Crossed. Abbreviation : M.I. R.c.

For working directions of these Increases *see* pages 290–292.

The Decreasing Units in Fig. 171 are so used that the upper stitch of each Decrease falls over to continue the chain line of the Bias stitches. This is correct, and Fig. 171 should be consulted as an example for all single-width Bias Fabric, as the units do their work correctly and without being obtrusive.

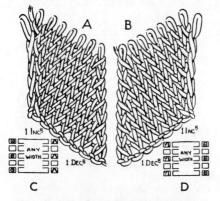

FIG. 171A, B, C and D.—Right and Left Bias Fabric or Diagonal Knitting.

RIGHT DIAGONAL BIAS. *Fig. 171A and* C.

Also known as DIAG-ONAL KNITTING.

Cast On any number of stitches.

Row 1: K.2 tog. * Knit to last stitch but one, * M.I (R.c.). Slip last stitch without knitting it.

Row 2: Purl.

Repeat these 2 rows.

LEFT DIAGONAL BIAS. *Fig. 171* B *and* D.

Cast On any number of stitches.
    Row 1: S.1, M.1 (R.c.). * Knit the row, *
    ending S.1, K.1, p.s.s.o., on last 2 stitches.
    Row 2: Purl.

USES. Bias scarves. The fabric is diagonal, and rows of different colours introduced at intervals will appear as diagonal stripes. When varied in width and colour these stripes are most effective.

BIAS REPEAT PATTERN. *Figs. 172* A *and* B.

Bias units are also used in repeat to make pattern. Figs. 172**A** and **B** show "**B**" in Fig. 171 repeated in pattern, the units being now separated by 3 stitches. Fig. 172**A** shows the method of designing, the brackets linking each pair of Bias units. Only those stitches between the bracketed units will run at a Bias as in Fig. 172**B**. Those between the repeat will remain vertical and just ordinary Knit stitches, in rib formation.

Either **A** or **B** in Fig. 171 can be used in this way, and divided by a rib of any width.

When employing this fabric for garments, jumpers, etc., the effect is more symmetrical if the Bias sections forming the opposite half of the garment front run in the opposite direction. This will be done by repeating **A** in Fig. 171 at intervals, and will also equalise the "pull" of the Bias.

Cast On stitches divisible by 8 and 2 over.
    Row 1: K.1. * M.1 (L.a.), K.3, K.2 tog., K.3. * Repeat * to *,
    ending K.1 instead of K.3.

FIG. 172A.

Row 2: Purl.

The opposite to this (using **A** in Fig. 171) would be as follows :—

Cast On stitches divisible by 8 and 2 over.
    Row 1: K.1. *S.1, K.1, p.s.s.o., K.3, M.1 (R.c.), K.3. * Repeat * to *, ending K.1.

Row 2: Purl.

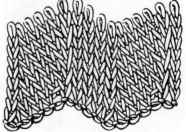

FIG. 172B.—Bias Repeat Pattern.

SUGAR-STICK RIBBING. *Figs. 173A and B.*

If Fig. 172B is knitted as a Round Fabric the result is not a vertical rib with Bias sections, but a spiral rib with Bias sections. This rib coils round the fabric like the markings of Sugar-stick

rock (*see* Fig. 173B). This is because there is only one Bias section used in the repeat. *See also* Fig. 184. The chart (Fig. 173A) shows the Bias units in Fig. 171B arranged in repeat.

In this way Sports, School, or Regimental scarves, or silk ties with diagonal markings, can be knitted round, using a second or even third colour for the Sugar-stick Rib. The second yarn is stranded or woven from rib to rib on the inside. The pattern is also effective in one colour only, as shown. The Rib, here 3 stitches wide, can be made to any width. If a wider or narrower background is required, increase or reduce the number of stitches between the bracketed units (*see* Fig. 173A). Directions for using two colour and solid Increases are given in the following :—

USING TWO COLOURS : Yellow Rib on black ground.

Cast On stitches divisible by 12, and arrange on 3 needles.

Round I : * (Black) S.1, K.1, p.s.s.o., K.6, M.1 into next stitch by knitting first into front and then into back. For this back stitch use yellow, and then K.3 yellow. * Repeat.

FIG. 173B.—Sugar-Stick Ribbing.

FIG. 173A.

Round 2: Knit, using black for the black stitches and yellow for the yellow stitches.

Repeat these 2 rounds.

USING ONE COLOUR :

For " dress " scarves the Over can be used as an Increase, instead of M.1, as it is a little less formal.   Can be knitted in one colour only as in Fig. 173B.

The directions will then read :—

Cast On stitches divisible by 12.
    Round 1: * S.1, K.1, p.s.s.o., K.6, O., K.3. *   Repeat.
    Round 2: Knit.

Repeat these 2 rounds.

————

BIAS CHEVRON FABRICS

To make a Bias Chevron Fabric of △ any width, both Bias fabrics, Fig. 171A and B, are joined.   The chart (Fig. 174A) shows this to be the charts Fig. 171C and D united, and in so doing it brings together two units of △ different Bias Motifs—the Decreases.

△ This adjacent position allows these units to be treated ornamentally as a Pair (*see* Fig. 297).

When the two Decreasing units are in the middle and the two Increasing units placed either side at the extreme edge of a fabric of any width, the Chevron so formed will be as in Fig. 174B, a jumper in yellow, with black chevrons.   The colours are still added in rows, two rows of black between six rows of yellow, but they take this chevron shape because of the Bias units.

Chevron sports colours on a scarf would be added in the same way.

△ The fabric between the units can be Stocking Stitch (the simplest) or as required.

BIAS CHEVRONS. *Figs. 174A and B.*

Cast On any even number of stitches.

> **Row 1:** S.1, M.1 (R.c.), knit to the centre 4 stitches of row, S.1, K.1, p.s.s.o., K.2 tog., now knit to last stitch but one, M.1 (R.c.), S.1.
>
> **Row 2:** Purl.

Repeat these 2 rows.

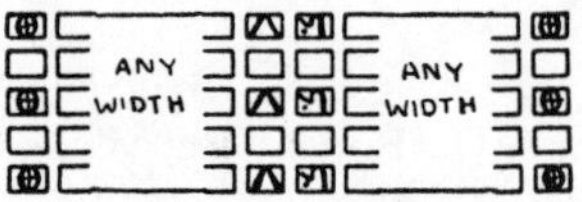

FIG. 174A.

FIG. 174B.—Bias Chevron Fabric.

VARIATION 1: Group 3 or 4 stitches between the two central Decreases, and so make a dividing rib of vertical stitches.

VARIATION 2: Instead of using two single Decreases in the middle, use one Double Decrease, choosing Central Chain Decrease (Fig. 296).

BIAS CHEVRONS REVERSED. *Figs. 175A and B.*

Fig. 175A shows that the Bias units are now reversed, so that the two increasing units are in the middle, while the decreasing units are placed either side. This will reverse the bias and also the point of the Chevron, which will now be as in Fig. 175B. This Chevron suggests a " V " neck.

The two adjacent units (Solid Increase) must be made as decorative as possible. △ Notice that though the units change positions, they never change their relationship, as one Increase and one Decrease still make one Bias Motif.

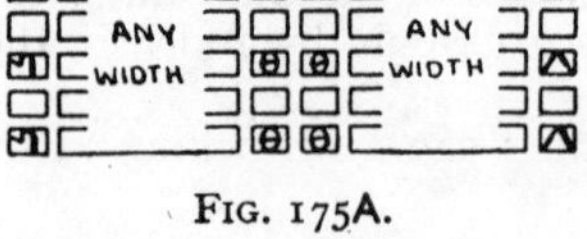

FIG. 175A.

FIG. 175B.—Bias Chevrons Reversed.

Cast On any even number of stitches.

Row 1: K.2 tog., knit to centre 4 stitches of row, M.1 (Bar), M.1 (Bar), now knit to last 2 stitches, and here S.1, K.1, p.s.s.o.

Row 2: Purl.

Repeat these 2 rows.

VARIATION: Group 4 or more stitches between the two Central Increases.

USES. For sports jumpers, etc., as shown, the fabric can be of any suitable Pattern.

DESIGNING CHEVRONS FANTASTIC

The Chevron Units can also be repeated in close formation to make pattern as in Figs. 176A, **B**, and **C**. Any decreasing or increasing units can be used.

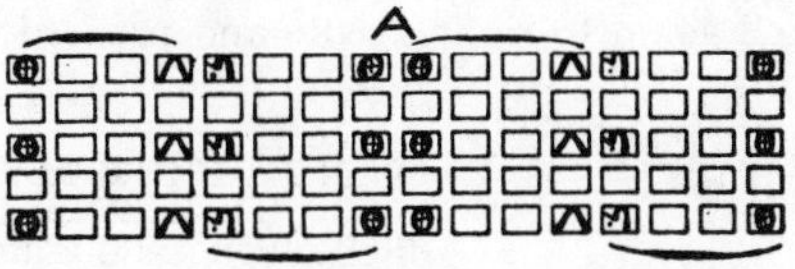

FIG. 176A.

Fig. 176A shows the units, Fig. 171A and **B**, as used in Fig. 174A now repeated closely together to form small Chevrons as in Fig. 176C.

CHEVRON FANTASTIC (SIMPLE). *Fig. 176A.*

Using Single Bias Units.

Cast On stitches divisible by 8 and 2 over.

Row 1: K.1. * M.1 (R.c.), K.2, S.1, K.1, p.s.s.o., K.2 tog., K.2, M.1 (R.c.). * Repeat * to *, ending K.1.

Row 2: Purl.

Repeat these 2 rows.

If wider Chevrons are required for sports colours, then the stitches between the units can be increased from 2, 4, or 6, or any number required, always remembering △ that 2 units are necessary for each Bias angle. The meeting units need not always be adjacent. If three or more stitches were left between them, at A, Fig. 176A, this would result in repeating Chevrons, divided by a vertical rib, of 3 ordinary plain stitches, as only the stitches between the units run at a bias, those outside remain vertical.

When two units of similar nature are repeated adjacently, as in Fig. 176A, it is often more decorative to unite them into a Double Decrease or Double Increase, as shown in Fig. 176B, and knitted in Fig. 176C.

△ The doubled units used in Fig. 176B are made as follows :—

The Double Solid Increase is (M.1 (L.), K.1 B., M.1 (L.a.)).

Knit into the head of the stitch below. Knit into the back of the stitch on needle and knit again into the head of the same stitch below. (This " same " stitch will now be the 3rd stitch down.) This is the most decorative version of a Double Solid Increase.

The Double Decrease is (K.2 tog. B. Double Reverse).

Knit 2 together through the back of the stitches. Put the resulting stitch back on the left needle, and pass the stitch beyond over it. Return the stitch again to right needle and proceed.

The written directions are as follows :—

CHEVRON FANTASTIC.
Figs. 176B and C.   FIG. 176B.

Using Doubled Bias Units.

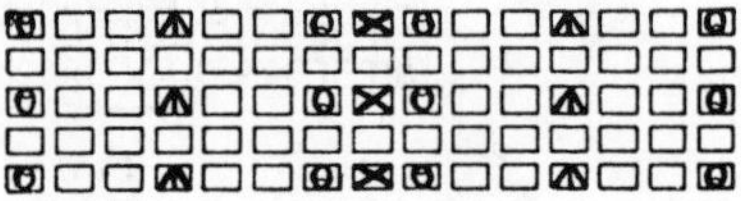

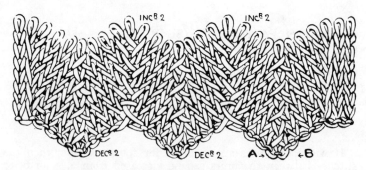

FIG. 176C.—Chevron Fantastic.

Cast On stitches divisible by 8 and 10 over.

Row 1: K.2, M.1 (L.a.), K.2. * (K.2 tog. B., Double Reverse),
K.2, (M.1 (L.), K.1 B., M.1 (L.a.)), K.2. * Repeat
* to *, ending (K.2 tog. B., Double Reverse), K.2,
M.1 (L.), K.1.

Row 2: Purl.

Repeat these 2 rows.

By courtesy of The Museum, Hove.

FIG. 177.—Knitted Bag in DIMPLE SHALE AND RIB PATTERN showing
how the undulated line, *see* Fig. 171, runs through the whole fabric.
For knitting directions *see* page 183.

INDENTED BASE LINE

The Bias tilt of the base line, already noted in Fig. 171, becomes
in Fig. 176, because of the repetition, a continuous line of indenta-
tions. The deep points are always below the vertical line of
Decreases. The high points, shown by the stitches released
from the needle, are those found above the vertical line of
Increases.

The wave of this indented line is decided by the width of
the Chevrons, and runs through the entire fabric, a fact better
appreciated when knitted in different colours, as in Fig. 177—a
small bag knitted in several shades of pink and in Dimple Shale

and Rib Pattern (*see* Fig. 190). It is a charming method of introducing an "ombre" colour scheme of any shade into any type of fabric designed on this principle. The following Fig. 178 shows that any horizontal row, or rows, of stitches can be given a waved or fantastic effect by using the same principle.

WELTING FANTASTIC.   *Figs. 178*A *and* B.

Six rows of Purl, a Welt (*see* Fig. 24), are here spaced at intervals between Chevron Fantastic (Fig. 176C), and in this way the Welt, instead of being straight, undulates in unison with the base line, even though it is knitted straight across the fabric, and omitting the Chevron units. Such intervals should not be too wide. Fig. 178A gives the method in chart form, using the simplest Bias units.

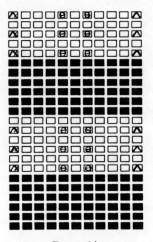

FIG. 178A.

If other horizontal Motifs, such as Double-Crested Garter Insertion Stitch (Fig. 124), or Ribbon Eyelet (Fig. 141), etc., are substituted for the Welt, they also will become Fantastic. Many lovely patterns can be made in this way, using the same colour yarns or contrast. The opposite to this in the vertical is Fig. 157, Rib Fantastic.

Cast On a multiple of 11 stitches.
    Row 1: Purl.
    Row 2: Knit.
    Row 3: Purl.
    Row 4: Knit.

FIG. 178B.—Welting Fantastic.

Row 5: Purl.
Row 6: Knit.
Row 7: * K.2 tog., K.3, (M.1 B.), K.1, (M.1 B.), K.3, K.2 tog. B. *
    Repeat.
Row 8: Purl.
Row 9: Same as Row 7.
Row 10: Purl.
Row 11: Same as Row 7.
Row 12: Purl.

Repeat from Row 1.

LACE FABRICS AND LACE

Designing Units—Overs and Decreases.

Lace Knitting depicts the height of the knitter's art, as it is inspired by the desire to reproduce as near as possible the art of the lace-maker. To this end, the old knitters used the finest of knitting needles and the finest of knitting yarns (*see* Fig. 179, a lace stitch sampler, utilised as a head scarf). The method of creating lace knitting patterns is most fascinating, and once the process is understood, it is possible to originate or reproduce any pattern on sight.

These fabrics make the most delightful garments, and, being Lace Fabrics, they should always be light and dainty, using fine yarns and needles. Shetland shawls are usually knitted on Size 14 (steel needles).

DESIGNING

The Lace Units are :—

    1. The Over.
    2. The Decrease.

Each unit is independent, but complementary to the other, but as one is an Increasing unit and the other a Decreasing unit, equality of each must be a consideration in order to keep the width of the fabric under control.

In some patterns one unit is used in excess of the other, so that the stitches often run plus or even minus for a row or several rows (*see* Figs. 190 and 140), in order to achieve a certain effect, but this is always corrected before the repeat by an excess of the other unit.

The Increase (Over) is the open lace-like unit, but the Decrease is the decorative unit, and in Lace Patterns this is also used to make form (*see* Fig. 185B, where the Decreases, being correctly paired, meet to form the diamond shapes). *See* Fig. 297 for pairing Decreases, and note there the angle made by the upper stitch of each Decrease. △ It is this upper stitch of the Decrease

170

By kind permission of Mrs. Hermann Tragy.

FIG. 179.—Lace Sampler arranged as a head scarf.   Early nineteenth century.

CHEVRON LACE STITCH. *Figs. 180A and* B.

Also known as BIAS LACE STITCH.

Fig. 180A shows both units in vertical arrangement, and the Decreases " smoothly " paired. Compare Figs. 176 with 180 and 181. The Charts show similar arrangements on paper, but different in effect because the Increase used is now the Ornamental Over.

Cast On stitches divisible by 13 and 1 over.

 Row 1: * K.1, O., K.4, K.2 tog., S.1, K.1, p.s.s.o., K.4, O. *
    Repeat, ending K.1.
 Row 2: Purl.

Repeat these 2 rows.

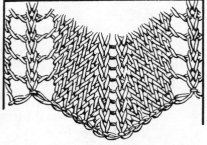

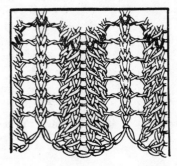

FIG. 180A.—Chart. Chevron Lace Stitch.

FIG. 180B.—Chevron Lace Stitch.

FEATHER PATTERN. *Figs. 181A and* B.

Fig. 181A shows the difference between this and 180A to be that the units are closer together, there being only one stitch instead of four between

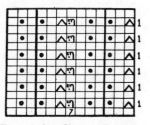

FIG. 181B.—Feather Pattern.

FIG. 181A.—Chart. Feather Pattern.

them; also that the Decreasing units have been reversed to "Reverse pairing". This breaks the clear vertical chain shown in Fig. 180B, and makes the "feathered" effect shown in Fig. 181B.

Cast On stitches divisible by 7.
>   **Row 1:** K.2 tog., K.1, O.   * K.1, O., K.1, S.1, K.1, p.s.s.o.,
>   K.2 tog., K.1, O.* Repeat * to *, ending K.1, O.,
>   K.1, S.1, K.1, p.s.s.o.
>   **Row 2:** Purl.

Repeat these 2 rows.

GATE AND LADDER PATTERN.   *Figs. 182A and* B.

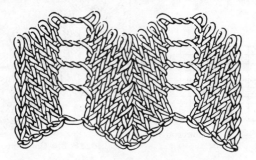

FIG. 182B.—Gate and Ladder Pattern.

The designing units are again arranged vertically, but this time two similar units are doubled. There is a Double Over, followed by a Double Decrease (K.3 tog.).

VARIATION: Change Double Decrease to Fig. 296, Central Chain Decrease.

Cast On stitches divisible by 9 and 1 over.

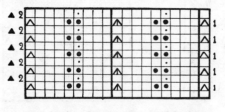

FIG. 182A.—Chart. Gate and Ladder
Pattern.

Row 1: K.2 tog. * K.3, O.2, K.3, K.3 tog. * Repeat * to *, ending K.2 tog., instead of K.3 tog.
Row 2: Purl, purling the first Over and knitting the second.

Repeat these 2 rows.

HORSESHOE IMPRINT. *Figs. 183A and B.*

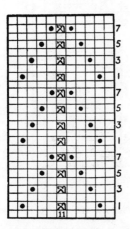

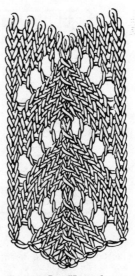

FIG. 183A.—Chart.
Horseshoe Imprint
Pattern.

FIG. 183B.—Horseshoe
Imprint Pattern.

Fig. 183A. In this pattern the two adjacent Decreases are united as one Double Decrease and remain vertical, while the two single Increases (Overs) travel diagonally to a converging point (*see also* Fig. 169).

Cast On stitches divisible by 10 and 1 over.

Row 1: K.1. * O., K.3, S.1, **K.2** tog., p.s.s.o., K.3, O., K.1. * Repeat * to *.

Row 2 and all even rows: Purl.

Row 3: K.1. * K.1, O., K.2, S.1, **K.2** tog., p.s.s.o., K.2, O., K.2. * Repeat * to *.

Row 5: K.1. * K.2, O., K.1, S.1, **K.2** tog., p.s.s.o., K.1, O., K.3. * Repeat * to *.

Row 7: K.1. * K.3, O., S.1, **K.2** tog., p.s.s.o., O., K.4. * Repeat * to *.

Row 8: Purl.

Repeat these 8 rows.

SCALE PATTERN. *Figs. 184A and B.*

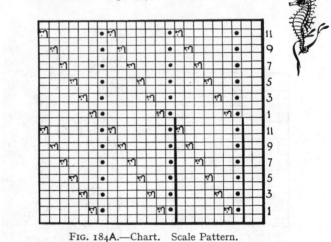

FIG. 184A.—Chart.   Scale Pattern.

The method of grouping the units is the reverse of Fig. 183. The stationary unit is now the Increase (Over), while the travelling unit is the Decrease. This moves one to the left in every Knit row, travelling diagonally and always in the same direction, which causes a Bias to the fabric as shown. Any single unit travelling always in the same direction will produce Bias

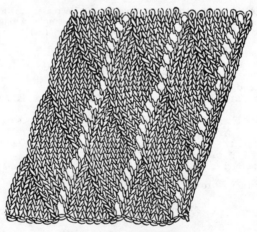

FIG. 184B.—Scale Pattern.

(*see* Fig. 173). Scale Pattern would have a similar spiral effect to this were it knitted as a Round Fabric. For garment use, one half of the front and back should be made to take the opposite Bias. To do this, the Decreasing Units must be arranged to take the opposite diagonal, thus forming large Chevrons. Don't forget that on this diagonal the Decrease will be K.2 tog. The pattern must first be charted and then rewritten as a whole.

In Scale Pattern this Bias is corrected by pressing.

Cast On stitches divisible by 7 and 4 over.
> **Row 1:** K.2. * O., S.1, K.1, p.s.s.o., K.5. * Repeat * to *, ending O., K.2 tog.
> **Row 2 and all even rows:** Purl.
> **Row 3:** K.2. * O., K.1, S.1, K.1, p.s.s.o., K.4. * Repeat * to *, ending O., K.2 tog.
> **Row 5:** K.2. * O., K.2, S.1, K.1, p.s.s.o., K.3. * Repeat * to *, ending O., K.2 tog.
> **Row 7:** K.2. * O., K.3, S.1, K.1, p.s.s.o., K.2. * Repeat * to *, ending O., K.2 tog.
> **Row 9:** K.2. * O., K.4, S.1, K.1, p.s.s.o., K.1. * Repeat * to *, ending O., K.2 tog.
> **Row 11:** K.2. * O., K.5, S.1, K.1, p.s.s.o. * Repeat * to *, ending O., K.2 tog.
> **Row 12:** Purl.

Repeat these 12 rows.

CANDLE-LIGHT PATTERN. *Figs. 185*A *and* B.

The travelling unit is again the Decrease, as in Scale Pattern, but there is no Bias in this pattern as there are 2 Decreases, and both travel diagonally and in contrary directions. Study how the Decreases are paired to accentuate the diamond outline. As there are two Decreases in each repeat, there must also be 2 Increases. These are arranged vertically in the middle of every diamond, and move on the half-drop principle. They let in the light " Candle-light " ! Also compare with Fig. 155A and note the Lace Principle of dividing the units.

Cast On stitches divisible by 12 and 1 over.
> **Row 1:** K.1. * O., S.1, K.1, p.s.s.o., K.7, K.2 tog., O., K.1. * Repeat * to *.
> **Row 2 and all even rows:** Purl.
> **Row 3:** K.1. * O., K.1, S.1, K.1, p.s.s.o., K.5, K.2 tog., K.1, O., K.1. * Repeat * to *.
> **Row 5:** K.1. * O., K.2, S.1, K.1, p.s.s.o., K.3, K.2 tog., K.2, O., K.1. * Repeat * to *.
> **Row 7:** K.1. * O., K.3, S.1, K.1, p.s.s.o., K.1, K.2 tog., K.3, O., K.1. * Repeat * to *.

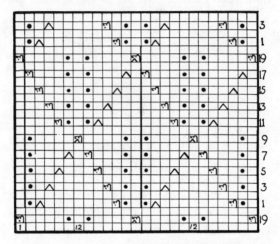

Fig. 185A.—Chart.   Candle-light Pattern.

Row 9: K.1. * O., K.4, S.1, **K.2** tog., p.s.s.o., K.4, O., K.1. * Repeat * to *.

Row 11: K.1. * K.3, K.2 tog., O., K.1, O., S.1, **K.1**, p.s.s.o., K.4. * Repeat * to *.

Row 13: K.1. * K.2, K.2 tog., K.1, O., K.1, O., K.1, S.1, **K.1**, p.s.s.o., K.3. * Repeat * to *.

Row 15: K.1. * K.1, K.2 tog., K.2, O., K.1, O., K.2, S.1, **K.1**, p.s.s.o., K.2. * Repeat * to *.

Row 17: K.1. * K.2 tog., K.3, O., K.1, O., K.3, S.1, **K.1**, p.s.s.o., K.1. * Repeat * to *.

Row 19: S.1, **K.1**, p.s.s.o. * K.4, O., K.1, O., K.4, S.1, **K.2** tog., p.s.s.o. * Repeat * to *, ending S.1, **K.1**, p.s.s.o. on last 2 stitches.

Row 20: Purl.

Repeat these 20 rows.

Fig. 185B.—Candle-light Pattern.

FALLING-LEAF PATTERN. *Figs. 186A and B.*

FIG. 186B.—Falling-Leaf Pattern.

In this pattern the 2 travelling units are the Increase (Over), and the 2 stationary units the Decrease, which are united to form 1 Double Decrease. The designing principle is the opposite to that of Fig. 185A. The comparison of these two charts will be helpful. Diamonds can be

FIG. 186A.—Chart. Falling-Leaf Pattern.

created on this plan to any size, by increasing the number of stitches between the unit, and correspondingly the number of rows. Also the centre of the diamond need not be solid, but decorated with Eyelets, and so make the fabric very open and lace-like.

Cast On stitches divisible by 10 and 1 over.
  Row 1: K.1. * O., K.3, S.1, K.2 tog., p.s.s.o., K.3, O., K.1. *
        Repeat * to *.

Row 2 and all even rows: Purl.
Row 3: K.1. * K.1, O., K.2, S.1, **K.2** tog., p.s.s.o., K.2, O., K.2. * Repeat * to *.
Row 5: K.1. * K.2, O., K.1, S.1, **K.2** tog., p.s.s.o., K.1, O., K.3. * Repeat * to *.
Row 7: K.1. * K.3, O., S.1, **K.2** tog., p.s.s.o., O., K.4. * Repeat * to *.
Row 9: S.1, **K.1**, p.s.s.o. * K.3, O., K.1, O., K.3, S.1, **K.2** tog., p.s.s.o. * Repeat * to *, ending S.1, **K.1**, p.s.s.o. on last 2 stitches.
Row 11: S.1, **K.1**, p.s.s.o. * K.2, O., K.3, O., K.2, S.1, **K.2** tog., p.s.s.o. * Repeat * to *, ending S.1, **K.1**, p.s.s.o. on last 2 stitches.
Row 13: S.1, **K.1**, p.s.s.o. * K.1, O., K.5, O., K.1, S.1, **K.2** tog., p.s.s.o. * Repeat * to *, ending S.1, **K.1**, p.s.s.o. on last 2 stitches.
Row 15: S.1, **K.1**, p.s.s.o. * O., K.7, O., S.1, **K.2** tog., p.s.s.o. * Repeat * to *, ending S.1, **K.1**, p.s.s.o.
Row 16: Purl.

Repeat these 16 rows.

MINIATURE-LEAF PATTERN.

Figs. 187A and B.

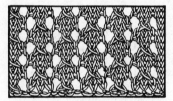

FIG. 187B.—Miniature-Leaf
Pattern.

FIG. 187A.—Chart. Minia-
ture-Leaf Pattern.

This is the smallest repeating Lace Unit or Motif, as the pattern consist of 1 Double Decrease and 2 Single Overs with an interval of 3 stitches. The units alternate in Row 3.

Cast On a multiple of 6 stitches and 2 over.
Row 1: K.1. * K.3, O., K.3 tog., O. * Repeat * to *, ending K.1.
Row 2: Purl.
Row 3: K.1. * O., K.3 tog., O., K.3. * Repeat * to *, ending K.1.
Row 4: Purl.

Repeat these 4 rows.

PINE TREES PATTERN. *Figs. 188A and B.*

FIG. 188B.—Pine Trees Pattern.

In all the previous lace designs 1 unit only has travelled, the other remaining stationary. Here both units are travelling simultaneously, and in parallel lines to a central point. The success of this pattern depends entirely on the strict pairing of the Decreasing unit, as these form the stitches which run obliquely across the fabric.

In this pattern the fabric between is often ornamented with Eyelets, and quite frequently 4 units are travelled instead of only 2.

Cast On a multiple of 12 and 1 over.
Row 1: * K.1, O., K.1, S.1, **K.1**, p.s.s.o., K.5, K.2 tog., K.1, O. *
Repeat, ending K.1.

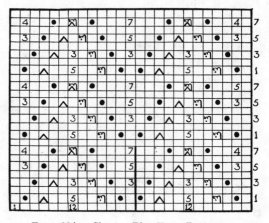

FIG. 188A.—Chart. Pine Trees Pattern.

Row 2 and all even rows: Purl.
Row 3: * K.2, O., K.1, S.1, **K.1**, p.s.s.o., K.3, K.2 tog., K.1, O., K.1. * Repeat, ending K.1.
Row 5: * K.3, O., K.1, S.1, **K.1**, p.s.s.o., K.1, K.2 tog., K.1, O., K.2. * Repeat, ending K.1.
Row 7: * K.4, O., K.1, S.1, **K.2** tog., p.s.s.o., K.1, O., K.3. * Repeat, ending K.1.
Row 8: Purl.

Repeat these 8 rows. Notice the Double Decrease in Row 7.

OLD SHALE. *Figs. 189A and B.*

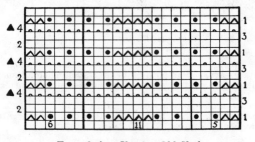

Fig. 189A.—Chart. Old Shale.

Both units are here grouped together in fours and arranged horizontally in the same row (*see* Fig. 189A).

Four Increases and four Decreases (4 and 4) have been used, but the number could be 6 and 6 or 7 and 7, just as desired. The number of inter-

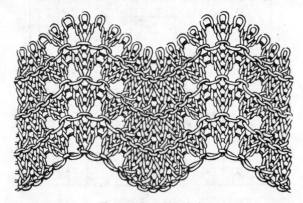

Fig. 189B.—Old Shale.

vening rows (three) can also be increased. The Purl row on the front of the fabric is optional, but it is legitimate as the units are in horizontal arrangement, also it does help to correct the " drooping " tendency of the knit fabric (*see* page 4).

This is an easy pattern to vary, and so many versions are found. It is also a very famous and well-known Shetland pattern, the name being inspired by the undulating waves left on the shale sands, and often corrupted to Old Shell.

Cast On stitches divisible by 11.
    Row 1: * K.2 tog., K.2 tog., O., K.1, O., K.1, O., K.1, O., K.2 tog., K.2 tog. * Repeat.
    Row 2: Purl.
    Row 3: Knit.
    Row 4: Knit.

Repeat these 4 rows.

DIMPLE SHALE AND RIB. *Figs. 190 and 177.*

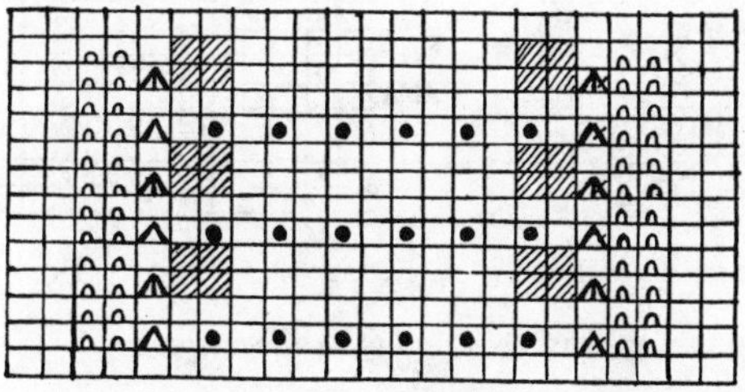

FIG. 190.—Chart. Dimple Shale and Rib.

A favourite variation of Old Shale Pattern is to delay the Decrease, *see* Fig. 190, where there are 6 Increasing units in Row 1, but only 2 Decreasing units. This makes the stitches in Row 2, 21, instead of 17, and a $\triangle$ plus pattern. In Row 3 there are 2 double Decreases and no Increases, so by Row 4 there are 17 again to the repeat. The pattern is also divided by a Purl rib. Another favourite device. For illustration *see* Fig. 177.

Cast On stitches divisible by 17 and 2 over.
    Row 1: * K.2, P.2, K.2 tog. B, (K.1, O.) 6 times, K.1, K.2 tog., P.2. * Repeat, ending K.2.
    Row 2: P.2. * K.2, P.15, K.2, P.2. * Repeat * to *.
    Row 3: * K.2, P.2, K.3 tog. B, K.9, K.3 tog., P.2. * Repeat, ending K.2.
    Row 4: P.2. * K.2, P.11, K.2, P.2. * Repeat * to *.

Repeat these 4 rows.

BEECH-LEAF LACE. *Figs. 191A and* B.

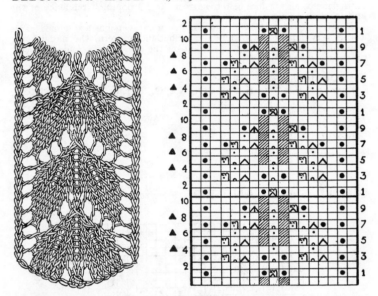

Fig. 191B.—Beech-Leaf Lace.   Fig. 191A.—Chart. Beech-Leaf Lace.

Eight units are used in this design, 4 Overs and 4 Decreases (*see* Fig. 191A).

Two of the Overs are arranged vertically either side. Two travel diagonally from Row 7, but link to Row 5. Two in Row 1 are ornamental, added to divide the leaf shapes. This makes it a plus pattern, as 14 stitches are cast on, but in Row 1 these become 16 because of the 2 extra Overs, and remain 16 until Row 5.

Extra stitches are often borrowed in this way for certain effects, or the design can run minus for several rows (*see* Fig. 140), but either must be corrected at the final row of the pattern, ready for the next repeat. Designs of this type can only be created on paper.

The 4 Decreasing units are arranged vertically until Row 7, and here they move inwards to the centre, running parallel with the Over, and so draw the leaf to a point. There is a cousin relationship between this pattern and Pine Trees (Fig. 188A). A feature of the design is the clever use of the Purl Stitch, arranged to form the central vein of the leaves and the central stalk.

This fabric has no background. The solid parts form a leaf, held in position by Lace stitches, so the design is no longer Lace Fabric, but Lace.

Cast On stitches divisible by 14 and 1 over.
   Row 1: * K.1, O., K.5, O., Sl.1, **K.2** tog., p.s.s.o., O., K.5, O. *
   Repeat, ending K.1.

Row 2: Purl.

Row 3: * K.1, O., K.1, K.2 tog., P.1, Sl.1, **K.1**, p.s.s.o., K.1, O., P.1, O., K.1, K.2 tog., P.1, Sl.1, **K.1**, p.s.s.o., K.1, O. * Repeat, ending K.1.

Row 4: P.1. * P.3, K.1, P.3, K.1, P.3, K.1, P.4. * Repeat * to *.

Row 5: * K.1, O., K.1, K.2 tog., P.1, Sl.1, **K.1**, p.s.s.o., K.1, P.1, K.1, K.2 tog., P.1, Sl.1, **K.1**, p.s.s.o., K.1, O. * Repeat, ending K.1.

Row 6: P.1. * P.3, K.1, P.2, K.1, P.2, K.1, P.4. * Repeat * to *.

Row 7: * K.1, O., K.1, O., K.2 tog., P.1, Sl.1, **K.1**, p.s.s.o., P.1, K.2 tog., P.1, Sl.1, **K.1**, p.s.s.o., O., K.1, O. * Repeat, ending K.1.

Row 8: P.1. * P.4, K.1, P.1, K.1, P.1, K.1, P.5. * Repeat * to *.

Row 9: * K.1, O., K.3, O., Sl.1, **K.2** tog., p.s.s.o., P.1, K.3 tog., O., K.3, O. * Repeat, ending K.1.

Row 10: Purl.

Repeat these 10 rows.

DROOPING ELM-LEAF PATTERN. *Figs. 192A and B.*

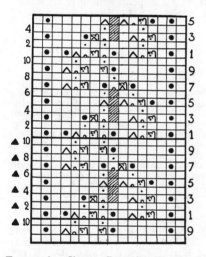

FIG. 192A.—Chart. Drooping Elm-Leaf Lace Pattern.

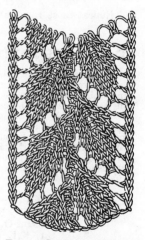

FIG. 192B.—Drooping Elm-Leaf Lace Pattern.

A favourite method of deriving unexpected patterns is to cut an existing chart and drop one half of it downwards, making the join where it best forms a new pattern. Fig. 192 shows Fig. 191 cut and dropped, so that the leaves now alternate either side of a central stem. Slight adjustments have been made, the Decreases either side of the central vein of the leaf have been reversed to give a rougher texture to the fabric which is more in keeping with the leaf of the Elm.

Such is an attempt at realism, and to this end the old Knitters always strived when naming their patterns. The texture of an Elm leaf is rough.

Cast On stitches divisible by 15 and 1 over.

Row 1: * K.1, O., K.1, S.1, **K.1**, p.s.s.o., P.1, K.2 tog., K.1, O., P.1, S.1, **K.1**, p.s.s.o., P.1, K.2 tog., O., K.1, O. * Repeat, ending K.1.

Row 2: P.1.   * P.4, K.1, P.1, K.1, P.3, K.1, P.4. *   Repeat * to *.

Row 3: * K.1, O., K1., S.1, **K.1**, p.s.s.o., P.1, K.2 tog., K.1, P.1, S.1, **K.2** tog., p.s.s.o., O., K.3, O. * Repeat, ending K.1.

Row 4: P.1.   * P.6, K.1, P.2, K.1, P.4. *   Repeat * to *.

Row 5: * K.1, O., K.1, O., S.1, **K.1**, p.s.s.o., P.1, K.2 tog., K.2 tog., K.5, O. *   Repeat, ending K.1.

Row 6: P.1.   * P.6, K.1, P.1, K.1, P.5. *   Repeat * to *.

Row 7: * K.1, O., K.3, O., S.1, **K.2** tog., p.s.s.o., P.1, O., K.1, S.1, **K.1**, p.s.s.o., P.1, K.2 tog., K.1, O. *   Repeat ending K.1.

Row 8: P.1.   * P.3, K.1, P.3, K.1, P.7. *   Repeat * to *.

Row 9: * K.1, O., K.5, O., S.1, **K.1**, p.s.s.o., K.1, S.1, **K.1**, p.s.s.o., P.1, K.2 tog., K.1, O. *   Repeat, ending K.1.

Row 10: P.1.   * P.3, K.1, P.2, K.1, P.8. *   Repeat * to *.

Repeat these 10 rows.

OGEE LACE PATTERN.   *Figs. 193A and B.*

This is the same principle of design as Fig. 226, only Faggot Stitch is used instead of a rib, and the background is decorated.   To do this the increasing unit is changed from invisible M.1 B. to visible (Over), and instead of this being hidden either side beneath the rib, as in Chart (Fig. 226), the Overs are brought out into the centre and used to form lace spaces.   These increasing units can be distinguished from the ornamental Eyelets, as they stand alone, and are not immediately preceded or followed by a Decrease.   As the shape narrows, the decreasing units are brought into the centre and grouped diagonally above each other to form the enclosing pear-shape lines of Knit stitches at the top of the Motif, seen in Figs. 193A and B.   (Compare the charts, Figs. 226A and 193A).

Cast On a multiple of 24 stitches and 1 extra.

Row 1: * K.2, O., K.2 tog., K.1, K.2 tog., K.3, O., S.1, **K.1**, p.s.s.o., O., P.1, O., K.2, O., S.1, **K.1**, p.s.s.o., K.1, S.1, **K.1**, p.s.s.o., K.1, S.1, **K.1**, p.s.s.o., O., K.1. * Repeat, ending K.1.

Row 2: P.1.   * P.7, O., P.2 tog. (that is, the Over and the next stitch), P.5, O., P.2 tog., P.8. *   Repeat * to *.

Row 3: * K.1, O., K.2 tog., K.1, K.2 tog., K.3, O., S.1, **K.1**, p.s.s.o., K.1, O., K.1, O., K.3, O., S.1, **K.1**, p.s.s.o., K.1, S.1, **K.1**, p.s.s.o., K.1, S.1, **K.1**, p.s.s.o., O. * Repeat, ending K.1.

Row 4: P.1. * P.6, O., P.2 tog., P.7, O., P.2 tog., P.7. * Repeat * to *.

Row 5: * K.3, K.2 tog., K.3, O., S.1, K.1, p.s.s.o., K.1, O., K.3, O., K.3, O., S.1, K.1, p.s.s.o., K.1, S.1, K.1, p.s.s.o., K.2. * Repeat, ending K.1.

Row 6: P.1. * P.5, O., P.2 tog., P.9, O., P.2 tog., P.6. * ·Repeat * to *.

Row 7: * K.2, K.2 tog., K.3, O., S.1, K.1, p.s.s.o., K.3, O., K.1, O., K.5, O., S.1, K.1, p.s.s.o., K.1, S.1, K.1, p.s.s.o., K.1. * Repeat, ending K.1.

Row 8: P.1. * P.4, O., P.2 tog., P.11, O., P.2 tog., P.5. * Repeat * to *.

Row 9: * K.1, K.2 tog., K.3, O., S.1, K.1, p.s.s.o., K.3, O., K.3, O., K.5, O., S.1, K.1, p.s.s.o., K.1, S.1, K.1, p.s.s.o. * Repeat, ending K.1.

Row 10: P.1. * P.3, O., P.2 tog., P.13, O., P.2 tog., P.4. * Repeat * to *.

Row 11: S.1, K.1, p.s.s.o. * K.3, O., S.1, K.1, p.s.s.o., K.1, S.1, K.1, p.s.s.o., O., K.2, O., K.1, O., K.2, O., K.2 tog., K.3, O., S.1, K.1, p.s.s.o., K.1., S.1, K.2 tog., p.s.s.o. * Repeat * to *, ending S.1, K.1, p.s.s.o. on last two stitches.

Row 12: P.1. * P.2, O., P.2 tog., P.15, O., P.2 tog., P.3. * Repeat * to *.

Row 13: S.1, K.1, p.s.s.o. * K.2, O., S.1, K.1, p.s.s.o., K.5, O., K.3, O., K.7, O., S.1, K.1, p.s.s.o., S.1, K.2 tog., p.s.s.o. * Repeat * to *, ending S.1, K.1, p.s.s.o.

Row 14: P.1. * P.1, O., P.2 tog., P.17, O., P.2 tog., P.1, K.1. * Repeat * to *.

Row 15: * P.1, O., K.2, O., S.1, K.1, p.s.s.o., K.1, S.1, K.1, p.s.s.o., K.1, S.1, K.1, p.s.s.o., O., K.3, O., K.2 tog., K.3, O., S.1, K.1, p.s.s.o., O. * Repeat, ending P.1.

Row 16: P.1. * P.2, O., P.2 tog., P.15, O., P.2 tog., P.3. * Repeat * to *.

Row 17: * K.1, O., K.3, O., S.1, K.1, p.s.s.o., K.1, S.1, K.1, p.s.s.o., K.1, S.1, K.1, p.s.s.o., O., K.1, O., K.2 tog., K.1, K.2 tog., K.3, O., S.1, K.1, p.s.s.o., K.1, O. * Repeat, ending K.1.

Row 18: P.1. * P.3, O., P.2 tog., P.13, O., P.2 tog., P.4. * Repeat * to *.

Row 19: * K.2, O., K.3, O., S.1, K.1, p.s.s.o., K.1, S.1, K.1, p.s.s.o., K.5, K.2 tog., K.3, O., S.1, K.1, p.s.s.o., K.1, O., K.1. * Repeat, ending K.1 .

Row 20: P.1. * P.4, O., P.2 tog., P.11, O., P.2 tog., P.5. * Repeat * to *.

Row 21: * K.1, O., K.5, O., S.1, K.1, p.s.s.o., K.1, S.1, K.1, p.s.s.o., K.3, K.2 tog., K.3, O., S.1, K.1, p.s.s.o., K.3, O. * Repeat, ending K.1.

Row 22: P.1. * P.5, O., P.2 tog., P.9, O., P.2 tog., P.6. * Repeat * to *.

Row 23: * K.2, O., K.5, O., S.1, K.1, p.s.s.o., K.1, S.1, K.1, p.s.s.o., K.1, K.2 tog., K.3, O., S.1, K.1, p.s.s.o., K.3, O., K.1. * Repeat, ending K.1.

Row 24: P.1. * P.6, O., P.2. tog, P.7, O., P.2 tog., P.7. * Repeat
* to *.

Row 25: * K.1, O., K.2, O., K.2 tog., K.3, O., S.1, K.1, p.s.s.o.,
K.1, S.1, **K.2** tog., p.s.s.o., K.3, O., S.1, **K.1,** p.s.s.o.,
K.1, S.1, **K.1,** p.s.s.o., O., K.2, O. * Repeat, ending K.1.

Row 26: P.1. * P.7, O., P.2 tog., P.5, O., P.2 tog., P.8. * Repeat
* to *.

Row 27: * K.2, O., K.7, O., S.1, **K.1,** p.s.s.o., S.1, **K.2** tog., p.s.s.o.,
K.2, O., S.1, **K.1,** p.s.s.o., K.5, O., K.1. * Repeat,
ending K.1.

Row 28: P.1. * P.8, O., P.2 tog., P.1, K.1, P.1, O., P.2 tog.,
P.9. * Repeat * to *.

Repeat these 28 rows.

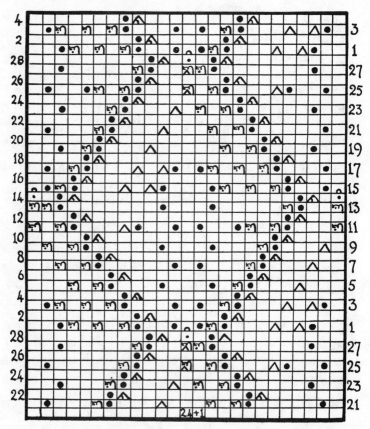

FIG. 193A.—Chart. Ogee Lace Pattern.

FIG. 193B.—Ogee Lace Pattern.

KNITTED LACE

Figs. 179–193 have shown in progressive order the structural and ornamental development of Lace fabrics, and ultimately lace itself, but as these patterns progress to greater complications, the designing units are used on every row, instead of on front rows only (*see* Fig. 169A), and then the fabric can be truly classified as LACE, and not just lace fabric.

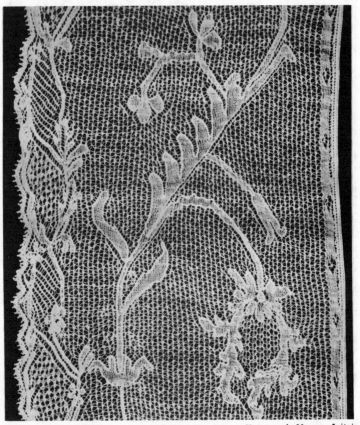

Kunstgewerbe Museum, Leipzig.

FIG. 194.—Knitted Lace, eighteenth to nineteenth century.
Freehand design.

The quest is endless, but fascinating, and ultimately leads to Freehand designs such as in Fig. 194.

Here, with the help of the previous examples, it is possible to follow the plan and development of this masterpiece.

The lines, no longer geometric, flow in flower-like forms, and the units travel in freehand outline, though still adhering to all the rules of technique and design, as explained. Such patterns would need pages to describe, though this single example will show to what degree of beauty knitted lace can ultimately achieve, and so act as an inspiration.

It shows how a master knitter could create pattern on paper. Technique is thoroughly understood, even to the twist of a leaf, which is done with a single Cable Cross. The leaf is midway in the left border.

The lace belongs to the grand period of WHITE KNITTING which flourished throughout the seventeenth to early nineteenth centuries.

This unique example is 5¾ inches wide, and 4 yards long. The solid parts of the leaves and flowers are in Stocking Stitch with needle-run outline. The background is in Lace Faggot. The left edge is finished with a Double Picot, and just within a waved insertion of Faggot. The lozenge shapes are filled alternately with Trellis Faggot and Double Eyelet patterns.

The large flower centre is in Miniature Leaf. The straight edge on the right is in Stocking Stitch with a Faggot Beading, and small Faggot Diamonds placed at intervals. Directions for all these patterns are contained in this book, and this photo should be studied as a classic.

FANCY LACE STITCHES

Designing Units—All Methods of Increasing and Decreasing.

Fancy ! The term really describes the coquettish, fancy-free, or syncopated use of the different Units and Motifs which have previously been selected and used in strict, almost scientific order.

These are really Purl Lace Fabrics, and as such might conclude the previous chapter, but having such individuality and being by popular consent regarded as " stitches ", they are treated separately.

The charts show the method of design and how simply yet ingeniously these patterns are constructed.

Most patterns consist of Ornamental units only, divided by a stitch or some repeating Motif. These are arranged in rows and on the Purl side of the fabric, which explains why they so often begin on the back of the work (*see* page 2). △ In chart-reading this must be remembered ; as it necessitates the first row being read from left to right, and the units as well as stitches must be " translated " (*see* page 6). An arrow is used to point this out. For symbols *see* Fig. 62.

Fancy fabrics are sometimes referred to as Garter Laces, because, like Garter Stitch, they are good width fabrics, frequently reversible, and preferably knitted on two knitting-pins. The patterns are often embossed or " knotty " in appearance, and popular because of their brief descriptions and good fabric width.

△ Needle sizes play an important part, as with larger needles ; sizes 6 or 7 (standard size 8 or 9), using a 3-ply yarn (wool) fabrics are open and lace-like, whereas on smaller needles, sizes 11 or 12 (Standard size 3 or 2), they appear almost solid and so quite different, and to the confusion of the knitter, will frequently bear a different name !

An experiment with different-size needles will yield much interest, the selection being made in proportion to the yarn, wool, silk, or cotton used.

DESIGN

Study anew all the different methods of Increasing (Visible and Invisible) and Decreasing (Single and Double, Knit and Purl) as shown on pages 290 to 300, as all can be used in making

192

these patterns. The fabrics are easy to design once the principle is appreciated. The units are not built up into geometric shapes as for Lace Patterns, but arranged as a sequence, and in Rows.

The method consists of selecting any two of these units (one Increase and one Decrease), with perhaps a Slip Stitch or a Cross Stitch as an extra Motif, which is placed between the Increase and Decrease, and so delays the action and makes pattern. Thus, instead of using O., K.2 tog., this may be O., S.1, K.2 tog., as in Fig. 195, or the Decrease can be still further delayed by more units or stitches. Sometimes the delay is a whole row, as in Fig. 206, where all the Decreases are together in one row, and the complementary Increase is not made until the next row. Again both the Increase and Decrease can be amalgamated, as in Fig. 204.

Another method is to arrange the units as a short sequence, the order of which is reversed in Row 3 to alternate the pattern, as for example Bramble Stitch :—

The designing units are Double Invisible Increase and Double Purl Decrease as follows :—

> (K.1, P.1, K.1.) into one stitch, P.3 tog.
> This represents the whole repeat.
> On the 3rd row the order is reversed as follows :—
> P.3 tog., (K.1, P.1, K.1) into one stitch.

Many different arrangements of units are shown in the following examples, and it will be noticed how, by a change of one unit, or even a slight variation in the sequence, an entirely different fabric is produced. The Brioche family have been treated in this way as an example.

BRIOCHE STITCH OR ENGLISH BRIOCHE.
*Figs. 195*A, B, *and* C.

Also known as SHAWL STITCH, REVERSE LACE STITCH, ORIENTAL RIB STITCH, and in France as POINT D'ANGLETERRE ! In this country it is known by a French name—BRIOCHE !

Designing Units—Over, Knit Decrease, divided or delayed by a Slip Stitch.

The success of any Brioche Pattern depends on the correct order in which the stitch and Over (K.2 tog.) are knitted (or purled together) (*see* Fig. 195B), which shows the action of the entire pattern : " Over, S.1, K.2 tog." The Over passes in front of the slipped stitch and then over the needle. In the next row the 2 stitches which are knitted together are the Over and the slipped stitch.   △ The Over at the beginning of the row is made as before a Knit Decrease, as the intervening Slip stitch is a auxiliary Motif, so it is slipped purlwise according to Pattern Principle, *see* Fig. 95.   The pattern consists of these 3 units which are repeated in every row, so the fabric is alike on both sides.

FIG. 195A.

FIG. 195B.—Brioche Technique.

Row 1 is preparatory and common to all Brioche patterns, and begins on the back of the fabric.   To obtain a lace-like fabric, use large needles. On small needles the fabric is " solid " and quite different.

FIG. 195C.—Brioche Stitch.

Cast On stitches divisible by 2.
    Row 1 (Preparation): Back of Fabric.   * Yarn forward, S.1 (purl-
           wise), K.1. *   Repeat.   (Briefly this row is: O., S.1, K.1.)
    Row 2: * O., S.1 (purlwise), K.2 tog. *   Repeat (*see* Fig. 195B).

Repeat Row 2 only for length required.

To cast off, knit one row plain, and then cast off.

USES.   Both sides are alike, and so successful for shawls, pram-covers, or any article where the back and front of the fabric must show.   Also garments.

TURKISH BRIOCHE STITCH. *Fig. 196.*

Units—O., Purl Decrease, divided by a Slip Stitch.

The same effect as Brioche, only the position of the slipped stitch is changed and the Decrease reversed (P.2 tog.).

FIG. 196.

Cast On stitches divisible by 2.

Row I (Preparation): Back of Fabric. * O., S.1, K.1. * Repeat.

Row 2: Yarn to front. * S.1, O. (*i.e.*, take yarn over needle and to front again), P.2 tog. * Repeat.

Δ Repeat Row 2 for required length.

SYNCOPATED BRIOCHE STITCH. *Figs. 197A and B.*

This combines the use of English and Turkish Brioche, and so gives a broken ribbed effect. The fabric is the same both sides.

FIG. 197A.

FIG. 197B.—Syncopated Brioche.

Cast On stitches divisible by 2.

Row 1 (Preparation): Back of Fabric. * Over, S.1 (purlwise), K.1. * Repeat.

Row 2: * Over, S.1 (purlwise), K.2 tog. * Repeat.

Rows 3–7: △ Repeat Row 2.

Row 8: Yarn to front. * S.1 (purlwise), O., P.2 tog. * Repeat.

Rows 9–13: △ Repeat Row 8.

Pattern repeats from △ Row 2.

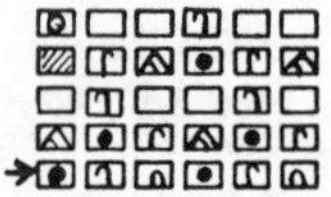

FIG. 198A.

DOUBLE ENGLISH BRIOCHE STITCH. *Figs. 198A and B.*

Units—Purl Decrease, Slip Stitch, and Over.

FIG. 198B.—Double English Brioche Stitch.

Knit on large needles if a lace-like fabric is required. On smaller needles, Size 12 (or standard 4), the fabric has a pretty, close, honey-cell effect and is almost a Solid Fabric.

The yarn is to the front in the Purl position throughout the whole pattern. △ The front and back of fabric are *not* alike. *See also* Double Rose Fabric, page 206).

Cast On an even number of stitches.

Row 1 (Preparation): Back of Fabric. * Yarn forward, O., S.1 (purlwise), K.1. * Repeat * to *.

Row 2: * S.1 (purlwise), O., P.2 tog. (*i.e.*, stitch and Over). * Repeat * to *.

Row 3: P.1. * S.1 (the Over), P.2. * Repeat * to *, ending S.1, P.1.

Row 4: * P.2 tog. (stitch and Over), S.1, O. * Repeat * to *, ending P.2 tog., S.1. The Over is omitted and made at beginning of next row, leaving this row a stitch short (*see* Fig. 198A).

Row 5: △ Yarn to back to make Over as before Purl Stitch, P.2 * S.1 (the Over), P.2. * Repeat * to *.

Repeat from Row 2.

PLAITED BRIOCH E STITCH.

Figs. 199A and B.

Units—Crossed Stitch, Over, and Purl Decrease.

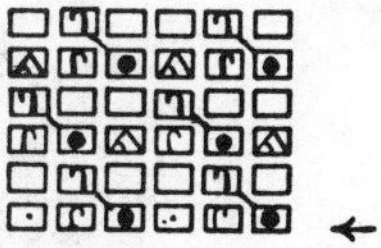

Begin on △ front of fabric, as there are 2 preparatory rows.

FIG. 199A.

FIG. 199B.—Plaited Brioche Stitch.

Cast On an even number of stitches.

Row 1: * O., S.1 (purlwise), K.1. * Repeat * to *.

Row 2: P.1. * Slip Over, P.2. * Repeat * to *, ending S. Over, P.1.

Row 3: * P.2 tog. (stitch and Over), O., S.1. * Repeat * to *.

Row 4: △ * Miss the stitch and slip the Over purlwise over this stitch, now Purl the stitch, P.1. * Repeat * to *.

Row 5: Yarn to back. * O., S.1, P.2 tog. (stitch and Over). * Repeat * to *.

Row 6: △ P.1. * Slip Over as before, P.2. * Repeat * to *, ending S.1, P.1.

Repeat from Row 3.

RIBBON BRIOCHE STITCH. *Figs. 200A and B.*

Also known as DOUBLE KNITTING.

Units—Double Knit Decrease and Elongated Stitch, △ *amalgamated and used as an Increase. To make a Throw, see Fig. 117.*

FIG. 200B.—Ribbon Brioche Stitch.

Cast On an even number of stitches.

Row 1: (F. of F.), S.1. * Insert needle into next stitch and throw yarn twice round the point of pin and then knit it. * Repeat on every stitch.

Row 2: S.1. * K.2 tog. △ This will include the long second throw and a stitch. Insert the needle through both these and then throw the yarn twice round the point of the needle and knit them together. * Repeat all along the row.

FIG. 200A.

△ Repeat the second row for length required.

To cast off, knit one row plain and then cast off.

USES. Both sides of the fabric are alike. Is very pretty on the ends of wide scarves, hems of children's frocks, etc., as it extends the base. Makes a thick all-over reversible fabric, with good width, when knitted on smaller needles.

OPEN STAR STITCH. *Figs. 201*A, B, *and* C.

Also known as LATTICE STITCH.

Units—Overs and delayed Slip Decrease.

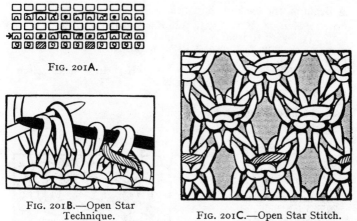

FIG. 201A.

FIG. 201B.—Open Star
Technique.

FIG. 201C.—Open Star Stitch.

Fig. 201A. The pattern consists of 4 rows, the units being alternated in the 1st and 3rd rows. The first row on chart represents the Cast-on stitches.

Cast On stitches divisible by 3 and 3 edge stitches.

△ Begin on the back of the fabric.

Row 1: K.2. * Over, K.3. △ Then insert the left needle into the first of these 3 Knit stitches (as in Fig. 201B) and lift it over the other 2 stitches and off the needle. * Repeat * to *, ending K.1.

Row 2: Knit, including the Overs.

Row 3: K.1. * K.3, take the first over the other two. Over. * Repeat * to *, ending K.2.

Row 4: Knit.

Repeat from row 1.

USES. Pretty in cotton yarns for jumpers, gloves, hats, etc.

BRAMBLE STITCH. *Figs. 202A and B.*

Also known as BLACKBERRY STITCH and TRINITY STITCH.

Units—Double Increase and Decrease.

The units of the 1st and 3rd rows are alternated to form an all-over pattern. Edge stitches not shown on Chart.

Cast On stitches divisible by 4 and 4 edge stitches.

△ Begin on the back of the fabric.

Row 1: K.2. * (K.1, P.1, K.1) into next stitch, making 3. Pass yarn to front of work and P.3 tog., pass yarn to back again. * Repeat * to *, ending K.2.

Row 2: Purl.

Row 3: K.2. * P.3 tog. (K.1, P.1, K.1) into next stitch. * Repeat * to *, ending K.2.

Row 4: Purl.

USES. Jumpers, borders, hats, bags.

FIG. 202A.

FIG. 202B.—Bramble Stitch.

SPIDER STITCH.

Units—Double Increase and Decrease.

Similar in appearance to Bramble Stitch (*see* Fig. 202), only units are reversed so that knitting is begun on the △ front of the fabric. More convenient in Round Knitting.

Cast On stitches divisible by 4 and 4 edge stitches.

Row 1: K.2. * (P.1, K.1, P.1) into next stitch, making 3. S.1, K.2 tog., p.s.s.o. * Repeat * to *, ending K.2.

Row 2: Knit.

Row 3: K.2. * S.1, K.2 tog., p.s.s.o., (P.1, K.1, P.1) into next stitch. * Repeat * to *, ending K.2.

Row 4: Knit.

PICOT EDGING. *Fig. 203.*

When using Bramble or Spider Stitch for articles such as scarves, shawls, etc., where the edges show, it is prettier to decorate the sides with a Picot, as in Fig. 203.

Instead of beginning each row with two ordinary Knit stitches, begin every row as follows :—

" Yarn forward, K.2 tog ", as in Fig. 203. These are the 2 edge stitches. From here continue as for Fig. 202.

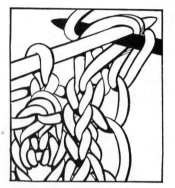

FIG. 203.—Picot Edging.

INDIAN PILLAR STITCH. *Figs. 204A and B.*

Also known as CLUSTER STITCH and MUSTER STITCH.

Units—Double Increase and Decrease amalgamated.

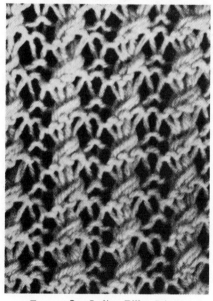

FIG. 204B.—Indian Pillar Stitch.

Cast On stitches divisible by 4 and 3 edge stitches.

Δ Begin on the back of the fabric.

FIG. 204A.

Row 1: K.2. * Insert needle purlwise into 3 stitches as if to purl together, but instead (P.1, K.1, P.1) into these 3 stitches as though they were one, K.1.* Repeat * to *, ending K.1.

Row 2: Purl.

Repeat these 2 rows.

BLUEBELL STITCH. *Figs. 205A and B.*

Units—Quintuplet Increase and Decrease and Elongated Drop Stitch.

Five stitches are knitted together and 5 are made into the next stitch. The 5th row is elongated.

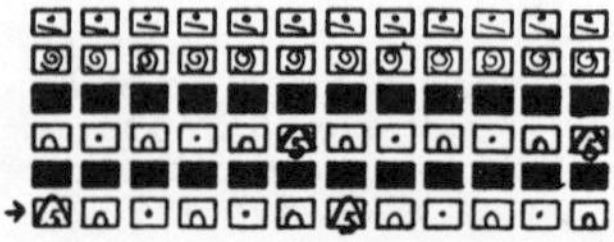

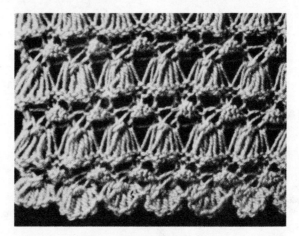

FIG. 205A.

FIG. 205B.—Bluebell Stitch.

Cast On stitches divisible by 6 and 2 edge stitches.
△ Begin on the back of the fabric.

Row 1: K.1. * P.5 tog. Into next stitch (K.1, P.1, K.1, P.1, K.1), before slipping it off needle. * Repeat * to *, ending K.1.

Row 2: Purl.

Row 3: K.1. * (K.1, P.1, K.1, P.1, K.1), making 5 into next stitch, P.5 tog. * Repeat * to *, ending K.1.

Row 4: Purl.

Row 5: * Insert needle knitwise into 1st stitch and Throw the yarn 3 times round point of needle and then knit stitch. * Repeat on every stitch.

In the next row this will lengthen the stitch.

Row 6: Knit, knitting the 1st of the treble Throws and dropping the other 2. Repeat on every stitch until the original number of stitches is again on the needle.

Repeat these 6 rows.

CORAL KNOT STITCH. *Figs. 206A and* B.

Also known as HONEYCOMB STITCH.

Units—Raised Increase and Knit Decrease but used on separate rows (see *Fig. 282*). *Edge stitches not on chart.*

FIG. 206B.—Coral Knot Stitch.   FIG. 206A.

Cast On an even number of stitches.

△ Begin on the right side of the fabric.

Row 1: S.1. * K.2 tog. * Repeat * to *, ending K.1.
Row 2: K.1. * K.1, pick up and K.1 on running thread. *
          Repeat * to *, ending K.1.
Row 3: Knit.
Row 4: Purl.

Repeat these 4 rows.

CORAL LOOP STITCH. *Figs. 207A and* B.

Units—Knit Decrease, Raised Increase, and Elongated Drop Stitch.

Similar to Coral Knot Stitch, only elongated in Row 2. To get the best effect knit loosely.

FIG. 207A.

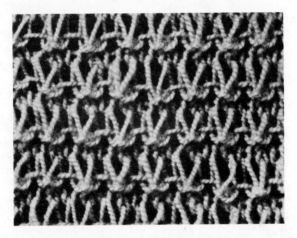

FIG. 207B.—Coral Loop Stitch.

Cast On an uneven number of stitches.

Begin on front of fabric.

Row 1: S.1. * K.2 tog. * Repeat * to *.

Row 2: * Insert right needle knitwise into 1st stitch and Throw the yarn twice round needle-point and draw through a double stitch. Pick up the running thread and knit this also with a double Throw. * Repeat for entire row.

Row 3: Knit, knitting the 1st of the long double stitches and Δ dropping the 2nd. This will restore the original number of stitches to needle.

Row 4: Purl.

Repeat these 4 rows.

LABURNUM STITCH. *Figs. 208A and B.*

Units—Woven Slip, amalgamated with Double Decrease, followed by Double Over. Edge stitches not on chart.

For O.2 Rev., *see* Fig. 289.

Cast On stitches divisible by 5 and 2 over.

Row 1 (Front of Fabric): P.2. * Keep yarn to front and S.1, yarn to back, K.2 tog., p.s.s.o. O.2 Rev. P.2. * Repeat * to *

FIG. 208A.

Row 2: K.2. * Purl into back of first Over and then into front of second Over, P.1, K.2. * Repeat * to *.

Row 3: * P.2, K.3. * Repeat, ending P.2.

Row 4: K.2. * P.3, K.2. * Repeat * to *.

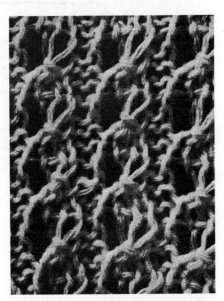

FIG. 208B.—Laburnum Stitch.

RAINDROP STITCH. *Figs. 209A and B.*

Units—Lifted Increase (M.1 L.), Slip Decrease.

Cast On stitches divisible by 8 and 1 over.

Row 1 (Front of Fabric): K.1. * Knit into head of stitch below. Return it to left needle and knit it again. Now knit the stitch on needle and pass the lifted stitch over this stitch and off the needle, K.3. * Repeat * to *.

Row 2: Purl.
Row 3: * K.3, M.1 L., and work as before. *
Repeat, ending K.1.
Row 4: Purl.

Repeat these 4 rows.

FIG. 209A.

FIG. 209B.—Raindrop Stitch.

ROSE FABRIC. *Fig. 210.*

Cast On an even number of stitches.
Row 1 (Front of Fabric): * K.1. For next stitch knit into stitch
below instead of stitch on needle. * Repeat.
Row 2: Purl.
Row 3: * Knit into stitch below, K.1. * Repeat.
Row 4: Purl.

Repeat these 4 rows.

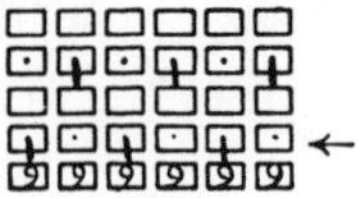

ROSE VARIATION.

Rows 2 and 4: Knit, instead of Purl.

FIG. 210.

DOUBLE ROSE FABRIC.

This fascinating fabric resembles Double English Brioche (Fig. 198) on the front, and Stocking Stitch on the back. Is often used with S.S. side uppermost as an extra cosy fabric for Cotton Gloves.

Cast On an even number of stitches.
Row 1: (F. of F.). * K.1. Knit into next stitch below that on
needle. * Repeat * to *.
Row 2: * P.1. Purl into next stitch below that on needle. *
Repeat * to *.

Repeat these 2 rows.

FIG. 211.—Albanian Socks, nineteenth century. Front and back view showing pointed Peasant Heel (*see also* page 270, Horizontal Openings). The white bands in Horizontal Tunisian Stitch,

TUNISIAN KNITTING

These are Eastern stitches, and the technique complies with the Eastern rules, which are the exact reverse of Western methods.

The stitches are knitted through the back, and the slip stitches are slipped knitwise, as a Pattern Principle.

There are two methods of work, Horizontal and Oblique Tunisian Stitch. △ Both begin on the back of the fabric, and the success of either depends on the correct order in which the Overs are knitted. If this is not strictly regarded it becomes quite impossible to form the fabric.

Make an experiment on six stitches before using these fabrics for any specific purpose.

These stitches are popular in the East for either solid or open fabrics, varying according to size of needles used.

They are often used to form a solid background and richly embroidered, as the fabric lends itself admirably to the addition of embroidery stitches.

In Fig. 212 the Horizontal Stitch is used to divide the elaborate pattern of the gay Albanian sock. Knitted thus on smallish needles it gives an embossed horizontal line shown white in the photograph. The white vertical lines are crossed Knit stitches (K.1 B.). The curious pointed heels of the socks are added afterwards according to Eastern methods (*see* page 270).

HORIZONTAL TUNISIAN STITCH. *Figs. 212*A *and* B.

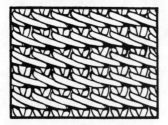

Fig. 212 B.—Horizontal Tunisian Stitch.

Fig. 212A.

Cast On any number of stitches.

△ Begin on the back of the fabric.

Row 1: * S.1 (knitwise), Over. * Repeat on every stitch
△ (*i.e.*, S.1, then bring the yarn forward between the
needles, and slip the next stitch. Take yarn over
needle and to front again and slip the next stitch, etc.).
△ End the row with an Over, and keep the left thumb
on it to retain it in position while turning to begin the
return row.

Row 2: * K.2 tog. B. * (*i.e.*, insert the needle through the back of
the last Over and the last slipped stitch and knit them
together). Do this all along the row, every stitch being
knitted together with the correct Over.

Repeat these 2 rows.

OBLIQUE TUNISIAN STITCH. *Figs. 213*A *and* B.

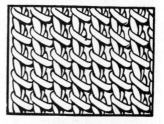

FIG. 213B.—Oblique Tunisian
Stitch.

FIG. 213A.

Cast On any number of stitches.

Begin on the back of the fabric.

Row 1: * Over, S.1 (knitwise). * Repeat △ (*i.e.*, yarn forward and over needle, slip the 1st stitch knitwise,
forward again between needles, S.1. Yarn over and
to front again, S.1 and so on. The Over is single). Be
sure to complete the last Over.

Row 2: * K.2 tog. B. * Repeat (*i.e.*, insert the needle through
the back of the slipped stitch and the last Over, and
knit them together. △ Keep the Overs strictly in
position with the left thumb and forefinger all along
the row, so that the last stitch is knitted together with
the last Over, *i.e.*, the one made at the beginning of the
row).

Repeat these 2 rows.

EMBOSSED MOTIFS AND PATTERNS

Designing Units—Casting-on, Increasing and Decreasing.

These patterns are very different from any others, as the blister-like Motifs are built up of extra stitches, "clustered" into the fabric at regular intervals quite independent of the original number of stitches cast on.

These extra stitches can be either cast on in mass or built-in to the fabric with Increasing units, wherever the Motif is inserted.

There are four distinct types of Embossed Motifs :—

1. Detached Motifs, Knots or Tufts.
2. Semi-detached Embossed Motifs.
3. Attached Blister, Embossed or Cloqué Motifs.
4. Embossed (Exchange Principle).

All four are explained under these headings.

Knitted Cloqué fabrics, like cloqué materials, have a heavy appearance, and, as such, are more suitable for coats, bedjackets, hats, bedspreads, pram-covers, or any article where the "quality" of weight will impart dignity.

DESIGN

All Motifs can be arranged vertically, horizontally, or as all-over repeat patterns, on the same principle as Eyelet Motifs. They can, and with good effect, be grouped into geometric shapes, such as squares, diamonds, chevrons, etc.

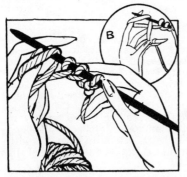

Two different methods of casting on are necessary for the detached and semi-detached Motifs :—

I. Right Needle Cast-on.

Fig. 214 shows method of casting on extra stitches on the right needle, when these are added in the middle of a row to form the basis of a Motif. The yarn is looped round the thumb, and then transferred to the needle.

FIG. 214.—Casting-on Right Needle.

2. Left Needle Cast-on.

Fig. 215 shows method of casting on extra stitches on the left needle, when these are added in the middle of a row, as a basis for a Motif. The stitches are knitted on. Knit a loop and transfer it from right to left needle. Repeat as required.

I. DETACHED MOTIFS

These include Picot Knot, Cheniel Tuft, and Detached Oval Cluster, all of which are loose Motifs only attached to the fabric by one stitch.

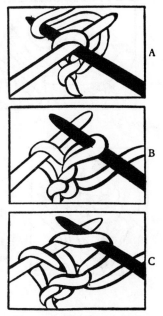

FIG. 215.—Casting-on Left Needle.

PICOT KNOT. *Figs. 216*A, B, *and* C.

DESIGN. The Knot is made and completed on one stitch, and so can be arranged in patterns on the same plan as for Eyelet Motifs (*see* Charts, substituting Knots for Eyelets). For an all-over repeat plan, *see* Fig. 57, substituting the Knot for the Purl stitch. When grouped in geometric shapes, the Knot can be repeated on every other stitch.

Working Method

On arriving at position for Knot cast 4 stitches on to left needle (*see* Fig. 216). (If larger Knot is required, cast on more stitches.) Insert right needle into stitch, shown black in Fig. 216A. Knit a new stitch and put this back on to left needle. Insert needle into the new stitch and knit another new stitch and put back again on to left needle. Make 4 new stitches in this way. Now knit the 4 new stitches just made, and then drop the 5th and original stitch shown black (*see* Fig. 216B).

FIG. 216A.

FIG. 216B.

FIG. 216C.

With the left needle lift stitch No. 3 over stitch No. 4 and off the needle. Do the same with stitches Nos. 2 and 1 (*see* Fig. 216C). This leaves the 4th stitch only on the right needle and completes the Knot.

The yarn is also in position to continue knitting, until the next Knot is needed.

CHENIEL TUFT. *Figs. 217*A, B, *and* C.

The Tuft, like the Picot Knot, also begins and ends on the same stitch, and follows the same rules of design.

Working Method

Insert the right needle into a stitch, knit a loop and put it back on left needle (*see* Fig. 217A), and then knit this new loop, which transfers it to the right needle.

FIG. 217A.

Insert the needle again into the same original stitch, shown black in Figs. 217A and B, and make another loop. Put it on the left needle and knit this. Repeat until there are 4 new stitches made in this way (*see* Fig. 217B). If larger Tuft is required, add more stitches. The original stitch (black) is then dropped.

With the left needle, lift stitch No. 3 over stitch No. 4, and off the needle.

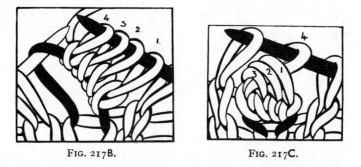

FIG. 217B.   FIG. 217C.

Now lift No. 2 over No. 4, and then No. 1. This leaves 1 stitch (No. 4) on the right needle (*see* Fig. 217C), and completes the Tuft.

Repeat as required.

DETACHED OVAL CLUSTER. *Fig. 218.*

DESIGN. This is a larger Motif, but also built up and completed on 1 stitch, as shown in Fig. 218. Such Motifs can be introduced at intervals of several stitches, and repeated all over a fabric. They are often used on fine cotton Lace Edgings, repeated in diamond formation, about 20 or so to the diamond, and are frequently seen arranged thus on old knitted bedspreads. Eyelet charts will again suggest patterns.

Working Method

Row 1: Six stitches are formed into 1 stitch as a basis for the Motif as follows: Yarn forward, insert needle knitwise into stitch, and K.1, Over, K.1, Over, K.1, all into this same stitch. Drop original (black) stitch.

Row 2: Turn and Purl these 6 stitches.

Row 3: Turn, S.1, K.5.

Row 4: Turn, S.1, P.5.

Row 5: Turn, S.1, K.5.

Row 6: Turn, P.2 tog., 3 times.

Row 7: Turn, S.1, K.2 tog., p.s.s.o.

This leaves 1 stitch on the right needle as in Fig. 218, and completes the Motif. The knitting is then resumed without further concern to the tuft so made.

FIG. 218.—Detached Oval Cluster.

An Oval Cluster can be based on fewer or more stitches, according to size of Motif required. It can be made either oblong or round by increasing the number of knitted rows to lengthen it or increasing the number of stitches forming the base to broaden it.

2. SEMI-DETACHED EMBOSSED MOTIFS

The principles of work are quite different, as the Motif is now " Built " in △ *between* two stitches, and starts from an *independent* base of cast-on stitches. The shape is built-in over several rows before completed. In this case certain pattern rows will contain considerably more stitches than originally cast-on, but these are gradually reduced to the original number as the Motif is completed.

△ The chosen Motif must be designed separately, *see* Fig. 219A, taking care to use the correct Decrease (left and right angle, *see* Fig. 297), in order to keep the outline of shape clean. The lined spaces represent no stitch (*see* Fig. 62). The favourite shape is " Bell " as designed in Figs. 219A and B. Other shapes are built on the same principle.

△ As the stitches forming such Motifs are all extra to those cast on, the only possible way of charting the pattern is to indicate by a vertical line the position on the chart where the Motif will be inserted (*see* Fig. 219A). Here two lines, four stitches apart, indicate that the Motif is to be repeated *between* every 4th stitch.

△ △ This same method of designing must be used for ATTACHED Embossed Motifs.

The Bell Motif needs fourteen rows to complete, so each vertical line must be fourteen rows high, as shown (Fig. 219). In Figs. 220 and 221 the Bell is shorter, so this line must be correspondingly shorter.

Take a large sheet of graph paper and indicate on this the design required. The Bell can be made as an all-over repeat, or to alternate, or the Bells can be arranged in Chevron shapes, or grouped in Diamond or any other geometric shape, according to the position of the vertical lines as indicated on the graph.

In order to throw the Bell or any other Motif into relief, the background should be arranged to contrast. In Fig. 219B the Bell is in Knit stitches on a Purl background, but any other background, such as Lace Faggot Stitch, can be used.

Bell Motifs, when repeated in rows, can be considered as an insertion, and given a Fantastic movement as in Fig. 178. The repeating Bells would then take the position of the Welt.

These patterns are most exciting to create and are exceedingly popular. They are often found in old lace patterns, and on knitted cotton bedspreads, grouped in different geometric shapes, a favourite method being to arrange them in diamond shapes and repeat this diamond all over the spread. Sometimes they are knitted in squares and afterwards joined on the community principle (*see* Fig. 240).

HOW TO WRITE THE DIRECTIONS

First design and chart out the Motif as in Fig. 219A (Bell Motif). Then write description of Motif only as on page 216, numbering the rows and placing the description in the middle of the paper. Now △ before and after this description write the number of stitches forming the background. Add repeat marks plus edge stitches. Do this in each row. △ Next decide how many rows shall divide the pattern before it is repeated, and then the description is complete.

△ Both semi-detached and attached Motifs are described in the same way. The following is a practical example :—

BELL MOTIF. *Figs. 219A and B.*

Written description of Bell Motif only is given first, but below this on page 216, is shown how to add the background stitches and repeat marks.

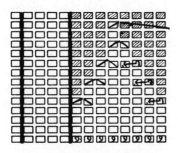

Fig. 219A

Fig. 219B.—Semi-detached Bell Cluster.

Row 1: **Cast On** 8 stitches.   (Right needle method, Fig. 214.)
Row 2:   Purl 8.
Row 3:   Knit 8.
Row 4:   Purl 8.
Row 5:   S.1, K.1, p.s.s.o., K.4, K.2 tog.
Row 6:   Purl 6.
Row 7:   S.1, K.1, p.s.s.o., K.2, K.2 tog.
Row 8:   Purl 4.
Row 9:   S.1, K.1, p.s.s.o., K.2 tog.
Row 10:   Purl 2.
Row 11:   K.2 tog.
Row 12:   Purl 1.
Row 13:   K.2 tog.

This last decrease will include the last stitch of the Bell and one
background stitch.   See Row 13 below when it is P.3 instead
of P.4.

Row 14: Purl.

BELL MOTIF IN REPEAT.   *Figs. 219A and* B.

The following description now incorporates the previous Bell Motif
description, this being here shown in brackets.   Placed before and after
this are the number of stitches forming the background and edge, also
repeat marks *.   The long vertical lines in Fig. 219A show that the Bell
Motif is repeated between every fourth stitch.   This also gives the number
of stitches to cast on, *i.e.*, " Stitches divisible by 4 " plus any edge stitches
needed.   The background must contrast to the Bell Stitches, so Purl Fabric,
the simplest, is chosen.

Cast On stitches divisible by 4, plus 4 for edge.
Row 1:   P.4.   * (Cast on 8 stitches), P.4. *   Repeat * to *.
Row 2:   * K.4, (P.8). *   Repeat, ending K.4.
Row 3:   P.4.   * (K.8), P.4. *   Repeat * to *.
Row 4:   * K.4, (P.8). *   Repeat, ending K.4.
Row 5:   P.4.   * (S.1, K.1, p.s.s.o., K.4, K.2 tog.), P.4. *   Repeat
                  * to *.
Row 6:   * K.4, (P.6). *   Repeat, ending K.4.
Row 7:   P.2.   * (S.1, K.1, p.s.s.o., K.2, K.2 tog.), P.4. *   Repeat
                  * to *.
Row 8:   * K.4, (P.4). *   Repeat, ending K.4.
Row 9:   P.4.   * (S.1, K.1, p.s.s.o., K.2 tog.), P.4. *   Repeat
                  * to *.
Row 10:   * K.4, (P.2). *   Repeat, ending K.4.
Row 11:   P.4.   * (K.2 tog.), P.4. *   Repeat * to *.
Row 12:   * K.4, (P.1). *   Repeat, ending K.4.
Row 13:   P.4.   * (K.2 tog.), P.3. *   Repeat * to *.
Row 14:   Knit.

Knit 2 rows of Stocking Stitch and repeat from Row 1, or, to
alternate the Bell for the next repeat, increase the number of edge
stitches from 4 to 6 in all odd-number rows.   This will automatically
increase the ending from 4 to 6 stitches in all even rows.

OLD ROUND SAMPLER

Fig. 220.   Here two different methods of grouping the "Bell" Motif in pattern are shown.

In "Bell-and-Rope Pattern" the Bell is repeated in rows divided by six stitches and an ornamental rib of one Crossed Knit stitch to represent the rope.   In the second, "Bell-Ringer's Peal Pattern", the Bell is grouped as a half-diagonal square, one half containing Bells, the other half Bell-ropes, represented by a 2 and 2 Rib of Cross Knit stitches, which give a better embossed effect to the rope.

BELL-AND-ROPE PATTERN. *Fig. 220.*

FIG. 220.—Knitted sampler bearing signature and date 1833 in bead knitting, and showing two designs in semi-detached Bell Motif. (1) Bell-and-Rope Pattern. (2) Bell-Ringers Peal Pattern.

The Bells are a little shorter in height than the Bell in Fig. 219, as the Decreases are made on both rows. For P.R. *see* Fig. 293. The stitches forming the Bell are enclosed in brackets.

Cast On stitches divisible by 5.

Row 1: P.2. * K.1 B., P.4. * Repeat * to *, ending K.1 B., P.2.

Row 2: K.2, P.1 B. * K.4, P.1 B. * Repeat * to *, ending K.2.

Row 3: P.2. * K.1 B., P.2. (Cast on 8 stitches), P.2. * Repeat * to *, ending K.1 B., P.2.

Rows 4 and 6: K.2, P.1 B. * K.2, (P.8), K.2, P.1 B. * Repeat * to *, ending K.2.

Row 5: P.2. * K.1 B., P.2, (K.8), P.2. * Repeat * to *, ending K.1 B., P.2.

Row 7: P.2. * K.1 B., P.2, (S.1, K.1, p.s.s.o., K.4, K.2 tog.), P.2. * Repeat * to *, ending K.1 B., P.2.

Row 8: K.2, P.1 B. * K.2, (P.2 tog., P.2, P.R.), K.2, P.1 B. * Repeat * to *, ending K.2.

Row 9: P.2. * K.1 B., P.2, (S.1, K.1, p.s.s.o., K.2 tog.), P.2. * Repeat * to *, ending K.1 B., P.2.

Row 10: K.2, P.1 B. * K.1, (K.2 tog., K.2 tog.), K.1, P.1 B. * Repeat * to *, ending K.2.

Repeat from Row 1.

BELL-RINGER'S PEAL PATTERN.

Figs. 220 and 221.

For illustration of this pattern *see* Fig. 220, and for plan of pattern, Fig. 221. The Bells are set into a background of Purl fabric. This is left plain on the chart so that the position of Bells can be seen. Each Bell falls between two Purl stitches and takes 8 rows to decrease. The Bell-ropes are in Cross Stitches.

For (K.2 B.) Knit through the back of each stitch; (P.2 B.) Purl through the back of each stitch.

Cast On stitches divisible by 26 and 4 edge Garter stitches. Knit 4 rows of Purl Fabric as a Welt, and then begin pattern.

Row 1: K.2. * P.3, O., K.2 tog., (P.3, K.2 B., P.2, K.2 B., P.2, K.2 B., P.2, K.2 B., P.2, K.2 B.). * Repeat * to *, ending K.2 as edge stitches. The brackets enclose the Ribbing.

Row 2: K.2. * (P.2 B., K.2, P.2 B., K.2, P.2 B., K.2, P.2 B., K.2, P.2 B., K.3). P.2—that is the Decrease and Over—K.3. * Repeat * to *, ending K.2, as edge stitches.

These two lines are given in full; from here on " rib in pattern " means repeat between the brackets. Always knit last 2 stitches of row.

The plan (Fig. 221) shows how the stitches forming the rib section are cut diagonally. As the number of Bells increases the ribbed stitches become fewer. On back (even) rows the ribbing stops at the Decrease which is one stitch before the Over. This will be clearly seen after knitting is commenced. Here the directions say " Purl the Decrease and Over ", or (P. dec. and O.)

From Rows 3–12 Bell stitches are enclosed in brackets.

Row 3: K.2. * P.4, O., K.2 tog. Rib in pattern as before. * Repeat * to *, ending K.2.

Row 4: K.2. * Rib in pattern. Purl dec. and O., K.4. * Repeat * to *, ending K.2.

Row 5: K.2. * P.4, (Cast on 8 for 1st Bell), P.1, O., K.2 tog. Rib in pattern. * Repeat * to *, ending K.2.

Row 6: K.2. * Rib in pattern. P. dec. and O., K.1, (P.8), K.4. * Repeat * to *, ending K.2.

Row 7: K.2. * P.4, (S.1, K.1, p.s.s.o., K.4, K.2 tog.), P.2, O., K.2 tog., Rib. * Repeat * to *, ending K.2.

Row 8: K.2. * Rib. P. dec. and O., K.2, (P.6), K.4. * Repeat * to *, ending K.2.

Row 9: K.2. * P.4, (S.1, K.1, p.s.s.o., K.2, K.2 tog.), P.3, O., K.2 tog., Rib. * Repeat * to *, ending K.2.

Row 10: K.2. * Rib. P. dec. and O., K.3, (P.4), K.4. * Repeat * to *, ending K.2.

Row 11: K.2. * P.4, (S.1, K.1, p.s.s.o., K.2 tog.), P.4, O., K.2 tog., Rib. * Repeat * to *, ending K.2.

Row 12: K.2. * Rib. P. dec. and O., K.3, (P.3 tog.), K.4. * Repeat * to *, ending K.2.

Row 13: K.2. * (P.4, Cast on 8) twice, P.1, O., K.2 tog., Rib. * Repeat * to *, ending K.2.

Row 14: K.2. * Rib. P. dec. and O., K.1, (P.8, K.4) twice. * Repeat * to *, ending K.2.

Row 15: K.2. * (P.4, S.1, K.1, p.s.s.o., K.4, K.2 tog.) twice, P.2, O., K.2 tog., Rib. * Repeat * to *, ending K.2.

Row 16: K.2. * Rib. P. dec. and O., K.2, (P.6, K.4) twice. * Repeat * to *, ending K.2.

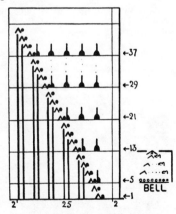

FIG. 221.—Plan for Bell-Ringer's Peal Pattern.

Row 17: K.2. * (P.4, S.1, K.1, p.s.s.o., K.2, K.2 tog.) twice, P.3, O., K.2 tog., Rib. * Repeat * to *, ending K.2.

Row 18: K.2. * Rib. P. dec. and O., K.3, (K.4, P.4) twice. * Repeat * to *, ending K.2.

Row 19: K.2. * (P.4, S.1, K.1, p.s.s.o., K.2 tog.) twice, P.4, O., K.2 tog., Rib. * Repeat * to *, ending K.2.

Row 20: K.2. * Rib. P. dec. and O., K.3, (P.3 tog., K.3, P.3 tog.), K.4 .* Repeat * to *, ending K.2.

This Double Decrease finishes the 2 Bells. The pattern repeats now with 3 Bells.

Row 21: K.2. * (P.4, Cast on 8) 3 times, P.1, O., K.2 tog., Rib. * Repeat * to *, ending K.2.

Rows 22 to 28: Same as Rows 14 to 20, only repeat Bell instructions 3 times instead of twice. *See* plan.

Beginning at Row 29; the Bell is repeated 4 times.

Row 29: K.2. * (P.4, Cast on 8) 4 times, P.1, O., K.2 tog., Rib. * Repeat * to *, ending K.2.

Rows 30 to 36: Same as Rows 14 to 20 only repeat Bell instructions 4 times. *See* plan.

Beginning at Row 37 the Bell is repeated 5 times.

Row 37: K.2. * (P.4, Cast on 8) 5 times, P.1, O., K.2 tog., Rib. * Repeat * to *, ending K.2.

Rows 38 to 44: Repeat Bell instructions 5 times.

Rows 45 and 47: Purl.

Rows 46 and 48: Knit.

Repeat these 48 rows.

BELL FRILLING. *Fig. 222.*

To form a frilling of little Bells, begin from the top of the Bell with one Knit Stitch on a background of Purl, and increase either side with an Over on every Knit row, to build out the shape. Cast off along the base line of the Bells.

USES. For collars, etc. A Picot cast-off forms a pretty finish to this frill. *See* Fig. 244.

FIG. 222.—Bell Frilling.

Cast On stitches divisible by 8 and 7 over.

Row 1:	* P.7, K.1. *	Repeat, ending P.7.
Row 2:	* K.7, P.1. *	Repeat, ending K.7.
Row 3:	* P.7, O., K.1, O. *	Repeat, ending P.7.
Row 4:	* K.7, P.3. *	Repeat, ending K.7.
Row 5:	* P.7, O., K.3, O. *	Repeat, ending P.7.
Row 6:	* K.7, P.5. *	Repeat, ending K.7.
Row 7:	* P.7, O., K.5, O. *	Repeat, ending P.7.
Row 8:	* K.7, P.7. *	Repeat, ending K.7.
Row 9:	* P.7, O., K.7, O. *	Repeat, ending P.7.
Row 10:	* K.7, P.9. *	Repeat, ending K.7.
Row 11:	* P.7, O., K.9, O. *	Repeat, ending P.7.
Row 12:	* K.7, P.11. *	Repeat, ending K.7.
Row 13:	* P.7, O., K.11, O. *	Repeat, ending P.7.
Row 14:	* K.7, P.13. *	Repeat, ending K.7.
Row 15:	* P.7, O., K.13, O. *	Repeat, ending P.7.
Row 16:	* K.7, P.15. *	Repeat, ending K.7.
Row 17:	* P.7, O., K. 15,O. *	Repeat, ending P.7.
Row 18:	* K.7, P.17. *	Repeat, ending K.7.
Row 19:	* P.7, O., K.17, O. *	Repeat, ending P.7.
Row 20:	* K.7, P.19. *	Repeat, ending K.7.

Cast off.   Use either plain or Picot cast-off (Fig. 244).

---

3. ATTACHED EMBOSSED MOTIFS

For these Motifs extra stitches are built into the background by first using an Increasing Unit, and then taken away by using a Decreasing Unit. Both must be arranged to pair right and left (*see* Fig. 297). The Motif looks like a Blister (*see* Fig. 223B). The method can be better appreciated by studying the chart in Fig. 223A. Each black vertical line indicates where the Motif (charted at the side) will be clustered in between these stitches over 18 rows. Blisters of this type can be any shape. In Fig. 223A the plan is a triangle, and produces the shape shown in Fig. 223B, but the Motif can be built out in both directions to form embossed circles, ovals, leaves or diamonds, as required (*see also* Fig. 240). The Motif must be designed separately and then spaced △ between the background stitches.   It is an extra, and so not calculated in the number of stitches cast-on (*see* page 215 for method of charting and writing directions).

FUCHSIA PATTERN.   *Figs. 223A and* B.

The Motif is gradually built up on the Over increase for 12 rows, and then from Rows 13 to 18 is decreased away again on both rows, thus giving it a quick slanting line.   *See* Chart in Fig. 223A.   One of the 8 stitches cast on is incorporated into this Embossed Motif.

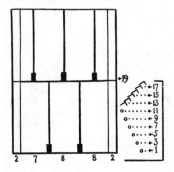

FIG. 223A.—Chart for Fuchsia Pattern.

Cast On stitches divisible by 8 and 11 over, 4 of which are edge stitches.

Row 1: K.2.   * P.7, K.1, O. *   Repeat * to *, ending P.7, K.2.
Row 2: K.9.   * Purl the Over, P.1, K.7. *   Repeat * to *, ending K.2.
Row 3: K.2.   * P.7, K.2, O. *   Repeat * to *, ending P.7, K.2.
Row 4: K.9.   * P.3, K.7. *   Repeat * to *, ending K.2.
Row 5: K.2.   * P.7, K.3, O. *   Repeat * to *, ending P.7, K.2.
Row 6: K.9.   * P.4, K.7. *   Repeat * to *, ending K.2.
Row 7: K.2.   * P.7, K.4, O. *   Repeat * to *, ending P.7, K.2.
Row 8: K.9.   * P.5, K.7. *   Repeat * to *, ending K.2.
Row 9: K.2.   * P.7, K.5, O. *   Repeat * to *, ending P.7, K.2.
Row 10: K.9.   * P.6, K.7. *   Repeat * to *, ending K.2.
Row 11: K.2.   * P.7, K.6, O. *   Repeat * to *, ending P.7, K.2.
Row 12: K.9.   * P.7, K.7. *   Repeat * to *, ending K.2.
Row 13: K.2.   * P.7, K.5, K.2 tog. *   Repeat * to *, ending P.7, K.2.
Row 14: K.9.   * P.2 tog., P.4, K.7. *   Repeat * to *, ending K.2.
Row 15: K.2.   * P.7, K.3, K.2 tog. *   Repeat * to *, ending P.7, K.2.
Row 16: K.9.   * P.2 tog., P.2, K.7. *   Repeat * to *, ending K.2.
Row 17: K.2.   * P.7, K.1, K.2 tog. *   Repeat * to *, ending P.7, K.2.
Row 18: K.9.   * P.2 tog., K.7. *   Repeat * to *, ending K.2.
Row 19: K.2, P.3, * K.1, O., P.7. *   Repeat * to *, ending K.1, O., P.3, K.2.
Row 20: K.5.   * P.2, K.7. *   Repeat * to *, ending P.2, K.5.

Row 21: K.2, P.3. * K.2, O., P.7. * Repeat * to *, ending K.2, O., P.3, K.2.
Row 22: K.5. * P.3, K.7. * Repeat * to *, ending P.3, K.5.
Row 23: K.2, P.3. * K.3, O., P.7. * Repeat * to *, ending K.3, O., P.3, K.2.
Row 24: K.5. * P.4, K.7. * Repeat * to *, ending P.4, K.5.
Row 25: K.2, P.3. * K.4, O., P.7. * Repeat * to *, ending K.4, O., P.3, K.2.

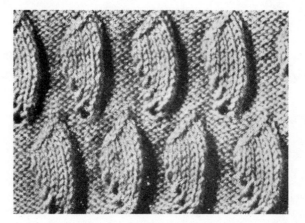

FIG. 223B.—Fuchsia Pattern.

Row 26: K.5. * P.5, K.7. * Repeat * to *, ending P.5, K.5.
Row 27: K.2, P.3. * K.5, O., P.7. * Repeat * to *, ending K.5, O., P.3, K.2.
Row 28: K.5. * P.6, K.7. * Repeat * to *, ending P.6, K.5.
Row 29: K.2, P.3. * K.6, O., P.7. * Repeat * to *, ending K.6, O., P.3, K.2.
Row 30: K.5. * P.7, K.7. * Repeat * to *, ending P.7, K.5.
Row 31: K.2, P.3. * K.5, K.2 tog., P.7. * Repeat * to *, ending K.5, K.2 tog., P.3, K.2.
Row 32: K.5. * P.2 tog., P.4, K.7. * Repeat * to *, ending P.2 tog., P.4. K.5.
Row 33: K.2, P.3. * K.3, K.2 tog., P.7. * Repeat * to *, ending K.3, K.2 tog., P.3, K.2.
Row 34: K.5. * P.2 tog., P.2, K.7. * Repeat * to *, ending P.2 tog., P.2. K.5.
Row 35: K.2, P.3. * K.1, K.2 tog., P.7. * Repeat * to *, ending K.1, K.2 tog., P.3, K.2.
Row 36: K.5. * P.2 tog., K.7. * Repeat * to *, ending P.2 tog., K.5.

Repeat from Row 1.

EMBOSSED RUCHING. *Fig. 224.*

An extra stitch is MADE before every stitch, using Raised Open Increase (Fig. 282), all along a row, and so doubles the number in the row. These extra stitches are knitted for 7, 9, or 11 rows, or depth of insertion required and in a contrasting fabric. Afterwards reduce to original proportion by decreasing all along the row. Use needles 2 sizes smaller for knitting these insertion rows. Change to larger size for background (*see* Fig. 224 for method of use).

FIG. 224.—Embossed Ruching.

Cast On any number of stitches.

Knit Stocking Stitch for 20 rows.

Change to smaller needles.

Row 1 (Pattern): On front of work. K.2. * M.1, (R.O.), K.1. * Repeat for entire row, ending K.2.

Knit 7 rows Garter Stitch or 7 rows in Purl Fabric.

Row 9: K.2. * P.2 tog. * Repeat * to *, ending K.2.

Row 10: Purl.

Change to larger needles.

Continue in Stocking Stitch until next insertion.

---

4. EMBOSSED MOTIFS (Exchange Principle)

The Embossed effect of the Pattern shown in Fig. 226, is obtained by quite another principle of design, and not by clustering in extra stitches as before, but by an exchange of stitches and designing units.

The simplest way to explain the principle is to assume the chart in Fig. 226, as representing a box of bricks, coloured white on one side, and black on the other.

In rows 1 and 2 the pattern begins with a Rib of 1, 3, and 11, that is 1 Purl Stitch, 3 Knit Stitches on a ground of 11 Purl Stitches, or, 1 black block, 3 white and 11 black. In Row 3, these 3 white blocks have been pushed one block to the left, and the empty space filled with a black block which thus makes an exchange of position. As in Knitting it is quite impossible to pick out one stitch, and replace it 3 stitches to the right or left; the effect is gained by making an extra stitch, M.1 B., to fill the empty space in Row 3, and then taking this stitch away again by a Decrease, after knitting the Rib of 3 Knit Stitches. Study the Chart.

The Pattern continues in this way, the same 3 white blocks (3 Knit Stitches) being pushed in all 5 blocks to the left, and then moved back again to their original position by Row 21.

To make the Ogee Shape, the next Rib of 3 Knit Stitches, is pushed in the opposite direction. As it is the same 3 Knit Stitches which are being moved all the time, they become embossed because the Increasing Unit used has been solid (M. 1 B.). Should the Ornamental Over have been chosen for this purpose, the Embossed effect would have been lost, as it allows a space. Since the Ribs are embossed the Purl background must recede, so when the fabric is reversed, the opposite effect is revealed, as in Fig. 225.

These Patterns are fascinating to create, and offer much scope for originality. The Pattern in Fig. 227 is built on the same principle, but is not so embossed because of the Trellis Lace sections introduced in between. Here too it should be noted that the single Ribs in Cross Knit Stitch help to give the embossed effect.

Another version of the same Pattern Principle is shown in Fig. 193, only here instead of waving left and right a Rib of 3 Knit Stitches, a vertical Insertion of Faggot Stitch is waved. Also, the Solid Increase which is used to push the Rib right and left, in Fig. 226, is in Fig. 193 changed to the Ornamental Over, and brought out into the middle of the Ogee Shape, to form decorative Lace Spaces. The Decreasing Units above still take the inverted V shape, but now brought 2 blocks inwards towards the middle, to make the inclosing Pear-like Shape at the top of the Pattern. Compare the two Charts, and notice how 6 extra Eyelets are used to make a more open flower-like pattern, in addition to the Lace building Overs.

This Pattern has no embossed effect, because, as explained, the Building Increase is open, so the comparison of the two patterns makes an instructive object lesson in the vast differences which can be achieved by the use of different Increasing Units, Solid or Visible.

PARQUET CLOQUÉ PATTERN.

Fig. 225.

This fabric is the reverse side of Fig. 226 (Waved Embossed Ribbing). As the directions are long, they are not repeated, but the fabric can be obtained by commencing the instructions for Fig. 226 on the back of the work.

FIG. 225.—Parquet Cloqué Pattern.

Each Motif is highly embossed, and the fabric would make excellent use for sport wear, or for knitted cushions, covers, etc.

One of the chief fascinations of creating Embossed Patterns in the Exchange Principle is that the reverse side often produces some such unexpected novelty fabric, especially when solid Increases are used as one of the Building Units.

WAVED EMBOSSED RIBBING. *Figs. 226*A *and* B.

The principle of design (Fig. 226A) is the same as Fig. 193A, only a rib of 3 stitches is waved left and right instead of a vertical row of Faggot Stitch. Also the background is solid and not lace. Compare the two charts and read Exchange Principle.

▲ For P.1, (M.1 B.), Purl 1 stitch, and then Knit into the back of this same stitch to make an Increase. For P.2, (M.1 B.), Purl two stitches and then knit into back of second stitch to M.1.

▲ For K.3, (M.1 B.), Knit 3 and M.1 into back of third Knit stitch
▲ after it is knitted.

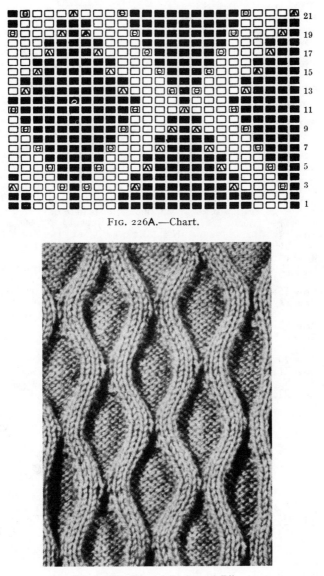

FIG. 226A.—Chart.

FIG. 226B.—Waved Embossed Rib.

Cast On stitches divisible by 18 and 1 over.

Row 1: * P.1, K.3, P.11, K.3. * Repeat, ending P.1.

Row 2: K.1.   * P.3, K.11, P.3, K.1. * Repeat * to *.

Row 3: * P.1, (M.1 B.), K.3, P.2 tog., P.7, P.2 tog., K.3, (M.1 B.). * Repeat * to *, ending P.1.

Row 4: K.2.   * P.3, K.9, P.3, K.3. * Repeat * to *, ending K.2 last stitches.

Row 5: P.2.   * (M.1 B.) (into back of 2nd P. stitch), K.3, P.2 tog., P.5, P.2 tog., K.3, (M.1 B.), P.3. * Repeat * to * ending P.2.

Row 6: K.3.   * P.3, K.7, P.3, K.5. * Repeat * to *, ending K.3.

Row 7: P.3. *(M.1 B.), K.3, P.2 tog., P.3, P.2 tog., K.3, (M.1 B.), P.5.* Repeat * to *, ending P.3 instead of 5.

Row 8: K.4.   * P.3, K.5, P.3, K.7. * Repeat * to *, ending K.4.

Row 9: P.4. *(M.1 B.), K.3, P.2 tog., P.1, P.2 tog., K.3, (M.1 B.), P.7. * Repeat * to *, ending P.4 instead of 7.

Row 10: K.5.   * P.3, K.3, P.3, K.9. * Repeat * to *, ending K.5.

Row 11: P.5.   * (M.1 B.), K.3, P.3 tog., K.3, (M.1 B.), P.9. * Repeat * to *, ending P.5 instead of 9.

Row 12: K.6.   * P.3, K.1, P.3, K.11. * Repeat * to *, ending K.6.

Row 13: P.4.   * P.2 tog., K.3, (M.1 B.), P.1, (M.1 B.), K.3, P.2 tog , P.7. * Repeat * to *, ending P.4 instead of 7.

Row 14: K.5.   * P.3, K.3, P.3, K.8. * Repeat * to *, ending K.5.

Row 15: P.3.   * P.2 tog., K.3, (M.1 B.), P.3, (M.1 B.), K.3, P.2 tog., P.5. * Repeat * to *, ending P.3 instead of 5.

Row 16: K.4.   * P.3, K.5, P.3, K.7. * Repeat * to *, ending K.4.

Row 17: P.2.   * P.2 tog., K.3, (M.1 B.), P.5, (M.1 B.), K.3, P.2 tog., P.3. * Repeat * to *, ending P.2 instead of P.3.

Row 18: K.3.   * P.3, K.7, P.3, K.5. * Repeat * to *, ending K.3.

Row 19: * P.1, P.2 tog., K.3, (M.1 B.), P.7, (M.1 B.), K.3, P.2 tog. * Repeat * to *, ending P.1.

Row 20: K.2.   * P.3, K.9, P.3, K.3. * Repeat * to *, ending K.2.

Row 21: P.2 tog.   * K.3, (M.1 B.), P.9, (M.1 B.), K.3, P.3 tog. * Repeat * to *, ending P.2 tog. on last 2 stitches.

Row 22: * P.3, K.11, P.3, K.1. * Repeat * to *.

Repeat from Row 3.

CLUSTERING

Fig. 227 shows that the Waved Rib pattern in Fig. 226 can be further enriched by "tying" the ribs together at their point of contact with several turns of the yarn, made as in Figs. 228A and B. This is called Clustering, and in repeat makes a little embossed Dot.

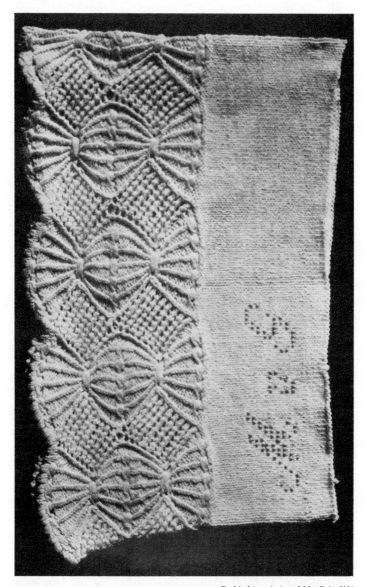

FIG. 227.—Early nineteenth-century sock top, in Hour-Glass Pattern with initials in Bead Knitting, showing the use of Clustering Tie Stitch.

In Fig. 227 the sock-top begins with a tiny picot hem.† In joining as a hem, the stitches are also " tied " into little groups, and so give an impression of Hemstitching. The Ribs in Cross Knit Stitch are designed on the same principle as Fig. 226, and are Clustered together at their nearest approach with this same Tie Stitch.

CLUSTERING TIE STITCH. *Figs. 228A and B.*

Three or more stitches are Clustered together as in Fig. 228. The stitches are first knitted and then transferred to a separate needle

FIG. 228A.—Clustering Tie Stitch.

as shown, and the yarn wound round them three or more times. The 3 stitches so treated are then returned to the right needle and the knitting continued until the next Cluster is made.

FIG. 228B.—Clustering Tie Stitch.

The effect of a completed Cluster is shown in Fig. 228B, the arrows indicating the final round of the yarn and its connection to the next stitch.

FIG. 229.—Fine knitted Doyly, showing how Clustering Tie Stitch can be used in pattern.

PATTERNS AND SMOCKING

Clusters made as in Fig. 228 can be repeated at intervals all along the row, with several rows of plain knitting between each pattern row. In the next repeat the Motif should alternate with those in the row beneath (*see* Fig. 229). This shows a beautiful little circular mat knitted in finest cotton yarn, so that the Clustered Motifs have the additional charm of appearing solid against a transparent background. Here the yarn is wound some six times, so that the Dot is very pronounced. *See also* Fig. 130A.

A separate and contrasting colour can be used for tieing by stranding or weaving the second colour from Cluster to Cluster on the back of the fabric. Repeated as an all-over diamond

effect, it has a pretty " SMOCKED " appearance, especially if
the tieing is kept a little tight.   Clustering has a practical as well
as decorative use, as, arranged at the base of a vertical opening,
neck-fastening, etc., it will considerably strengthen and guard
the base.

EMBOSSED MOTIFS ON EDGINGS

Embossed Motifs, such as Picot Knot, Cheniel Tuft, or Large
Oval Cluster, can be arranged on edgings made as in Figs. 230
and 231, as they have weight.

The plain middle portion would then be decorated with a
Blister Motif, such as Fuchsia (Fig. 223).   Also a vertical line of
Oval Clusters could be used instead of the Faggot Stitch, or be
grouped in diamond formation on the solid parts.   These edgings
look most effective arranged round pram-covers, cot-spreads,
etc.

SERRATED EDGE. *Fig. 230.*

The point is built out with the increasing unit, using an Over or solid
Increase as convenient.   The Building Increase is made on every front row,
as shown by the four black spots.   The same number of stitches (4) thus
added are then cast off *en bloc* on the △ back of the edging.   If a wider
edge is required, continue and make 7 or 9 Building Increases thus,
then the number cast off would be 7 or 9, respectively.   This edge
used without decoration is usually knitted in Garter Stitch, as directed,
since it keeps the points from curling.   The Faggot Stitches are optional,
and so bracketed.   Ordinary Knit Stitches can be used if preferred.   This
would make Row 1 K.6, O., K.1.

More elaborate Faggot Stitch insertions can be
chosen from Figs. 160–166.

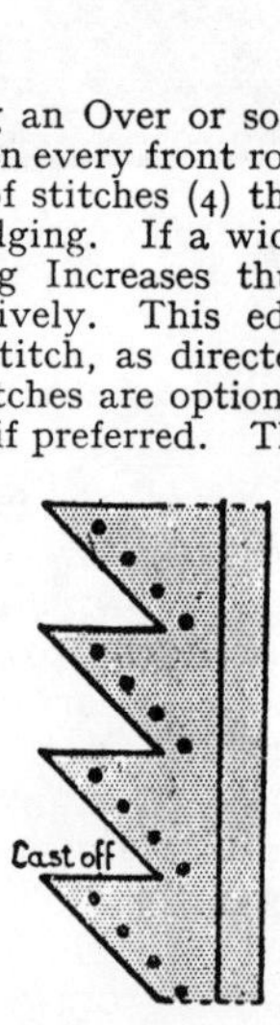

Cast On 7 stitches.
   Row 1: K.1, (O., K.2 tog.) K.3, O., K.1.
   Row 2: Knit.
   Row 3: K.1, (O., K.2 tog.), K.4, O., K.1.
   Row 4: Knit.
   Row 5: K.1, (O., K.2 tog.), K.5, O., K.1.
   Row 6: Knit.
   Row 7: K.1, (O., K.2 tog.), K.6, O., K.1.
   Row 8: Cast off 4, K.6. (7 stitches on needle).

Repeat these 8 rows.

Fig. 230.—Ser-
rated Edge.

SERRATED EDGE AND PICOT KNOT

Same edge (Fig. 230) built on same principle, but decorated with Picot Knot (Fig. 216) on a Stocking Stitch Fabric broken by 2 rows of Purl. The points have been lengthened using 5 increasing units, and so 5 stitches are cast off.   The S.S. Fabric can be made more lace-like by introducing 4 or 5 Eyelets grouped in diamond shape.   The Faggot Stitch Edge is also reversed.

(P.) = Picot Knot (*see* Fig. 216).

Cast On 9 stitches.
    Row 1: K.1, K.2 tog., O., K.3, O., (P.), K.1.
    Row 2: Knit.
    Row 3: K.1, K.2 tog., O., K.4, O., (P.), K.1.
    Row 4: Purl.
    Row 5: K.1, K.2 tog., O., K.5, O., (P.), K.1.
    Row 6: Purl.
    Row 7: K.1, K.2 tog., O., K.6, O., (P.), K.1.
    Row 8: Purl.
    Row 9: K.1, K.2 tog., O., K.7, O., (P.), K.1.
    Row 10: Cast off 5, K.8 (9 stitches on needle).

Repeat from Row 1.

TURRETED EDGE. *Fig. 231.*

The edge is built outwards in steps, extra stitches for these being cast on right needle at the △ end of a front row.   For the receding steps the same number of stitches are cast off again at the △ beginning of a back row.   In this way the edging can be made to any depth.   The fabric when undecorated is generally in Garter Stitch, as this prevents rolling, but the edge is effective when decorated with Embossed Motifs, one example being given in Bobble Edging.   The plan of pattern and numbered rows will enable other Motifs—Eyelets, Faggot Stitch, etc.—to be used in the same way.

The following directions introduce a central decorative pleat of Stocking Stitch between a Garter Stitch Fabric.

Cast On 6 stitches.
    Rows 1, 2, and 3: Knit.   (Cast on 3 stitches at end of 3rd row.)
    Rows 4, 5, 6, and 7: Knit.   (Cast on 3 stitches at end of 7th row.)
    Rows 8 and 9: Knit.
    Row 10: Purl.
    Row 11: Knit.
    Row 12: Purl.
    Rows 13, 14, and 15: Knit.
    Row 16: Cast off 3, K.9.
    Rows 17, 18, and 19: Knit.
    Row 20: Cast off 3, K.6.

Repeat these 20 rows.

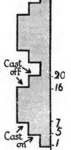

FIG. 231.—Turretted Edge.

TURRETED BOBBLE EDGE

(O.C.) = Oval Cluster, *see* Fig. 218.

Cast On 6 stitches.
  Row 1: K.4, (O.C.), K.1.
  Row 2: Knit.
  Row 3: K.6.   Cast on 3.
  Row 4: P.9.
  Row 5: K.7, (O.C.), K.1.
  Row 6: K.9.
  Row 7: K.9.   Cast on 3.
  Row 8: Knit.
  Row 9: K.10, (O.C.), K1.
  Row 10: Purl.
  Row 11: K.10, (O.C.), K1.
  Row 12: Purl.
  Row 13: K.10, (O.C.), K.1.
  Row 14: Knit.
  Row 15: Knit.
  Row 16: Cast off 3.   K.9.
  Row 17: K.7, (O.C.), K.1.
  Row 18: Purl 9.
  Row 19: K.9.
  Row 20: Cast off 3.   K.6.

Repeat these 20 rows.

MEDALLION KNITTING

Building Units—Increases or Decreases.

Medallions can be knitted, (1) Round on four, five, or six needles, or (2) Flat, on two knitting-pins, the work being one of the most fascinating forms of knitting, once the principle of forming shape is understood.

Medallion knitting enjoyed a tremendous vogue in the 18th and 19th centuries, when cotton-knitting was at its best, with bonnets the fashion for everyone, and knitted bedspreads the treasured heirlooms of every family.

Fig. 232 is an early 18th-century sampler of bonnet-backs, a rare treasure. Every one is different, and each a little gem, and is still fashionable today. Only about half the number contained in the sampler is shown in the photo, as it is difficult to photograph a long strip to advantage.

Such medallions were used for the backs of bonnets or doylys, also a number were joined to form large articles, such as bed-spreads, covers, cushions and so forth.

MEDALLIONS IN ROUND KNITTING

There are two methods of work in Round Knitting :—

Method 1. Commence from the centre of the medallion and gradually increase to the circumference, as for the bonnet-backs in Fig. 232. This is the more usual way. The Building Unit is then the Increase, which can be solid or open.

Method 2. Commence from the circumference and diminish to the middle; the Building Unit is then the Decrease, and must be paired.

In knitting a beret, both methods are used, as the crown is built outwards from the centre, and beneath is diminished to the head-band.

CASTING-ON AND NEEDLE ARRANGEMENT

It is easier to cast the stitches first on to one needle, using method as in Fig. 215, then rearrange them on other needles as necessary, according to shape. It is difficult to accommodate more than four needles at first, so in the case of a Pentagon, where five needles are suggested, and ten stitches are cast on, three needles can be used as follows. Transfer four stitches to one needle and four to a second needle; this will leave two on the original needle. These two stitches will also constitute one-fifth section of the Pentagon, and so give the number for all the following .sections, and the position of the Building Units. An odd needle like this is also helpful in denoting end of round, etc. As the shape grows larger, five needles will be necessary and a sixth for knitting.

After casting-on, always knit first Round into the back of all stitches, as this flattens them. Any hole in the centre of medallion left by the cast-on can be drawn together afterwards with a few sewing or embroidery stitches, using the long cast-on end of yarn left in centre for this purpose. If the square is to form a pocket, Buttonhole Stitch is smart and often used to finish a centre.

△ To cast-off, draw yarn end through last stitch and then through the first loop to close Round correctly.

YARNS AND NEEDLES

Yarn and needle sizes are a consideration when knitting all medallion shapes, and should be correctly balanced. If for some particular purpose a thicker yarn is being used with small needles, and the medallion becomes frilly, knit extra plain rounds between the Building Rounds. On the other hand if it becomes tight, subtract a plain round. This will bring the Building Rounds nearer and so increase the size of the medallion. Either method should be repeated throughout to maintain balance of design.

MEDALLION SHAPES

A Medallion when knitted on four or more needles can be square, pentagonal, hexagonal, octagonal, or circular. It can be small (more usual) or exceedingly large, being one method of making a shawl.

The shape is formed by arranging the Building Units in different geometric order, according to the shape required, as in Figs. 233–237. These Building Units are indicated by the black spots,

By courtesy of Mrs. Hermann Tragy.

FIG. 232.—Early eighteenth-century Sampler of Bonnet
Backs in Medallion Knitting.

and when the shape is knitted from the centre outwards, the
spots represent Increasing Units, but when the shape is knitted
from the circumference inwards, they must be read as Decreasing
Units.

There are two distinct ways of building all these medallion
shapes :—

1. Geometric or Straight.
2. Swirl or Bias.

When a Geometric shape is required, there must be △ two
Building Units grouped at each point. *See* Fig. 233, Square,
and 236, Pentagon.

When a Swirl is required, there is only △ one Building Unit at each point. *See* Fig. 237, Hexagon.

△△ Any Increasing Unit can be used as a Building Unit, and each will have a different effect, though the two in general use are M.1 Bar, when a solid shape is required, and O. (Over) when a lace-like effect is required. In using these it must be remembered :—

1. That the Over is made △ before the stitch, in which case the Increase on the next Round will come before the Stitch.

2. That when using M.1 Bar the Increase occurs △ after the parent stitch. △△ So, for correct balance on each needle, " M.1 Bar at the beginning and end of each needle " will mean M.1 into the first stitch on the needle, and into the last stitch but one on the needle. In this way the Increase will occur one stitch in from either end of the needle and be in the correct position.

3. In M.1, R.O. the Increase is made △ between the stitches, so can be used successfully at beginning and end of all needles.

4. M.1, L. The Increase is made before stitches, while for M.1, L.a. the Increase is usually after the stitch, so these can be used at beginning and end of all needles.

In using an Over to build a Geometric shape such as Pentagon the Double Increase at each of the five corners can be made in two ways :—

1. O. before first and last stitch on needle.
2. O.2 before first stitch.

In this case both Overs will be knitted.

Sometimes, for certain effects, O.2 is used at the beginning of the needle when making a Swirl, but in the next Round the second Over is dropped, because a Swirl needs only one Building Unit at each point. The object in using the O.2 is to form a wider open space. In the same way O.3 or O.4 can be used as the shape grows larger, and wider lace spaces may be required, then the extra two or three Overs will be dropped, and the Building Over only, be knitted.

For certain effects the Building Units can be made on the second or third stitch from the beginning and end of the needle. Either position must be maintained throughout to keep a regular shape, as these units are not ornamental but structural, even though they can be made to △ look ornamental by using the Over as a Building Increase.

The following Figs. 233–237 make this quite clear, and the directions are given for knitting each shape in Stocking Stitch, using the solid Increase so that the method can be understood.

Afterwards, for experiment, reknit the shape using the Over as the Increasing Unit, and see the difference.

Once shape is mastered, ornament can be added, so that the fabric △ between the Building Units becomes lace-like, instead of Stocking Stitch. Embossed Motifs are particularly favoured, as they can be inserted with such good effect. Eyelets and Faggot diamonds are other suggestions.

Directions for writing out Embossed Motifs are given on page 215.

In charting, first arrange the Building Units. These are permanent, and make shape. Then add the Ornamental Units, which are quite independent, and make pattern, so must never be confused with Building Units.

Make 1 (M.1) Bar (*see* Fig. 277).

SQUARE MEDALLION (GEOMETRIC). *Fig. 233.*

There are 4 sides to a square, so CAST ON 8 stitches, double the number of sides.

Eight building units are necessary to make a square, 2 at each corner. 1 arranged at the beginning and end of every needle (*see* Fig. 233).

Use 4 needles and knit with a fifth.

Cast On 2 stitches on each of 4 needles, making 8 in all.
  Round 1: Knit into back of all stitches.
  Round 2: M.1 (Bar) into every stitch.
  Round 3: Knit. △ All odd rounds knit plain.
  Round 4: M.1 at the beginning and end of each needle.

Repeat Rounds 3 and 4 until the required size.

Cast off, drawing yarn end through last stitch and then through the first loop to close correctly.

For Decrease Method:—

Cast On 20 stitches on each of 4 needles.

At the beginning of each needle K.2 tog., and at the end of each needle S.1, K.1, p.s.s.o. Knit one plain round, and then a decreasing round. Read the

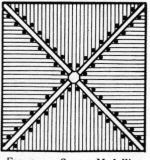

Fig. 233.—Square Medallion.

chart from the circumference inwards, and all the black spots as Decreases. △ This applies to all shapes.

USES. Squares of this description using solid Increases and knitted in Stocking Stitch make pretty patch pockets on cardigans, etc.   Also for mats, cushions, etc.

WINDMILL MEDALLION (SQUARE).

Work as for Fig. 233, only to continue move the Building Units 3 stitches inwards from the beginning and end of each needle, *i.e.* :—

Round 6: M.1 into second stitch from the beginning and third stitch from the end of each needle.

Continue thus for all even rounds.

MALTESE CROSS MEDALLION (SQUARE).   *Fig. 234.*

The same 8 building units as in Fig. 233 are used to form this square, but they are now moved from the corners and grouped together on the centre 2 stitches of each needle, or for variety 1 either side of the centre 2 stitches, which is prettier.

FIG. 234.—Maltese Cross Medallion.

This change begins on the 4th Round, using Bar Increase, otherwise the instructions given for Fig. 233 remain the same.

Placed thus in the centre they permit of a Motif being introduced at the four corners, as in Fig. 235, instead of in the middle of a side, as in Fig. 233.

FIG. 235.—Knitted Doyly. Modern Danish.

Fig. 235.—This beautiful little doyly is modern Danish knitting. The Building Unit is the Over, Visible Increase, which is more in keeping with the lace design of the pattern.   The mat begins as a Maltese Medallion, and then finishes with eight points.

SQUARE MEDALLION (SWIRL)

One Building Unit only is arranged at each of the four corners (beginning of each needle), but in order to keep the square a good flat shape, the Building Units must be repeated in △ every round.   Directions suggest the use of the Over, which has better expansion than the Made Stitch as the Building Unit.

For technique *see* Fig. 285 (Selvedge Over).

Cast On 8 stitches. Use 4 needles and arrange 2 on each needle, and knit with fifth.

Row I: Knit, knitting into back of stitches.

Row 2: O. at beginning of all 4 needles.   In the next round the Over is knitted and so becomes an Increase.

Repeat Round 2 as required.

NOTE.—A triangle (cast on 6 stitches) is made in same way, but using O.2 (*see* Fig. 283), at beginning of all 3 needles and on every round.   On next Round, Knit one Over, and drop the second.

PENTAGONAL MEDALLION (GEOMETRIC). *Fig. 236.*

There are five sides to a Pentagon, so 10 stitches (double the number of sides) are cast on.   It also needs 10 increases in each Building Round for a Geometric Pentagon, so it is better to arrange an alternate extra Round between the Building Rounds as detailed, to prevent it becoming frilly.   Yarn, needles and tension are a consideration.   With thicker yarn, these extra Rounds might be omitted.   Experiment.

Use five needles and knit with a sixth (or else knit 2 sections on one needle).   *See* arrangement, page 236.

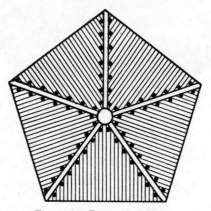

FIG. 236.—Pentagonal Shape.

Cast On 10 stitches, 2 on each needle.
  Round 1: Knit.
  Round 2: M.1 into every second stitch.
  Round 3: Knit.
  Round 4: M.1 at beginning and end of all 5 needles.
  Round 5: Knit.
  Round 6: Knit.
  Round 7: M.1 at beginning and end of all 5 needles.
  Round 8: Knit.

Repeat from Round 4.

PENTAGONAL MEDALLION (SWIRL).

One Building Increase is used and arranged at each of the five points, making five Increasing Units in a Round, with one plain Round between. The Increasing Unit can be solid (M.1 Bar) or open. O.1 or O.2 can be used. If O.2 is used, drop the second Over in the next Round, or the figure will become Geometric and not Swirl. If arranged on 3 needles, the Increase is made before the first and before the middle two stitches on each needle containing two sections.

Cast On 10 stitches.
> **Round 1:** Knit in back of stitches.
> **Round 2:** M.1 into first stitch of all 5 needles.
> **Round 3:** Knit.

Repeat Rounds 2 and 3.

HEXAGONAL MEDALLION (GEOMETRIC).

There are 6 sides to a Hexagon and so 12 stitches are cast on. There will now be 12 Increases in each Building Round, 2 at each point, so 2 Rounds plain are better arranged between. ▲ Two sections are knitted on each needle. With thinner yarn, 3 Rounds plain between each Building Round may be necessary, instead of only 2 as given.

Cast On 12 stitches and use 3 needles. Arrange 4 stitches on each and knit with a fourth.
> **Round 1:** Knit all stitches through the back.
> **Round 2:** M.1 into every other stitch.
> **Round 3:** Knit.
> **Round 4:** M.1 into first and last stitch, also into middle 2 stitches of each needle.
> **Rounds 5** and **6:** Knit.

Repeat Rounds 4, 5 and 6.

HEXAGONAL MEDALLION (SWIRL). *Fig. 237.*

One Unit is now arranged at each of all six points, and one Round plain knitted between each Building Round. The Building Increase can be solid or open. The Over is used here.

Cast On 12 stitches. Use 3 needles and arrange 4 stitches on each and knit with a fourth.
> **Round 1:** Knit all stitches through the back.
> **Round 2:** O. before 1st and 3rd stitches on each needle.
> **Round 3 and all odd rounds:** Knit.

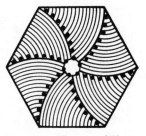

FIG. 237.—Hexagonal Shape.

Round 4: O. before 1st and 4th stitches of each needle.
Round 6: O. before 1st and 5th stitches of each needle.
Round 8: O. before 1st and 6th stitches of each needle.
Round 10: O. before 1st and 7th stitches of each needle.

Continue in this way for size required.

NOTE.—The reason why the Increase moves one to left in every Round is because only 3 needles are used. If 6 were used (rather inconvenient) it would always be before the first stitch on each needle.

OCTAGONAL MEDALLION (GEOMETRIC).

There are 8 sides to an Octagon, so cast on 16 stitches, but as this will make rather a larger central hole, 8 can if desired be cast on, and 16 established in second round by M.1 into each stitch. This is optional but convenient. To make the Octagon, 16 Building Increases are necessary. These can be arranged in two different ways.

(1) Arranged all in one Round as before, grouping two together at each of the 8 points, and knitting Δ 4 Rounds plain between each Building Round.

(2) They can, as shown here, be alternated, arranging 8 in one Round, and 8 in the following second Round. In this case there is only one plain Round between each Building Round.

Both order of Units have their special designing value when extra Ornamental Units are being introduced to form patterns. Two sections are knitted on each needle.

Cast On 8 stitches. Arrange 2 on each of 4 needles and knit with fifth.
Round 1: Knit into back of all stitches.
Round 2: M.1 into each stitch (16 now on needle).
Round 3: Knit.
Round 4: M.1 into 1st and 3rd stitch of each needle.
Round 5: Knit, and all odd Rounds Knit.
Round 6: M.1 into 3rd and last stitch of each needle.
Round 8: M.1 into 1st and 4th stitch of each needle.
Round 10: M.1 into 5th and last stitch of each needle.
Round 12: M.1 into 1st and 6th stitch of each needle.
Round 14: M.1 into 7th and last stitch of each needle.
Round 16: M.1 into 1st and 8th stitch of each needle.
Round 18: M.1 into 9th and last stitch of each needle.
Round 20: M.1 into 1st and 10th stitch of each needle.

Continue in this way as required.

OCTAGONAL MEDALLION (SWIRL).

One Building Unit is here arranged at each of the 8 points, and this can be sold (M.1) or open (Over) as desired. If 16 stitches are cast on, then after knitting one Round plain, follow on from Round 4. Two sections are arranged on each needle. The directions are the same as for a Hexagonal Swirl, as the 4th needle gives the extra two sides. Also solid Increases are suggested.

Cast On 8 stitches. Arrange 2 on each of 4 needles and knit with a fifth.

Round 1: Knit into back of all stitches.
Round 2: M.1 into each stitch (16 stitches now on needle).
Round 3: Knit, and all odd Rounds, Knit.
Round 4: M.1 into 1st and 3rd stitch of each needle.
Round 6: M.1 into 1st and 4th stitch of each needle.
Round 8: M.1 into 1st and 5th stitch of each needle.
Round 10: M.1 into 1st and 7th stitch of each needle.
Round 12: M.1 into 1st and 9th stitch of each needle.

Continue in this way for size required.

For illustration of an Octagonal Swirl, *see* Fig. 232, Bonnet Top No. 3 in line 3.

CIRCULAR MEDALLIONS

This is the most popular shape, so there are many different methods of design. Three are shown here, each having its own peculiar value as a background upon which Ornamental Units can be introduced in different order. The descriptions are for Solid Circles in Stocking Stitch suitable for berets, etc.

No circle should contain less than 8 Building Increases in any one Building Round, though it can contain more, as shown. When 8 only are used, then a Building Round must be repeated every second round, with $\triangle$ one plain Knit Round between. When more than 8 Building Units to the Round are used the number of plain rounds between must be correspondingly more, unless a frilly surface is particularly required.

CIRCULAR MEDALLION (DISC).

Eight Building Units are used in each Building Round but so distributed that their positions are invisible and the result a perfect flat Disc of solid fabric.

Cast On 8 stitches arranged on 4 needles, and knit with a fifth.
  Round 1: Knit in back of all stitches.
  Round 2: M.1 into each stitch on all needles.
  Round 3: Knit. All odd Rounds Knit.
  Round 4: M.1 into each 2nd stitch on all needles.
  Round 6: K.2, M.1 and into next 3rd stitch.
  Round 8: M.1 into every 4th stitch.
  Round 10: K.2, M.1 and into next 5th stitch.
  Round 12: K.1, M.1 and into next 6th stitch.
  Round 14: K.5, M.1 and into next 7th stitch.
  Round 16: K.2, M.1 and into next 8th stitch.
  Round 18: K.1, M.1 and into next 9th stitch.
  Round 20: K.6, M.1 and into next 10th stitch.

Continue in this way, arranging each Increase so that it alternates with that in the previous Round. This is done by varying the number of stitches at beginning of needle as shown.

CIRCULAR MEDALLION (RADIANT).

The Building Increases are arranged so that they radiate from the centre. After the sixth Round, there are 16 Increases in each Building Round, divided by 3 Rounds.

Cast On 8 stitches. Use 4 needles and knit with a fifth.
  Round 1: Knit in back of all stitches.
  Round 2: M.1 into each stitch (16 stitches).
  Rounds 3 to 5: Knit.
  Round 6: M.1 into each stitch.
  Rounds 7 to 9: Knit, and continue to knit 3 Rounds plain between every Building Round.
  Round 10: M.1 into every 2nd stitch.
  Round 14: M.1 into every 3rd stitch.
  Round 18: M.1 into every 4th stitch.
  Round 22: M.1 into every 5th stitch.
  Round 26: M.1 into every 6th stitch.
  Round 30: M.1 into every 7th stitch.

Continue in this way as required.

CIRCULAR MEDALLION (TARGET). *Fig. 238.*

The Building Increases are here arranged in concentric circles as for a target.

Cast On 8 stitches, arranging 2 on each needle.   Use 4 needles and knit with a fifth.
Round I: Knit into back of all stitches.
Round 2: M.1 into every stitch.
Rounds 3, 4, 5: Knit.
Round 6: M.1 into every stitch.
Rounds 7 to 11: Knit.
Round 12: M.1 into every stitch.
Rounds 13 to 19: Knit.

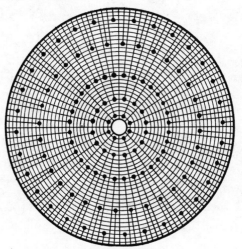

FIG. 238.—Circular.

Round 20: M.1 into every 2nd stitch.
Rounds 21 to 25: Knit.
Round 26: M.1 into every 3rd stitch.
Rounds 27 to 31: Knit.
Round 32: M.1 into every 4th stitch.

Continue in this way knitting 5 Rounds plain and then an Increasing Round, the next being M.1 in every 5th stitch and so on.

Fig. 239 shows a very beautiful circular lace doyly, knitted in a modern design. It is exceedingly fine and reveals a promising future for modern knitting.

FIG. 239.—Knitted Doyly, modern Bavarian.

FINISHING A DOYLY

Figs. 235 and 239 show the modern method of finishing the surrounding edge of a doyly with a chain of crochet. Several stitches are crocheted together in a group (the number depends on pattern), then seven chain or as many as necessary are made, and the next group is crocheted together. In certain places where pattern demands each stitch may be crocheted separately. This forms a freer and more dainty finish than casting off, especially when the pattern is in lace, as in Figs. 235 and 239.

When the pattern is in more solid fabric, the stitches can be cast off in Picot (*see* Fig. 244) or a separate lace edging added, as follows :—

Transfer all the stitches of doyly on to a length of yarn. Take two needles and cast on the required number for the lace edging, and at the end of every △ even row take one stitch of the doyly and knit it together with the last stitch of the lace edging. Continue in this way until the lace edging surrounds the doyly.

MEDALLIONS IN FLAT KNITTING

Also known as GOSSIP KNITTING and COMMUNITY KNITTING.

Most of the shapes as just described could be made with two knitting-pins, but not so conveniently. In Flat Knitting the most popular shapes are the square and the circle.

Fig. 240. Each square is made separately on △ two knitting-pins, and when several are made they are joined together as shown, in this case to form a bedspread. The work is small and easily carried about, and so squares can be made in odd moments and big articles ultimately created.

MAKING A SQUARE

Each square is commenced at one corner and built outwards to the diagonal, and then decreased again to a point. The following directions are for knitting a square in Garter Stitch :—

Cast On 2 stitches.
Row 1 : M.1 (Bar) into each stitch.
Row 2 : Knit.
Row 3 : M.1 into the 1st stitch of the Row, afterwards Knit the Row.

Repeat Row 3, *i.e.* :—

Continue to M.1 on the 1st stitch of △ every row until the diagonal is reached. Then decrease :—

K.2 tog. at the △ beginning of △ every row until 2 stitches remain. Cast off.

By building up a square from one corner in this way, a number of squares when joined will form alternating diamonds of different design as shown in Fig. 240A. Garden-Plot Square, which is a much more elaborate presentation of the same method of making a square. To join as a spread the squares can be overcast together or joined with crochet as shown. *See also* Fig. 266.

THE GARDEN-PLOT SQUARE. *Figs. 240A and B.*

Here the Building Unit is the Over, made at the beginning of every row (*see* Figs. 240A and B). The pattern commences at one corner with one Blister Motif of leaf design on a purl background (*see* centre of photograph, and, for principle, page 221). The leaf is clustered in either side of the central stitch, using 2 visible Increases (Over). To point the leaf, the Decreases are paired either side (*see* Fig. 240B). The pattern then changes to Welts, followed by a band of Blister Motifs. This again changes back to Welts, but now decorated with a row of Reverse Eyelets along the centre (*see* Fig. 241B). The directions for the Blister Motifs are bracketed.

The entire bedspread (Fig. 240A) is made of these squares, and then joined together with crochet. This particular model is finished with a surrounding border of Ruffle Feather Stitch (Fig. 276), and an insertion of Blister Motifs, to knit which the knitter must have cast on something like 1000 stitches ! A deep lace edging of fairly solid design would serve and give a good finish.

For S.2, K.1, p.2.s.s.o., *see* Fig. 296.   Central Chain Decrease.
For Reverse Over (O.(R.)), *see* Fig. 289.

Cast On 3 stitches.
  Row 1: O., K.3.
  Row 2: O., K.4.
  Row 3: O., K.2, (O., K.1, O.), K.2.
  Row 4: O., K.2, (P.3), K.3.
  Row 5: O., K.3, (K.1, O., K.1, O., K.1), K.3.
  Row 6: O., K.3, (P.5), K.4.
  Row 7: O., K.4, (K.2, O., K.1, O., K.2), K.4.
  Row 8: O., K.4, (P.7), K.5.
  Row 9: O., K.5, (K.3, O., K.1, O., K.3), K.5.
  Row 10: O., K.5, (P.9), K.6.
  Row 11: O., K.6, (K.4, O., K.1, O., K.4), K.6.
  Row 12: O., K.6, (P.11), K.7.
  Row 13: O., K.7, (K.5, O., K.1, O., K.5), K.7.
  Row 14: O., K.7, (P.13), K.8.
  Row 15: O., K.8, (S.1, K.1, p.s.s.o., K.9, K.2 tog.), K.8.
  Row 16: O., K.8, (P.11), K.9.
  Row 17: O., K.9, (S.1, K.1, p.s.s.o., K.7, K.2 tog.), K.9.
  Row 18: O., K.9, (P.9), K.10.
  Row 19: O., K.10, (S.1, K.1, p.s.s.o., K.5, K.2 tog.), K.10.
  Row 20: O., K.10, (P.7), K.11.
  Row 21: O., K.11, (S.1, K.1, p.s.s.o., K.3, K.2 tog.), K.11.
  Row 22: O., K.11, (P.5), K.12.
  Row 23: O., K.12, (S.1, K.1, p.s.s.o., K.1, K.2 tog.), K.12.
  Row 24: O., K.12, (P.3), K.13.
  Row 25: O., K.13, (S.2, K.1, p.2.s.s.o.), K.13.
  Row 26: O., Purl the whole row.
  Rows 27–70: Welts.
  Row 27: O., P.29.
  Row 28: O., Knit.
  Row 29: O., P.31.

By courtesy of Dr. Marie Schuette.

FIG. 240A.—Close-up of Knitted Squares Forming Part of Bedspread.
White Knitting of the Early nineteenth century showing the Garden-
Plot Square Pattern.

Row 30: O., Knit.
Row 31: O., K.33.
Row 32: O., Purl.
Row 33: O., K.35.
Row 34: O., Purl.
Rows 35–70: Continue in this way, knitting 5 more Purl Welts, *i.e.*, 4 rows of Purl Fabric, followed by 4 rows of Stocking Stitch, always remembering to make an Over at the beginning of every row.

Now begin the 10 repeating Leaf Motifs. These are clustered in either side of a central stitch and placed 6 stitches apart on a Purl background with one exception—between leaves 5 and 6 there are 7 stitches. This must be remembered until Row 87.

Row 71: O., K.4. * (O., K.1, O.), P.6. * Repeat * to *, remembering to P.7 between 5th and 6th leaves throughout, ending K.4.
Row 72: O., K.4. * (P.3), K.6. * Repeat * to * (K.7 between 5th and 6th leaves), ending K.5.
Row 73: O., K.5. * (K.1, O., K.1, O., K.1), P.6. * Repeat * to *, ending K.5.
Row 74: O., K.5. * (P.5), K.6. * Repeat * to *, ending K.6.
Row 75: O., K.6. * (K.2, O., K.1, O., K.2), P.6. * Repeat * to *, ending K.6.
Row 76: O., K.6. * (P.7), K.6. * Repeat * to *, ending K.7.
Row 77: O., K.7. * (K.3, O., K.1, O., K.3), P.6. * Repeat * to *, ending K.7.
Row 78: O., K.7. * (P.9), K.6. * Repeat * to *, ending K.8.
(Row 78 is widest part of square. From here on decrease.)
Row 79: S.1, K.1, p.s.s.o., K.6. * (S.1, K.1, p.s.s.o., K.5, K.2 tog.), P.6. * Repeat * to *, ending K.6, K.2 tog.
Row 80: K.7. * (P.7), K.6. * Repeat * to *, ending K.7.
Row 81: S.1, K.1, p.s.s.o., K.5. * (S.1, K.1, p.s.so., K.3, K.2 tog.), P.6. * Repeat * to *, ending K.5, K.2 tog.
Row 82: K.6. * (P.5), K.6. * Repeat, * to *, ending K.6.
Row 83: S.1, K.1, p.s.s.o., K.4. * (S.1, K.1, p.s.s.o., K.1, K.2 tog.), P.6. * Repeat * to *, ending K.4, K.2 tog.
Row 84: K.5. * (P.3), K.6. * Repeat * to *, ending K.5.
Row 85: S.1, K.1, p.s.s.o., K.3. * (S.2, K.1, p.2.s.s.o.), P.6. * Repeat * to *, ending K.3, K.2 tog.
Row 86: K.4. * (P.1), K.6. * Repeat * to *, ending K.4.
Row 87: S.1, K.1, p.s.s.o., P.69, K.2 tog.
Row 88: Knit.
Row 89: S.1, K.1, p.s.s.o., P.67, K.2 tog.

The pattern finishes in Welts composed of 5 rows of Stocking Stitch which always begins on the back of fabric, alternating with 5 rows of Purl Fabric, which begins on the front of the fabric, centred with Reverse Eyelet (*see* Row 97: O. (R.), P.2 tog.). (*See* Fig. 289 for special way of throwing yarn.)

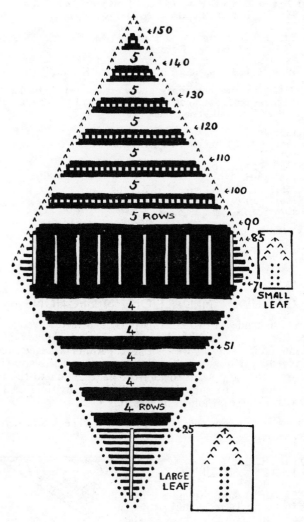

FIG. 240B.

Rows 90, 92, and 94: Purl.
Rows 91 and 93: S.1, K.1, p.s.s.o.   Knit, ending K.2 tog.
Row 95: S.1, K.1, p.s.s.o., Purl, ending K.2 tog.
Row 96: Knit.
Row 97: S.1, K.1, p.s.s.o. * P.1, O. (R.), P.2 tog. * Repeat
* to *, ending K.2 tog.
Row 98: Knit, knitting through △ back of Over.
Row 99: S.1, K.1, p.s.s.o. * Purl *, ending K.2 tog.

Repeat last 10 rows five times, always remembering to decrease
at the beginning and end of each △ front row.   The last Purl
Welt will end with one eyelet.

Row 150: Purl.
Row 151: S.1, K.1, p.s.s.o., K.5, K.2 tog.
Row 152: Purl.
Row 153: S.1, K.1, p.s.s.o., K.3, K.2 tog.
Row 154: Purl.
Row 155: S.1, K.1, p.s.s.o., K.1, K.2 tog.
Row 156: Purl.
Row 157: S.2, K.1, p.2.s.s.o.

Draw yarn through and finish.

CIRCULAR MEDALLION IN SECTIONS

A circle, as made on two knitting-pins, is formed of wedge-like
sections (*see* Fig. 241) achieved by "Turning". The advantage
of forming a circle in this way is that it permits of a lace edging
being added to a doyly as it is knitted. The disadvantage is
that there must be a seam to join the final section to the first
section. This can be somewhat overcome if Invisible Cast-on
is used † and the seam joined by Grafting.†

Each section is constructed in this way.   The fabric here is
Stocking Stitch.

Cast On 12 stitches.
Row 1: Knit, and all odd numbers
Knit.
Row 2: Purl.   Turn, leaving 2 stitches.
Row 4: Purl.   Turn, leaving 4 stitches.
Row 6: Purl.   Turn, leaving 6 stitches.
Row 8: Purl.   Turn, leaving 8 stitches.
Rows 10–12: Purl.

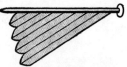

FIG. 241.—Section of
Circular Mat.

This forms one section.   Repeat from Row 1.

SUN-RAY DOYLY.

The following directions are for a circular mat with lace edging, knitted in sections and in cotton yarn.   Notice the use of the Purl Decrease.   It is prettier.

△ The number of stitches left at the end of the turn corresponds each time with the number of the row.

Cast On 25 stitches.
Row 1:   S.1, K.19, O., P.2 tog., K.1, O., K.2.
Row 2:   K.4, O., P.2 tog., K.18, Turn.   (2 stitches left.)
Row 3:   S.1, K.17, O., P.2 tog., K.2, O., K.2.
Row 4:   K.5, O., P.2 tog., K.16, Turn.   (4 left.)
Row 5:   S.1, K.15, O., P.2 tog., K.3, O., K.2.
Row 6:   K.6, O., P.2 tog., K.14, Turn.   (6 left.)
Row 7:   S.1, K.13, O., P.2 tog., K.2 tog., O.2, K.2, O., K.2.
Row 8:   K.6, P.1, K.1, O., P.2 tog., K.12, Turn.   (8 left.)
Row 9:   S.1, K.11, O., P.2 tog., K.8.
Row 10: Cast off 5, K.2, O., P.2 tog., K.10, Turn.   (10 left.)
Row 11: S.1, K.9, O., P.2 tog., K.1, O., K.2.
Row 12: K.4, O., P.2 tog., K.8, Turn.   (12 left.)
Row 13: S.1, K.7, O., P.2 tog., K.2, O., K.2.
Row 14: K.5, O., P.2 tog., K.6, Turn.   (14 left.)
Row 15: S.1, K.5, O., P.2 tog., K.3, O., K.2.
Row 16: K.6, O., P.2 tog., K.4, Turn.   (16 left.)
Row 17: S.1, K.3, O., P.2 tog., K.2 tog., O.2, K.2, O., K.2.
Row 18: K.6, P.1, K.1, O., P.2 tog., K.2, Turn.   (18 left.)
Row 19: S.1, K.1, O., P.2 tog., K.8.
Row 20: Cast off 5, K.2, O., P.2 tog., K.2, (O., K.2 tog.) 8 times, K.2.

This forms one section of mat as shown in Fig. 241.   Repeat from Row 1 (16 sections are needed for one doyly).

TURNING

When the directions say " Turn, leaving 2 stitches ", Purl to the last 2 stitches on left needle and then stop.   Now slip one of these 2 last stitches from left to right needle without knitting it, and take the yarn round this stitch and to the back, and return the slipped stitch to left needle again.   Turn the work and knit back.   By Wrapping the yarn round the stitch in this way prevents a gap.

PICOT POINT KNITTING

Designing Units—Casting-on and Casting-off.

Picot Point Knitting is purely decorative, and a frank imitation of Irish Crochet done on knitting-needles. It is chiefly used for knitted flowers, lace edgings, insertions, hats, bonnets, etc. The work is fascinating, and once the technique is mastered, affords much scope for originality.

FIG. 242.—Bonnet in Picot Point Knitting.

Fig. 242 shows a baby's bonnet in Picot Point Knitting. The back consists of a central medallion flower, made as in Figs. 246 and 247, surrounded by other similar flowers. The front is also outlined with flowers, and between is a strip of lacis prepared as for the edge of the lace in Fig. 248.

Picot Points can also be used as a decorative method of finishing a straight edge instead of an ordinary cast-off.

MAKING A PICOT POINT. *Fig. 243.*

Fig. 243A. Make a loop in the yarn, put this on left needle and cast 2 more stitches on left needle (*see* Fig. 215), making 3 in all.

Fig. 243B. Knit and cast off 2 of these 3 stitches, which leaves 1 on the needle.

FIG. 243.—Making a Picot Point.

This in detail reads: knit 2 stitches, lift the first over the second and off the needle. Knit the third stitch and lift the second over the third and off the needle. This forms 1 picot and leaves 1 stitch on the right needle.

Transfer this remaining stitch to left needle and repeat—*i.e.*, cast on 2 more stitches, and cast them off as before.

Continue in this way, and so make a long chain of Picot Points as in Fig. 244.

The picot can be made larger and to any size by working as follows: Make a loop and

Cast on 3, cast off 3, or

Cast on 4, cast off 4,

and so on.

PICOT POINT CHAIN

FIG. 244.—Picot Point Chain.

Fig. 244 shows a chain of narrow Picot Points, made as just described (Cast on 2, cast on 2). These chains form the basis of the work, and can be joined as a lacis, as for bonnet (Fig. 242), or used to join medallions together, as in Fig. 248, also to make flower centres, or as an edging. By making a long chain, and then picking up the loops on the plain edge, a pretty Cast-on is made. Most practical of all, the same method will form a delightful Cast-off.

PICOT POINT CAST-OFF.

This cast-off makes a pretty finish to the top straight edge of an article, such as a pram-cover, etc., etc.

To make the other 3 sides of article similar in decoration, pick up the loops along the sides or base, on left needle, and cast off on Picot Points. Keep strict note to tension, especially the sides. First read "Making a Picot Point".

METHOD. Insert the needle through the first stitch of the row to be cast off and here: * Cast on 2 stitches, knit and cast off 2 stitches. Knit the next stitch. There are 2 stitches now on right needle, knit and cast off 1. Return remaining stitch to left needle. * Repeat * to *, all along the row. If the effect is too frilly, knit and cast-off another stitch, before repeating second Picot.

VARIATION. B. of F. * Cast on 2 stitches. Lift second stitch over first and off needle. Lift a third stitch over and off needle. Transfer remaining stitch to right needle. K.1. Two stitches now on right needle. Lift second over first and off the needle. Return remaining stitch to L.N. * Repeat * to *.

CROWN PICOT

The method of work is different, as the stitches are first cast on the needles in the ordinary way, so it is made by the △ width, but it can be used as an Edging, or a Cast-off, or to form a lacis.

CROWN PICOT EDGING.

Fig. 245.

Cast On stitches divisible by 5 for
△   width   required.
(This can be 30, 60, or
100, as necessary.)

Row I: Knit.

Row 2: On the first stitch * Cast on 2, cast
off 2.   (This forms a Picot Point,
see Fig. 243.)   Transfer remaining
stitches to left needle. *   Repeat
* to * 3 more times.   This will
form 4 picots, as in Fig. 245.   Now
knit and cast off 4 stitches in the
ordinary way (*see* Fig. 245).   This
completes one Crown Picot.

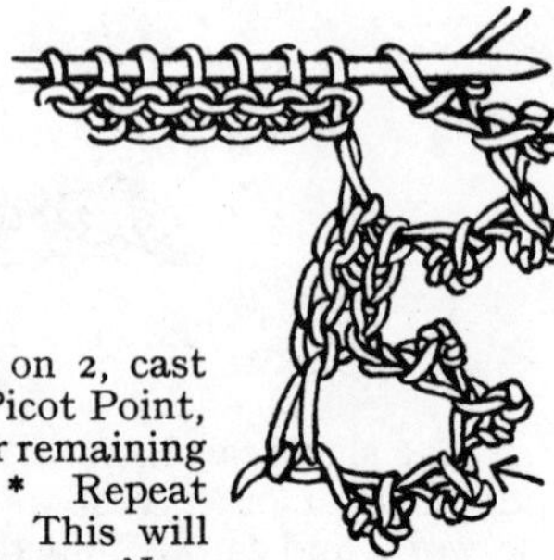

FIG. 245.—Crown
Picot.

On the next stitch make another Crown of 4 picots, as before,
and then cast off 4 more stitches.

Continue in this way until all the stitches cast on are
finished, and only 1 stitch remains on the needle.   If desired
as an Edging or Cast-off, draw yarn through and finish.

When making a lacis, this Edging becomes the foundation,
and is referred to as a STRIP, and not a row.   In this case, the
last stitch is required to continue the work.

CROWN PICOT CAST-OFF.

Crown Picot Edging also makes a decorative method of casting off.
Work in the same way as in Fig. 245.   △ The number of stitches
cast off △ between the Crown loop will be determined by the number
contained in the row being cast off.   They can be any number.

MAKING A PICOT POINT LACIS

Picot Lacis is an all-over open-lace fabric, such as the lattice
part of the bonnet in Fig. 242.   The Lacis can be of any width
and used for an entire garment if desired.

Cast on sufficient stitches divisible by 5 for width required.
Begin by making a series of Crown Picots, as in Fig. 245, until the
row is finished.   This is used as a foundation, and called a STRIP.
Now add a second strip as follows:—

There is 1 stitch left on right needle. Transfer to left needle. Make 4 picots. Join to centre of Crown Picot in first strip (*see* arrow, Fig. 245), by picking up and knitting a stitch between 2 picots. Cast off 1. Transfer stitch to left needle and make another 4 picots and join to centre of next Crown Picot.

Continue in this way, making a series of Crown Picots until the end is reached.

Turn and repeat for another strip. Continue for required depth. (*See also* lacis for Fig. 248.)

FLORAL MEDALLION. *Figs. 246 and 247.*

These medallions are used in much the same way as Crochet wheels. Several can be joined together to make jumpers, spreads, etc. They are used to make the lace edge in Fig. 248. Also the bonnet in Fig. 242.

The flower centre can be composed of more picots than 5 if required, which will necessitate a corresponding number of extra petals. The picots can also be larger by making the unit Cast on 4, cast off 4, or 5 and 5, or 6 and 6, etc.

CENTRE. *Fig. 246.*

This consists of a Picot Chain of 5 points as in Fig. 243, but using 3 stitches instead of 2.

Make a loop, put on left needle. Cast on 3, cast off 3.

Repeat 5 times.

Join in a circle as in Fig. 246, ready for petals, by picking up and knitting a stitch. Cast off 1. Transfer remaining stitch to left needle, and begin a petal.

FIG. 246.—Centre.

PETALS. *Fig. 247.*

One stitch now on left needle. Cast on 1, making 2.

Row I: K.1, M.1 in second stitch by knitting into the back as well as the front before slipping it off needle.
Row 2: K.3.
Row 3: K.2. M.1 into last stitch as before.
Row 4: K.4.
Row 5: K.3. M.1 into last stitch (5 stitches).
Rows 6, 7, 8, and 9: Knit 5.
Row 10: Cast off 1, K.3.

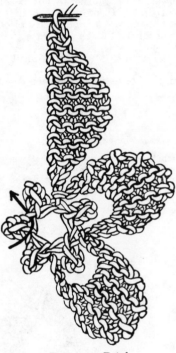

FIG. 247.—Petal.

Row 11: K.4.
Row 12: Cast off 1, K.2.
Row 13: K.3.
Row 14: Cast off 1, K.1.
Row 15: K.2.

Cast off 1.

This leaves 1 stitch on the needle, and the petal now appears as in Fig. 247.

With right needle pick up and knit a loop between the picots, △ as shown by arrow. Cast off 1.

Repeat from Rows 1 to 15 to make next petal.

When all the petals are complete, this will form a medallion such as is used for the lace in Fig. 248.

KNITTED FLOWERS

Flowers for buttonholes are knitted in the same way as just described. Knit a medallion (*see* Figs. 246 and 247).

When this is completed add a second and a third series of petals, each above the other, graduating the size, like a rose.

Fill in the centre with extra picots, knitting round and round, until it is solid and embossed as follows :—

Make picot, pick up and knit stitch to attach, cast off 1. Repeat.

BUDS. Knit one petal (Fig. 247), and fold into a bud.

LEAVES. Work as for a petal. Fold and overcast to form a central vein. Mount on wire as required.

Knitted flowers look best done in very fine cotton yarns and on very fine needles.

WASHING. If knitted in white cotton yarn, the flowers can be washed in frothy soap flakes. Afterwards dip in rice-water to stiffen, and shape the centre and petals with the fingers before they are allowed to dry.

PICOT POINT LACE. *Fig. 248.*

Make a Floral Medallion as described in Figs. 246 and 247, only with 6 Picot points and 6 petals.

This is then surrounded with a chain of Picot Points made as in Fig. 243 to form a wheel (*see* Fig. 248).

Each wheel is made separately (as in crochet), and then linked together and finished on one side with a long chain of Picot Points to form a lace as shown in Fig. 248.

FIG. 248.—Picot Point Lace.

1ST ROUND. When the flower medallion is completed, join cotton to the centre of a petal tip. * K.1, make 4 picot points. (Cast on 2, cast off 2 for each picot.) After making the 4th picot join to the centre tip of next petal. * Repeat * to * all round the flower. The medallion must lie flat; if a wider " span " than 4 picots is necessary, then make 5.

Now surround with a series of festoon loops.

2ND ROUND. Make 4 picots and join between 2nd and 3rd picot of previous span in 1st Round. This will make a festoon loop. Make another 4 picots and join again between 2 picots. Repeat these loops all round.

3RD ROUND. * 4 picots and join between 2nd and 3rd loop of previous Round. * Repeat * to * all round.

4TH ROUND. There are now 12 surrounding loops. These are now joined to form a wheel, using 4 picots to a span.

△ Ten of these points in joining are also ornamented with a CREST OF PICOTS, as follows :—

Join cotton between 2nd and 3rd picot of a loop. Make * 3 picots and join into same place to make Crest. Now make 4 picots and join between 2nd and 3rd picot of previous loop. * Repeat * to *, making 10 Picot Crests. Then complete the wheel omitting two Crests. * 4 picots, join. *

This completes one wheel Motif.

Make several of these, sufficient for length required, and then join with a lacis as follows:—

LACIS

Row 1: Join cotton to crest of 10th picot, marked " **A** " in Fig. 248.
　　　　* Make 6 picots, join, repeat twice and then join into
　　　　△ Crest of picots, marked " **B** " in Fig. 248. * Repeat
　　　　* to *, until all the wheel Motifs are joined.

Row 2: Return journey. Join cotton to centre of first loop.
　　　　* Make 6 picots, join to centre of next loop. * Repeat
　　　　to end.

Row 3: To form the straight edge, join cotton to centre of first
　　　　loop. * Make 4 picots, join to centre of next loop. *
　　　　Repeat to end, and finish by drawing thread through
　　　　last loop.

INSERTION

To form an insertion work another lacis (Rows 1, 2, and 3) on the opposite side, having previously omitted 2 of the Picot Crests, Nos. 5 and 6, in last surround of wheel as was done before between **A** and **B**.

FILET LACE

Designing Units : Double Overs, Double Decrease
(Binding), Casting-on, Casting-off.

Filet Lace is a distinctive form of knitting, planned to produce a square mesh, as in netting.

The solid parts of the Lace (*see* Fig. 251B) suggest the pattern, which were it embroidery would be darned upon a foundation of Filet net. The fabric needs to be crisp and well tensioned to get the best effect, and this is better obtained in fine cotton yarns.

DESIGNS

These are made on the same principle as the embroidery designs created for Filet Darning. The pattern is composed of BLOCKS and SPACES, the Blocks being the solid parts of the pattern, and the Spaces the open parts (*see* Figs. 251A and B).

The fabric is in Garter Stitch, so all rows are Knit, plus the Designing Units.

WORKING METHOD

BLOCKS

These are the solid parts, and consist of three Knit stitches in width and four rows in depth for every block.

SPACES

These are the open parts of the design, knitted as follows: O.2, Bind 2, K.1. *See* Figs. 249A, B, and C, where this abbreviation is shown progressively in six movements and in three diagrams as follows :—

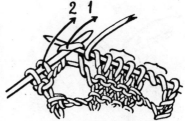

FIG. 249A.—Space Movements, 1 and 2.

Fig. 249A (Movements 1 *and* 2). After completing a

263

block, or the edge stitch, as the case may be, bring the yarn forward, take it over the needle and to the front again. (This is O.2.) On the next three stitches work as follows :—

(1) Slip the first stitch knitwise.
(2) Slip a second knitwise.

Fig. 249B (Movements 3 and 4).

(3) Take the first slipped stitch over the second and off the needle to " bind " it.
(4) Slip a third stitch.

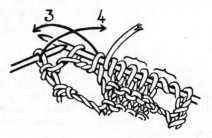

FIG. 249B.—Space Movements, 3 and 4.

Fig. 249C (Movements 5 and 6).

(5) Bind again by taking the second stitch over the third and off the needle (*see* arrow).
(6) Knit the remaining stitch by inserting left needle into it and knitting it in ordinary way.

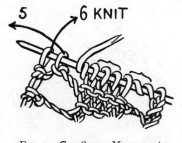

FIG. 249C.—Space Movements, 5 and 6.

△ The whole of the six movements is referred to as SPACE.

There are now three loops on the needle, again composed as follows : two Overs and one stitch.

On the return row the first of the two Overs is knitted and the second is purled. In this way three stitches are again restored to the needle.

CHANGING FROM BLOCKS TO SPACES

When a block changes to a space, as in centre of Row 17, Fig. 251, the three stitches of the block are then treated as a space movement, Figs. 249A, B, and C.

△ SQUARING THE BLOCK

This is done by knitting two rows and then repeating them, △ four rows being necessary to square each mesh vertically. This means that Rows 3 and 4 will be the same as Rows 1 and 2 Rows 7 and 8 same as 5 and 6, and so on.

CASTING ON

To obtain the number to cast on, count the number of squares contained in the bottom row of the design. In Fig. 251A the number is 3 (1 Block and 2 Spaces equal 3). For every square cast on 3 stitches. 3 × 3 = 9. Edge stitches are extra.

In Fig. 251B there is only one edge stitch, as, being a lace edging, there is only one edge to consider. On an Insertion there will be edge stitches on both sides. Any number of edge stitches can be used as desired, but they must be considered as extras, as they are not charted and do not concern the pattern, though there must be one edge stitch before the knitting can commence.

FILET LACE INSERTION. *Fig. 250.*

The Insertion is 5 squares wide, plus 5 edge stitches, 3 at the beginning and 2 at the end (2 only are necessary at the end, as the last stitch of pattern balances the number). These edge stitches are enclosed in brackets so that they can be recognised.

1 square = 3 stitches.

Cast On 15 plus 5 edge stitches = 20 (cast on 20 stitches).

Rows I and 3: (K.3 edge) 2 spaces, K.3, 2 spaces, (K.2 edge).

Row 2 and all even Rows: Knit, purling the second Over.

Rows 5 and 7: (K.3) 1 space, K.3, 1 space, K.3, 1 space, (K.2).

Rows 9 and 11: Same as Rows 5 and 7.

Rows 13 and 15: Same as Rows 5 and 7.

Rows 17 and 19: (K.3), 2 spaces, K.3, 2 spaces, (K.2).

Rows 21 and 23: (K.3), 1 space, K.3, 1 space, K.3, 1 space, (K.2).

Row 24: Knit, purling the second Over.

Repeat these 24 rows.

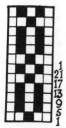

FIG. 250.—Filet Lace Insertion.

LACE MESH

When knitting a Filet Lace edge such as shown in Figs. 251A and **B**, the work is a little different, as the left edge is either accumulating extra meshes to form the points, or meshes are being eliminated.

When additional meshes have to be added to form points, △ these are cast on at the △ end of the third row and consolidated in the next.

For example *see* Fig. 251A. Row 5 will require six extra stitches. These are prepared in advance in Row 3, by casting on six stitches. Again, a further three stitches will be cast on in Row 7, ready for the extra mesh in Row 9. Use right needle cast-on (Fig. 215).

When the number of meshes has to be reduced, the stitches are cast off at the △ beginning of the fourth row (last row in the mesh), and the remaining stitches are knitted as before.

FILET LACE EDGING.   *Figs. 251A and B.*

The lace begins with 3 squares, plus 1 edge stitch.
1 square = 3 stitches.
Follow the chart; it simplifies the instructions.   The Fabric is in Garter Stitch.

Cast On 10 stitches.
  Row 1: (K.1), 1 space, K.3, 1 space.
  Row 2: Knit.   Knit the first Over and purl the second.
  Row 3: Same as Row 1, △ then make 2 extra meshes by casting on 6 stitches.
  Row 4: Knit.
  Row 5: (K.1), 1 space, K.3, 3 spaces.
  Row 6: Knit.
  Row 7: Same as Row 5.   △ Cast on 3 for extra mesh.
  Row 8: Knit.
  Row 9: (K.1), 1 space, K.3, 1 space, K.3, 2 spaces.
  Row 10: Knit.
  Rows 11 and 12: Repeat Rows 9 and 10.
  Row 13: (K.1), 1 space, K.12, 1 space.
  Row 14: Knit.
  Rows 15 and 16: Same as Rows 13 and 14.
  Row 17: (K.1), 1 space, K.3, 1 space, K.3, 2 spaces.
  Row 18: Knit.
  Row 19: Same as Row 17.
  Row 20: Cast off 3, K.16.
  Row 21: (K.1), 1 space, K.3, 3 spaces.

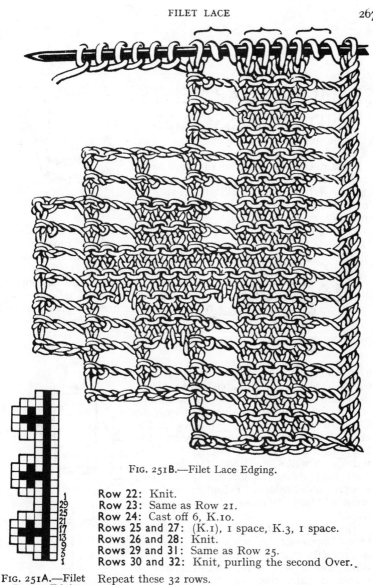

FIG. 251B.—Filet Lace Edging.

FIG. 251A.—Filet Lace Edging Chart.

Row 22: Knit.
Row 23: Same as Row 21.
Row 24: Cast off 6, K.10.
Rows 25 and 27: (K.1), 1 space, K.3, 1 space.
Rows 26 and 28: Knit.
Rows 29 and 31: Same as Row 25.
Rows 30 and 32: Knit, purling the second Over.

Repeat these 32 rows.

USES.   For towel-ends, borders, mats, edges, etc.

SEAMLESS GARMENTS
AND ACCESSORIES

Peasant Garments are so simple in shape that all attention can be given to beautifying the fabric, which will often glow in colour or sparkle with beads, sequins, or embroidery (*see* Fig. 211).

Peasant patterns are traditional, and their repeating Motifs often bear a religious sentiment, such as the Sacred Heart, the Cross, the Anchor of Faith, the Crown of Glory, etc. These are planned out in squares on scraps of paper or wood, and even on tables. They may be borrowed or copied from another garment, but never written down. This is unthinkable! The fabric they knit is round, and so seamless, and the human body the garment must fit is regarded as a series of cylinders, in the same way as the armourer considers the body (*see* Fig. 252). Nothing could be simpler. One large cylinder for the body. Two long cylinders for the legs. Two shorter and smaller cylinders for the arms. One cylinder for the head (cap).

The elasticity of the fabric was allowed to accommodate fit, whereas modern use of elasticity is to promote style. But their ways and means were, and still are, so ingenious that much can be learnt from them, as will be shown.

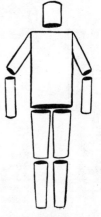

FIG. 252.—The Cylindrical Body.

268

SEAMLESS GARMENTS

The sack, with a hole cut for the head and two slits for the armholes, provides the earliest model for a knitted pullover, or vest, as it was called. The method is shown in Fig. 253, and as still used in the Faroe Islands, and far European countries.

Ribbing is used at the hips, and a "cylinder" shape is knitted straight up to the shoulder, a few extra stitches being added in at the sides for greater width. These are "made" on the background of the pattern, and thus avoid disturbing the design. When the necessary depth has been knitted the "cylinder" is folded flat and joined either side for the shoulder. This can be done in three different ways:—

1. Turn the garment inside out and join with a slip and bind cast-off—*i.e.*, take a stitch from the back needle over a stitch on the front needle, knit the remaining stitch. Do the same with the next two stitches, knit this and then cast off and continue.

2. The stitches are grafted together with matching wool.†

3. The stitches are joined in a herringbone movement, using a blunt-pointed needle. Begin on the △ left and take the needle first through a stitch off the back needle and then through one on the front, and continue so.

FIG. 253.—Working Method.

NECK. The middle stitches are left, and on these a smaller "cylinder" is knitted for the neck, making either a polo, stand or sailor-man collar, as required.†

The "sack"-like shape is then cut either side for the armholes, dropping one stitch and cutting to a "Platform Stitch" (*see* page 100). The edges are turned under and sewn as in Fig. 253.

The sleeves are seamless and knitted upwards, beginning at the cuffs and increasing for greater width. They finish quite straight at the top and without a crown. The stitches are not cast off, but sewn into the armhole stitch by stitch, or knitted in stitch by stitch, as preferred.

This completes a SEAMLESS garment.

Note.—Sleeves finishing straight at the top in this way will not " cup " the shoulder, as in the modern way, but, since the shoulder line itself is straight, this will overlap the shoulder top, and so meet the sleeve in comfort.

OTHER GARMENTS

The method of making other garments is just as simple and ingenious, and it matters little to these clever knitters whether socks are knitted upwards from the toe (it is considered more lucky to knit towards the heart) or downwards from the top. Socks or mittens are seamless, and heels or thumbs are added afterwards by means of a horizontal opening. It is all so simple. They laugh at modern methods ! This is how they do it.

HORIZONTAL OPENINGS

When a peasant desires to add a heel to a sock, a thumb to a glove, or a pocket to a sweater, she uses the same method of preparation for all three.

First decide on the position of either by measurement.

FIG. 254.—Horizontal Opening.

Knit to this position, and then take a length of contrasting coloured yarn, and with this knit the number of stitches required for $\triangle$ width, stranding the other yarn (or yarns) across at the back. For a heel, half the number in a round is knitted. For a thumb, about ten to fourteen stitches. For a pocket, 4 inches to 5 inches of stitches. Now leave the contrasting yarn and continue in pattern with the original yarn or yarns. When the garment is finished, return to this coloured yarn, remove it (*see* Fig. 254), pick up the stitches along the top on one needle and along the bottom on a second needle, and knit the heel (shaped like a toe, *see* Fig. 211) or the thumb to a glove, or a pocket to a sweater.† The method is most successful, particularly for pockets.

VERTICAL OPENINGS

These are made by dropping three or four stitches from top to bottom of the cylinder, as in Fig. 255. The resulting strands are then cut two at a time and tied. If the pattern is in colour and in Stranded or Woven Knitting,† the stitches cannot be dropped in this way, and so the two or several yarns are held together and wound some six or eight turns round the needle at place for opening and the knitting is continued in pattern. On the next round these "turns" are dropped off the needle, and another six or eight turns made, and so on. When the cylinder is finished, there will be a series of wide, ladder-like strands arranged vertically above each other, similar to when stitches are dropped. These are cut in pairs and tied as before. In this way the round fabric is opened.

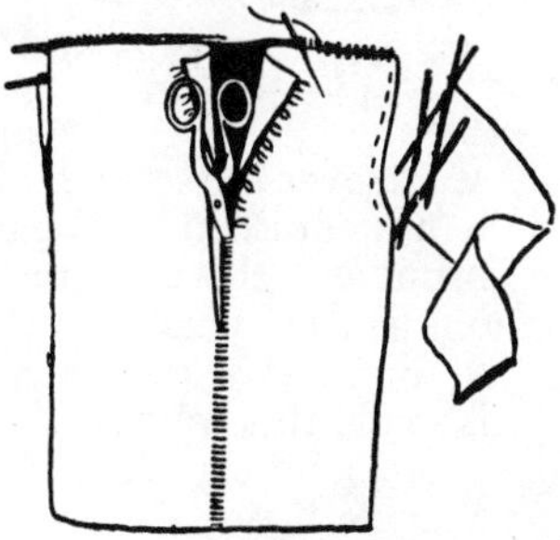

FIG. 255.—Vertical Opening.

SEAMLESS COATS

Fig. 256. These are knitted round and opened vertically down the front, as described in Fig. 255. The edges and outline of neck are then finished with crochet, and perhaps embroidery stitches, and the coat tied with a string in front as shown. In all probability a lining is also added. Children's and adults' coats (men and women) are all made in the same way, though the colours and patterns of the fabric will differ. Patterns can cover the entire coat, or a band of bead knitting can be introduced as shown.

FIG. 256.—Seamless Coat.

SEAMLESS CAP

Just as the sack is the model for a sweater, so is the bag a model for the knitted cap. Take the measurements of the head and knit a cylinder 8 inches in depth. Fold and join as a hem. Knit another 3 inches. Turn inside out, and join and cast off at the same time as for the toe of a sock—*i.e.*, divide the stitches

FIG. 257A.—A Bag-cap and Stocking Cap.

on two needles, hold these together. With a third needle insert through a stitch on the front needle and one on the back, and knit them together. Repeat on next two stitches, and then lift the first

FIG. 257B.— Seamless Cap.

stitch over the second. Cast off all stitches in this way. The cap is now finished, and can be worn with a roll or turned-back brim, and the two top corners turned over, as in Fig. 257A, or one corner finished with a tassel and the other tucked in, as in Fig. 257B, and in a dozen other ways. The cap in Fig. 256 is made this way but in Looped Knitting.†

Stocking caps (Fig. 257A) take a longer cylinder and finish with a single tassel.

SEAMLESS BAGS

These are made exactly like a cap and joined together in casting-off. The △ cast-on edge thus becomes the top opening of the bag and handles and linings are added. The bag is actually knitted upside down, so any pattern, initials, etc., would also need to be knitted upside down.

SEAMLESS CUSHIONS

These are only longer and bigger bags, joined in the same way, and the cushion pad inserted at the cast-on end and sewn in. Fig. 40 is a cylinder cushion shape, in Moss Stitch, the depth of the cylinder forming the width of the cushion.

SEAMLESS SCARVES

These are round and seamless, and in gay colours or in Sugar-Stick ribbing (*see* Fig. 173). The ends are finished with a tassel or a Knotted-in Fringe (Fig. 258).

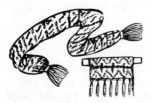

FIG. 258.—Seamless Scarves and Knotted-in Fringe.

SQUARES OR CIRCLES

For bonnet backs, Tam-o'-Shantèrs, etc., *see* Medallion Knitting, page 235.

MODERN GARMENTS AND ACCESSORIES

The modern knitter, unlike the peasant, does not regard the body as a cylinder, but as a flat, open shape, as in Fig. 259, and knits the garment accordingly.

This idea has introduced a new feature to knitwear, namely style, and because the separate sections which are now seamed together can be more conveniently made on two knitting-pins than on five, it has given Flat Knitting the star rôle in the modern world, and practically reduced the use of Round Knitting to socks or glove-making.

The secret of the peasants' success in knitting was the simplicity of the seamless shape, which was so easily understood that all attention could be paid to the beauty of the fabric.

If this same comprehension of shape can be allied to modern methods, then the same graceful use of stitch and fabric which characterises peasant work will naturally follow. For sheer beauty of fabric *see* Fig. 68, but the shape is peasant.

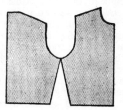

FIG. 259.—The Plan of a Body.

SEAMED GARMENTS

The shape shown in Fig. 259 is the simplest and fundamental shape in dressmaking—a Block or Master Pattern. This is cut to the shape and size of the body only, void of all style lines and without extra allowance for seam turnings. So, it can be used as an accurate means of measurement by laying each section of the garment as it is being knitted, on the pattern and shaping it accordingly. In this way modern shape can be known beforehand as easily as peasant shapes, and the knitter can be free to create her own styles, or fabrics, as she pleases. The pattern can also be used as a check for shape and size when working from written directions.

No two bodies are ever the same size or shape, and so each person must cut and keep her own Master Pattern. Full directions for doing this, with simplified shoulder line, as required for knitting, are given. By this means all figures, small or large, can be accurately fitted. Ordinary dressmaking patterns are not suitable, as they have fullness, seam allowances, and often too acute shoulder lines. They can be adapted when the figure is normal.

The block also serves for other purposes, as a basis for original design, accurate placing of pockets, neck-lines, etc. Blocks of this description can be cut as guide for all garments, children's and adults', see also *First Knitting Book.*

HOW TO TAKE YOUR OWN MEASUREMENTS. *Figs. 260*A, B, *and* C.

Body. Four measurements only are necessary : (1) Bust; (2) back length; (3) back width; (4) waist.

Allow a second person to take your measurements. The bust and back measurements are important, as the pattern is constructed on these. Take the bust measurement round fullest part of figure, adjusting tape across front, under arms and across back. Make the measurement easy, and write down the figure and decimal recorded. For back length: tie a piece of string round waist, push well down to hips and small of back. Measure from nape-bone of neck to string. The back width is measured across the **△** shoulder-blades, and **△** not across the shoulders. Waist: round body at depression above hips.

Sleeve. Three measurements are made: (1) inner arm, measured from arm-pit to wrist-bone; (2) elbow, taken round elbow with arm bent; (3) wrist, taken round palm of hand with thumb and fingers straight.

The shape in Fig. 260A is cut to the following measurements: bust, 36 inches; back length, 15 inches; back width, 13 inches; waist, 30 inches (armhole of pattern 16 inches); inner arm, 18 inches; elbow, 12 inches; wrist, 8 inches.

Pattern to be cut out of brown paper or cutting-paper squared with inch measurements.

BLOCK OR MASTER PATTERN. *Fig. 260*A.

Pattern must be planned as half front and half back only, so the two width measurements, bust and shoulder, must be halved. To do this, locate measurement on tape and fold in half. (Do this for all decimal measurements.) Experiment by first cutting pattern in miniature on squared paper, allowing ¼ inch to equal 1 inch. The method will thus be more easily grasped and applied to a full-size pattern.

CONSTRUCTIONAL LINES OF PATTERN

The following letters are given in the order in which the lines should be ruled on the paper.

A, A' = half total bust measurement.
A, B = total length of garment required + 1 inch. (Number of inches below waist vary with garment. Here 5 inches are given, suitable for jersey or short coat.)
A, C = 1 inch.
C, D = back length to waist level.
E = midway to C, D.
F = midway C, E.

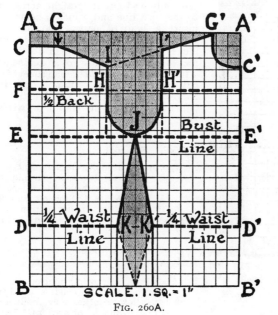

Fig. 260A.

Drafting a Block or Master Pattern.

PATTERN LINES

C, G = one-third half back width.
F, H = half back width.   Rule a perpendicular line.
H, I = C, G measured on perpendicular line.   Rule in back shoulder, G, I.
A', G' = C, G.   Rule a dotted line from G to I.
A', C' = A, G' + $\frac{1}{2}$ inch.

$G', I' = G, I$. (Both shoulder measurements equal.) Drop a vertical line from I'.

J = a point mid-way armhole. Drop a vertical dotted line from J. Repress each side of this surplus measurement until D, K and D', K', each equal quarter waist measurement. Continue straight to basque line or as suggested by dotted line for fuller hip.

The lines are now all ruled and complete, so cut out the pattern which will consist of a half front and half back as in Fig. 260.

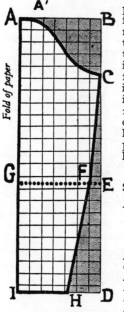

Fold of paper

FIG. 260B.
Drafting a Sleeve.

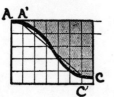

FIG. 260C.
Sleeve Top.

This very simple method of planning a pattern now needs a little adjustment, as the front needs to be a little longer, in order to make a better fit. Take the front of the pattern only and cut it straight across, parallel to the bust line and 2 inches below it. Here insert a strip of paper, allowing depth as follows : For a bust measurement of under 36 inches allow extra 1 inch in depth; over 36 inches allow 1½ inches; over 40 inches allow 2 inches. Now take a second sheet of squared cutting paper. Fold it and lay the two halves of pattern (front and back) to fold of paper and cut out the complete pattern, and keep it!

SLEEVE. *Fig.* 260B.

A, B = half of armhole measurement, — 1 inch. (This measurement can only be made after front and back of pattern are cut out, as it is made round the armhole of total paper pattern.)

B, C = quarter armhole of pattern + ½ inch.

C, D = inner arm length.

E = midway C, D.

F, G = half elbow width.

H, I = half wrist width.

A, A' = 1 inch.

C, C' = 1 inch. Draw in armhole.

Top of sleeve when it is cut will measure 1 inch to 2 inches more in circumference than armhole of pattern. This to be eased in between I' and H'.

Note.—The line between C and H is not one straight line, but drawn in two sections : one from C to F, the second from F to H.

The curve to the crown of the sleeve is a freehand line, drawn like an elongated "**S**", as shown in Fig. 260C. Mark the point A' and C' on line of graph. Drop A' ⅛ and higher C' ⅛.

Rule line from these points, and draw in " S " shape. Cut sleeve pattern. Now place the half sleeve to fold of paper as shown, and cut the whole sleeve pattern.

DESIGNING

Many hesitate to create original designs because they cannot draw. This does not matter. Merely indicate on paper the

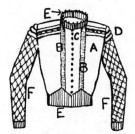

FIG. 261.—Rough Design.

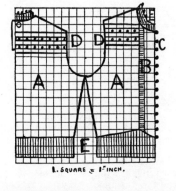

L. SQUARE = 1 INCH.

different style lines required, as in Fig. 261, and then transfer these to your own Block Pattern, either the full block or half block, which is sufficient in order to find the correct position, as in Fig. 262.

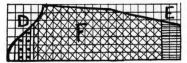

FIG. 262.—Design transferred to Block Pattern.

TRANSFER TO BLOCK. *Fig. 262.*

Do not design on the original block, but place this over a second piece of paper and draw round the edges and cut a second pattern and design on this, so as to leave Block intact. If sectional paper with eight or ten squares to 1 inch (according to gauge) is used, this will also denote measurements and position for Decreases, and so save time.

Any measurements made on the Block Pattern will be equivalent to making a measurement on yourself, as the pattern is a plan of yourself.

If the ribbing is to be 3 inches in depth, measure off 3 inches below waist line on block, and draw a horizontal line, or if a " V " neck of 4 inches depth is required, measure down 4 inches from neck and rule in the two lines.†

Choose and letter the different fabrics. Afterwards write the names of the fabrics out in full below, as follows :—

(The same principle can be applied to all garments, accessories, or articles of any shape.)

SPORTS JUMPER IN WOOL. *Figs. 261 and 262.*

A = Stocking Stitch.

B = Vertical Insertion of Faggot.

C = Picot Tufts (Fig. 216), to simulate buttons.

D = Welts (Fig. 24), to broaden shoulder, with picot knots arranged between on the Stocking Stitch for ornamentation.

E = Ribbing, 2 and 3 (K.2, P.3). Collar finished with Picot cast-off (Fig. 243).

F = Bramble Stitch, for sleeves done on same needles, so as to make solid knobbly fabric. This gives a waistcoat effect, and can be in contrasting colour to emphasise this if desired.

When the design is complete, take the selected yarn and needles, knit a tension square 4 inches + 4 inches, and count the number of stitches to the inch. If the number is 8 and the width of garment is 16 inches, then 8 multiplied by 16 will be 120. Cast on 120 stitches. The pattern in Fig. 262 increases in width 1½ inches either side to armholes. If 8 stitches equal 1 inch, this will be 12 extra stitches to be increased either side. These increasing rows will be spaces as Block directs. The same principles apply to shaping the sleeves.

Begin with something simple. One experiment will show how the method works. The next experiment can be more adventurous.

WEALTH OF FABRIC

Designing knitted fabric for garments differs considerably from designing woven fabric, as style lines, vertical and horizontal, must be considered with the fabric. For this reason the construction of each fabric, vertical or horizontal, is given throughout this book, which suggests width and uses of the fabric. The idea is to make the appropriate choice and use each as and when required. To the designer everything is a Motif of which he or she is the master (*see* Fig. 62). To associate any one particular Motif with any one design is unnecessary limitation. Units such as the Increase and Decrease need not necessarily be confined to pattern repeats. These can be used to accentuate style lines, and this is something new and rich in possibilities to a clever designer.

Discrimination is necessary when mixing vertical and horizontal fabrics, because, as pointed out, horizontal fabrics " take up ", whereas vertical fabrics have length. This is also noted throughout the book, together with little sketches which suggest different effects and uses of special motifs or fabrics.

TEXTURE

This is also an important feature of design, as some fabrics have a rough " sporting " appearance, some a slick, " tailored " appearance, and others a soft, dressy effect. The correct choice of either will aid in making the design more successful, and emphasise style. Suggestions as to texture and use of different fabrics will be found noted, and for this reason.

GLOVE IN COTTON YARN. *Fig. 263.*

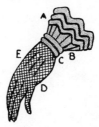

The same rules apply to gloves, etc. Design the effect required. Think of the style lines in knitted fabrics, vertical and horizontal.

A = Welting Fantastic (Fig. 178).
B = 6 and 3 Rib (K.6, P.3).
C = Welt (Fig. 24).
D = Purse Stitch (Fig. 168).
E = Vertical Glove marking in
     Wheat-Ear Stitch (Fig. 73).

FIG. 263.—Design for Glove.

Begin the gauntlet with a hem which will give a bolder extension to top.

BAG IN SILK YARN. *Fig. 264.*

A = Square Medallion (Fig. 234).
B = Leaves clustered into background (Fig. 240).
C = Handle and surround in Cable Rib (Fig. 84).

Fabrics created in this way provide endless fascination to the designer and complete satisfaction when finished.

A modern use of colour is suggested by the jumper in counter checks, Fig. 265.

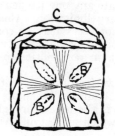

FIG. 264.—Design for Bag.

FIG. 265.—Modern Use of Colour.

All that is said about Gauges and Tension in the *First Knitting Book* should be read with care, also advice on needles, as these are the knitter's " machine ".

Keep a full range of needles as suggested, so that the gauge (size of stitch) can be changed as required, and so knit, as the Scots say, " a good cloth ".

BY THE WAY

EMBROIDERED KNITTING

Additional colour can be added to a finished knitted fabric in the following way, the method being similar to Tambour Work.

TAMBOUR STITCH. *Figs. 266A, B and C.*

Take a yarn of contrasting colour and hold it in the left hand beneath, and at the back of the fabric. Insert a crochet hook through the middle of a stitch from △ front to back, and draw the yarn through to the front in a loop as in Fig. 266A.

Now insert the hook through this loop and also through the stitch above, and hook through another loop. Continue in this way. The yarn should be of the same ply, or a little thicker than that used for the fabric itself.

The method is useful, as the stitch can be worked horizontally as in Fig. 266B, or diagonally as in Fig. 266C.

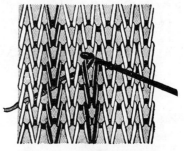

FIG. 266A.—Tambour Stitch. Vertical.

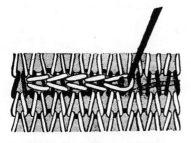

FIG. 266B.—Tambour Stitch. Horizontal.

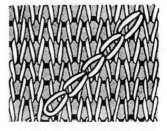

FIG. 266C.—Tambour Stitch. Diagonal.

281

USES. As a means of giving additional finish to articles, such as glove-markings or decorations to gauntlets, outline to a collar, cuffs, etc., etc. Is often used to convert an ordinary fabric of Stocking Stitch into a plaid or tartan of different colours. Can be used as a means of joining two fabrics together by placing the two selvedges side by side and inserting the hook first through a loop in one selvedge and then through a loop in the other selvedge, joining in a zig-zag line, which, evenly done, can form an additional ornament. The work has the advantage of being easily unpicked, and so easily corrected.

Can be used on other fabrics besides Stocking Stitch.

EYELET EMBROIDERY. *Fig. 267.*

Each eyelet is overcast with a matching or contrasting yarn as shown. A fabric such as Spot Eyelet treated in this way is most successful.

FIG. 267.—Eyelet Embroidery.

FILET DARNING. *Fig. 268.*

The work is similar to that done on Filet net, and can be used on open knitted fabrics of Eyelets, Filet, etc.

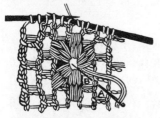

FIG. 268.—Filet Darning on Cane Stitch.

CANE STITCH. *Fig. 268.*

Cast On stitches divisible by 3, plus 2 for edge.

Row 1: K.1. * S.1, K.2 tog., p.s.s.o., O.2. * Repeat * to *, ending K.1.

Row 2: * Purl *, (knit the second Over).

Row 3: Knit.

Repeat these 3 rows.

Fig. 267 shows the method of embroidering the fabric. Thread the needle with double yarn of matching or contrasting colour. Silk yarn on a wool fabric is effective.

Tie the end through an eyelet, which then becomes the centre of a flower-like shape. Then insert the needle to the right, as shown through one eyelet (at *A*), and bring it out through the next (at *B*). Now insert the needle through the centre eyelet and out again at *B*, in at *A*, and out at *B*, in at centre and out at *B*. Continue in this way until the Motif is complete.

KNITTING LUXURIES AND HUMOUR. *Figs. 269, 270, 271, 272, 273.*

Knitting-sticks were once in common use, and peasants still knit by the aid of wooden knitting-sticks or pads fashioned with an aperture for holding the needle.†

This is girdled round the waist, and the pin held thus is stationary, and so encourages speed. Fig. 269 shows an elaborate knitting-stick of other days, carved in ivory, the needle being here inserted in the mouth of the fish, the leather belt being buckled through the back. Fig. 270 is a knitter's silver chatelaine, designed for drawing-room use and for carrying the finest needles,

FIG. 269.—Carved Ivory Knitting Stick.

as used for lace. When the knitting is removed, the right end is inserted into the left, and the two birds meet as an orna-

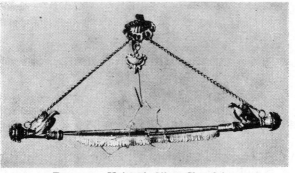

FIG. 270.—Knitter's Silver Chatelaine.

ment. The hook above carries the ball of cotton, and behind is a broader hook for tucking into the waist-belt. Luxuries of this kind characterised the knitting hours of the wealthier families throughout the 18th and early 19th centuries.

Among the many "affectations" of the early Victorian era was that of knitting in gloves (Fig. 271). Why is not known, unless it was to accentuate the pretty poise of the fingers which Medallion Knitting, because it was so small and light, permitted. (*See* page 235).

Lewis Carroll of *Alice in Wonderland* fame must have been very familiar with the occupation and terms of knitting.

FIG. 271.

FIG. 272.   FIG. 273.

He made Alice "Increase", Fig. 272, and "Decrease", Fig. 273, all over the place! He also describes the "old sheep" as bristling with needles, and as knitting in the boat with fourteen pairs of needles at once! This is not so fantastic as it sounds if she were knitting a petticoat, since sixteen needles were commonly needed for knitting a pullover. Can you wonder that the old knitters treasured their needles? Carroll's humour may have been inspired at the expense of his great contemporary, Addison, who in his spare time often knitted.

THICK AND THIN KNITTING

So called because two different yarns of different ply are used —one thin, say wool (2-ply), and one Fancy (3- or 4-ply). The garment is knitted in the 2-ply with an occasional 3 or 4 rows of the thicker yarn introduced as horizontal bands. The two yarns can be of the same colour, and the thicker yarn looks effective in a silk and wool mixture.

SILK WINDING. *Fig. 274.*

This shows how one person can wind a skein of silk on to a cardboard base. First loop the skein over the thumb, then take

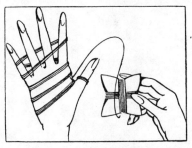

FIG. 274.—Silk Winding.

one side of the skein and wind it round the palm, and finish with the loop over the forefinger as shown.

TRANSCRIBING A PATTERN. *Figs. 275 and 276.*

A pattern written for Round Knitting can be adapted to Flat Knitting (or vice versa) in the following way :—

The process differs according to the number of Rounds comprising the entire pattern.

When the pattern has an even number of rounds, such as 2, 4, 6, or 8, etc., and every second round is a plain Knit round with no Designing Units, the process is simple. The only change will

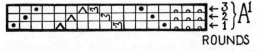

ROUNDS

FIG. 275A.—Chart. Ruffle Feather. Round Fabric.

occur on the second or △ back row, which in Flat Knitting will be purled instead of knitted.

When the pattern has an △ odd number of rounds, such as 3, 5, 7, etc., and every round carries Designing Units, as in Fig. 275A, the process is a little more complicated.

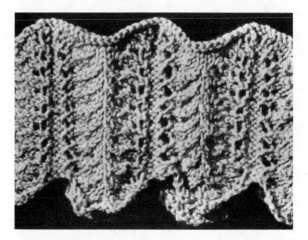

FIG. 275B.—Ruffle Feather.   Round Fabric.

The full pattern must first be charted.   △ This is absolutely necessary.

Ruffle Feather Pattern (Figs. 275 and 276A and B) is given as an example.

In Round Knitting this pattern takes seventeen stitches to the repeat and three rounds to make the pattern (*see* Fig. 275A).

In Flat Knitting it takes seventeen stitches, plus edge stitches, and six rows to complete it (*see* Fig. 276A), and for this reason.

In Fig. 275A every " round " is read from right to left, as directed by the arrows.

In Fig. 276A, Row 1 (front of fabric) is read from right to left, Row 2 (back row) from left to right, Row 3 (front row) from right to left.

This completes the pattern quite correctly, but leaves the yarn on the left, and the next row a back row, necessitating that Row 1 be now read from left to right, and all the directions and Decreases reversed.   In written directions this first row now becomes Row 4.   Row 2 becomes Row 5 and a front row, and Row 3 is now Row 6, a back row.   The arrows show the method of reading and the Decreases have been " translated " just to show what is meant.   The written directions for both versions are as follows :—

RUFFLE FEATHER PATTERN. *Figs. 275A and* B.

Round Fabric

Cast On a multiple of 17 stitches.
    Round I: * P.3, O., K.3, S.1, K.1, p.s.s.o., K.4, K.2 tog., K.3, O. *
        Repeat.
    Round 2: * P.3, K.1, O., K.3, S.1, K.1, p.s.s.o., K.2, K.2 tog.,
        K.3, O., K.1. * Repeat.
    Round 3: * P.3, K.2, O., K.3, S.1, K.1, p.s.s.o., K.2 tog., K.3, O.,
        K.2. * Repeat.

Repeat from Round 1.

RUFFLE FEATHER PATTERN. *Figs. 276A and* B.

Single Fabric

    Note P.R. Purl reverse decrease (*see* page 296).

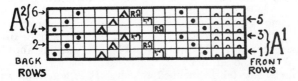

FIG. 276A.—Chart. Ruffle Feather. Single Fabric.
Rows 2, 4 and 6 show translated decreases.

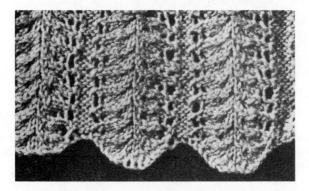

FIG. 276B.—Ruffle Feather. Single Fabric.

Cast On a multiple of 17 stitches, plus 3 for edge.
    Row I: * P.3, O., K.3, S.1, K.1, p.s.s.o., K.4, K.2 tog., K.3, O. *
        Repeat * to *, ending P.3.

Row 2: K.3.   * P.1, O., P.3, P.2 tog., P.2, P.R., P.3, O., P.1, K.3. *   Repeat * to *.

Row 3: * P.3, K.2, O., K.3, S.1, K.1, p.s.s.o., K.2 tog., K.3, O., K.2. *   Repeat * to *, ending P.3.

Row 4: K.3.   * O., P.3, P.2 tog., P.4, P.R., P.3, O., K.3. * Repeat * to *.

Row 5: * P.3, K.1, O., K.3, S.1, K.1., p.s.s.o., K.2, K.2 tog., K.3, O., K.1. *   Repeat * to *, ending P.3.

Row 6: K.3.   * P.2, O., P.3, P.2 tog., P.R., P.3, O., P.2, K.3. * Repeat * to *.

Repeat from Row 1.

The two photos are alike, which is as they should be ! But the charts are different, as are the directions.

WASHING WOOL

Knitted fabric of wool can be washed in either hot or cold water. If it is washed in hot water, then it must be dried in a warm atmosphere (not baked on a radiator or in an airing cupboard). If it is washed in cold water, then it must be dried in the open, and preferably in the wind ! The washing and drying atmospheres should not be mixed. This causes the trouble and makes the fabric inclined to felt. It is a felting process. When drying, garments should be hung, to retain their correct shape as much as possible, and flat objects, such as shawls, should be pegged out to correct shape on the ground.

WOOL, IRONING

Fancy fabrics knitted of wool should be dried, and then ironed between blankets. This process creates a kind of steam bath, and the fabric, being plastic, can be adjusted into shape by the fingers while it is still warm.

Never allow a patterned fabric to cool before attempting to adjust it, otherwise it looks flat and ironed. Ribbing and Welting can both be ironed in this way. Stretch the ribbing out flat, and pin it in this position, and iron under a blanket. Remove the blanket immediately and remove the pins, and then with the fingers gently adjust the ribbing to its correct accordion-pleated appearance while still hot. All the Ribbed and Welt fabrics shown in this book have been first ironed and treated in this way.

Cable and Plaited fabrics need careful ironing, or the Motifs crease and become flat at the junction where the stitches cross. Avoid, if possible, any pressure at these points.

YARNS

Choice of yarn plays an important part in knitted fabrics, but the more elaborate the stitch the better is this expressed in a simple yarn. Fancy yarns tend to disguise the stitch technique and give the appearance of woven fabric.

Yarns and process of making are fully described in the *First Knitting Book*, and should be read, as a knowledge of their manufacturing processes helps to determine the type of fabric each is best suited to express.

Silk and cotton yarns are more weighty than wool, and when used for garments will not " drop " so much if knitted in one of the Purl Fabrics (*see* page 15) or in any fabric designed in rows, as these " take up ", as explained (*see* page 4).

THE USE OF INCREASING AND DECREASING AS ORNAMENT

THE INCREASE AS ORNAMENT

The Increase as used in design is intended to show on the △ front of the fabric, therefore when an Increase is made on a back row it is the effect which it produces on the △ front of the fabric which makes ornament.

An Increase can be :—

    1. Solid or Invisible—*i.e.*, it leaves no open space.
    2. Open or Visible—*i.e.*, it leaves an open lace space.

SOLID OR INVISIBLE INCREASE

Extra stitches are "made" (Make 1 or M.1) directly on the needle, in such a way that no space is left beneath the extra stitch, and the fabric remains solid. There is one exception, Open Raised Increase. It is the Increase which makes design, and not the stitch out of which it is "Made", so in repeat the position of the Increase before or after the "Parent Stitch" must be a consideration.

There are several methods of work, each having its own peculiar designing value.

△ Made stitches must not be confused with Overs, which do **not** become stitches until the next row.

M.1 BAR (Knit). *Fig. 277.*

K.1 (M.1 B.). F. of F. Knit as usual into the front of a stitch, forming one loop, and then knit again into the back of this same stitch before slipping it off the needle. The Increase so made always comes △ after the Parent Stitch. **Abb.:** K.1 (M.1 B.).

Fig. 277.—Bar Increase, Knit.

Fig. 278.—Bar Increase, Purl.

M.I BAR (Purl). *Fig. 278.*

P.1 (M.1 B.).   B. of F.   Purl first into the front of a stitch, then into the back before slipping the stitch off the left needle.   On front of fabric, purl into front of stitch and △ knit into back.

Abb.: P.1 (M.1 B.).

M.I LIFTED (Knit). *Fig. 279.*

M.1 (L.).   Lift the stitch below the one on the left needle and knit it.   Then knit the true stitch on the needle.

Abb.: (M.1 (L.) K.1).

M.1 (L.a.).   Lift the stitch below △ after knitting the stitch on the needle.   This will now be the second stitch below.

Abb.: (K.1 (M.1, L.a.)).

△ These two form a pair on Knit Fabric (*see* Fig. 176C.).

FIG. 279.—Lifted Increase, Knit.

FIG. 280.—Lifted Increase, Purl.

M.I LIFTED (Purl). *Fig. 280.*

M.1 (L.) P.1.   Insert the right needle from back to front through the stitch △ below that on the needle and purl a new stitch.   After, purl the stitch on the needle.

Abb.: ((M.1 L.) P.1).

P.1, M.1 L.a.   Lift and purl the stitch △ after purling the stitch on the needle.   This will now be the second stitch below.

Abb.: (P.1 (M.1 L.a.)).

△ These two form a pair on Purl Fabrie.

M.I RAISED CROSSED (Invisible). *Figs. 281A and* **B.**

M.1 (R.c.).   Raise the running thread between two stitches with the

FIG. 281A.—Raised Increase, Invisible.

FIG. 281B.—Raised Increase, Invisible.

left needle. Insert the right needle into the △ back of this and knit a new stitch. This crosses the thread and makes an invisible increase. **Abb.**: M.1, R.c.

FIG. 282.—Raised
Increase. Open.

M.I RAISED (Open). *Fig. 282.*

M.1 (R.o.). Raise the running thread and knit a new stitch as shown. The Increase leaves an open space beneath, especially decorative in certain Fancy Patterns.
Abb.: M.1, R.o.

DOUBLE SOLID INCREASES

Solid Increases can be " Doubled ", though these are rarely used, but *see* Fig. 176C.

THE OVER

△ △ The method of making an Over varies according to the stitch (Knit or Purl), or Decrease (Knit or Purl), which △ succeeds the Over. This must be understood, △ as the abbreviation " O " does not vary. An Over is not converted into a stitch until the next row, when it then appears as a stitch, with a space beneath it.

△ The Over must be regarded as an △ Ornamental Increase only, *i.e.*, it is not used as a means of shaping a sleeve or garment. The Solid Increase is used for this purpose. △ △ Compare the " Over " with a " Throw ", Fig. 117.

OVER (Before a Knit Stitch or Knit Decrease). *Fig. 283.*

FIG. 283.—Over (before
a Knit Stitch).

Bring the yarn between the needles to the front, insert the needle knitwise into the next stitch or stitches, take the yarn △ over the needle and knit stitch. On the succeeding row the Over is purled, and then △ becomes an extra stitch with an open space beneath it. In repetition, this open space becomes the means of making Lace Patterns, etc. When used alone, and not immediately preceded or succeeded by a Decrease, it makes a LACE SPACE. **Abb.**: O.

O.2 or O.3 (Before a Knit Stitch or Knit Decrease).

For a Double or Treble Over begin as in Fig. 283, but take the yarn once (O.2) or twice (O.3) round needle △ before it is inserted to knit the next stitch.

△ Notice that in O.2 before a Knit Stitch the yarn encircles the needle once only, but passes " over " it a second time in knitting the stitch. On the succeeding row, Purl the first Over and Knit the second.

OVER (Before a Purl Stitch or Purl Decrease). *Fig. 284.*

Bring the yarn between the needles to the front (if the preceding stitch is purl it will already be in the front), take it over and round the needle and to the front again. Insert the needle purlwise into next stitch and purl it. On the succeeding row the Over will be knitted, unless specially instructed otherwise.

Abb.: O.

FIG. 284.—Over (before a Purl Stitch).

O.2 or O.3 (Before a Purl Stitch or Purl Decrease).

Begin as in Fig. 284, only take the yarn twice (O.2) or three times (O.3) over needle instead of only once.

△ In making O.2 before a Purl Stitch the yarn does encircle the needle twice (O.2) or three times (O.3).

OVER SELVEDGE (Knit). *Fig. 285.*

As used before a △ Knit Edge Stitch or Knit Decrease. **Abb.: O.**
Yarn forward, knit next stitch.
For O.2. Take yarn once round needle, insert in stitch and knit it.

FIG. 285.—Selvedge Over (Knit).

FIG. 286.—Selvedge Over (Purl).

OVER SELVEDGE (Purl). *Fig. 286.*

As used before a △ Purl Edge Stitch or Purl Decrease. **Abb.: O.**
Yarn to back, insert needle purlwise into stitch and purl it.

OVER (Before Crossed Knit Stitch or Knit Decrease). *Fig. 287.*

The actions are reversed.

The yarn is brought over and round the needle from back to front and the next stitch knitted through the back. On the next row the Over is purled through the back. **Abb.:** O.c.

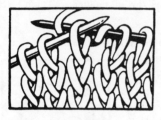

FIG. 287.   FIG. 288.

OVER (Before Crossed Purl Stitch or Purl Decrease). *Fig. 288.*

Take the yarn to the back. Insert needle purlwise through back of stitch, bring yarn over needle and purl it.

In next row the Over is knitted through the back. **Abb. :** O.c.

OVER (Reversed). **(Before a Purl Stitch or Purl Decrease.)** *Fig. 289.*

This Over shows to better advantage when the stitch preceding and succeeding it is Purl or a Purl Δ Decrease (*see* Figs. 141 to 143). It is a mixture of Figs. 288 and 292.

Working Method. Front of Fabric. In purling, the yarn is to the front. Take this between the needles to the back. Insert the needle purlwise through the next two stitches, bring the yarn Δ over the needle, and purl these two stitches together as shown. On the next row the Over is knitted (or purled according to pattern) through the Δ back, and not through the front, as is customary with other Overs.

FIG. 289.

Abb.: O. Rev.

O.2 (Reversed) (Before a Purl Stitch or Purl Decrease).

Take the yarn to the back as before, and bring it over and round to the back of needle again. Then insert needle into stitch and take yarn over the needle and purl the stitch or Decrease. This makes the second Over. On the succeeding row, purl the first Over through the back and Knit the second, or for special effect without Picot, purl into back of first Over, and into the front of second Over.

THE DECREASE AS ORNAMENT

The Decrease when promoted to a Designing Unit becomes Ornamental only when strictly paired with its opposite diagonal.

In knitting two stitches together, which is how a Decrease is formed, one stitch must lie over the other, either the left over the right (right diagonal) or the right over the left (left diagonal). This seems a small point, but an experiment will show that the repetition of these diagonals in design becomes ornamental and achieve their best effect when strictly paired.   Once this law is understood, it can be broken, and the Decrease used in other ways providing some definite effect is in view.

△ There are two methods of arranging these diagonals :—

(1) Right and left, so that the two diagonals meet as a pyramid (*see* Fig. 297).   This makes a SMOOTH pair.

(2) Left and right, so that the two diagonals point in opposite directions.   REVERSE or Rough pairing (*see also* page 300).

Either diagonal (right or left) can be formed on the front of the fabric or from the back, but it is the effect as seen on the front which makes ornament, so that a Decrease made on the back of the fabric must be chosen for its resulting effect on the front.

△ In the following diagrams the Signal drawing in the corner represents the diagonal made by the upper stitch as it appears on the △ FRONT of the fabric, whether it be a Knit Decrease (front of fabric) or a Purl Decrease (back of fabric).

A Purl Decrease made on the front of the fabric shows two stitches lying above each other and no angle.   This is often made a feature of design in Fancy Stitch patterns.

SINGLE DECREASE. This reduces two stitches to one. There are four different Single Decreases.

DOUBLE DECREASE. This reduces three stitches to one. There are nine different Double Decreases, two of which are rarely used.

△ △ **SLIP PRINCIPLE.** All stitches must be slipped knitwise when they form part of a Decrease. (If slipped purlwise they become crossed. Compare Decreasing Slip Principle with Pattern Slip Principle. Page 86.)

SINGLE DECREASES

KNIT or K.2 tog. *Fig. 290.* **(Right Diagonal.)**

Insert the needle knitwise through 2 stitches and knit them together.

S.1, K.1, p.s.s.o. *Fig. 291.* **(Left Diagonal.)**

Slip 1 stitch (K.w.) from left to right needle, knit the next. Insert the needle through the slipped stitch and pass it over the knitted stitch and off the needle.

△ These two Decreases form a pair. To obtain the same diagonals when worked on the back of fabric, knit as follows :—

FIG. 290.

FIG. 292.

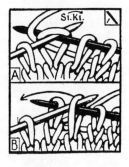

FIG. 291.

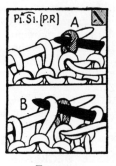

FIG. 293.

PURL, or P.2 tog. *Fig. 292.* **(Right Diagonal.)**

Insert the needle purlwise through 2 stitches and purl them together.

PURL REVERSE (P.R.). *Fig. 293.* **(Left Diagonal.)**

Purl 1 stitch. Return it to the left needle. Insert right needle through the stitch beyond and lift this over the purled stitch and off the needle. Return stitch to right needle.

△ These two Decreases form a pair.

SINGLE DECREASES IN DESIGN

When the Decreasing Unit is used on the front of the fabric only (every other row) the two Knit Decreases only are necessary, as these form a pair. When the units are used on all rows, front and back, all four Decreases are necessary, using the two right diagonals above each other, and the two left diagonals above each other, and so forming a continuous chain of pattern (*see* Fig. 140). *See also* Fig. 297.

DOUBLE DECREASES

The designer now has three stitches to play with and, as before, the upper stitch becomes a feature of design. There are nine different Double Decreases. Figs. 294–296 show these three stitches arranged in all possible methods, giving the technique on both the back and front of the fabric (Knit and Purl).

Fig. 294 (top).	Central Stitch vertical in middle. Left Stitch top.
(bottom).	Central Stitch vertical in middle. Right Stitch top.
Fig. 295 (top).	Central Stitch vertical in bottom. Left Stitch top.
	Central Stitch vertical in bottom. Right Stitch top.
Fig. 296.	Central Stitch top.

NOTE.—Working methods on both the front and the back of the fabric are given in brief in the drawings. For example, Fig. 294. K.3 tog. on front of fabric. On back of fabric P.3 tog. will give same effect in front. This is the simplest, others are more complicated and detailed here. ▲ The arrow on diagrams is a brief method of indicating p.s.s.o.

FOUR DOUBLE DECREASES AS IN FIG. 294.

K.3 tog. (Right Diagonal.)

(F. of F.) Insert the needle knitwise through 3 stitches and knit them together as 1 stitch.

D.S.D. (Double Slip Decrease). (Left Diagonal.)

(F. of F.) S.1, S.1, K.1, p.2.s.s.o. Slip 1 stitch from left to right needle, slip a 2nd (they must be slipped separately). Knit the 3rd stitch, pass the 2 slipped stitches over the knitted stitch and off the needle.

△ These two form a pair.

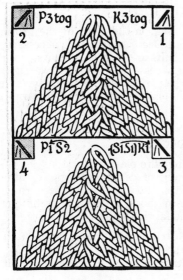

2 P3tog   K3tog 1

4 P1S2   (S1S1)K1 3

FIG. 294.

P.3 tog. (Right Diagonal.)

(B. of F.) Insert the needle purlwise through 3 stitches and purl them together.

D.P.R. (Double Purl Reverse). (Left Diagonal.)

(B. of F.) P.1, ret. L.N., p.2.n.s.o. Purl 1 stitch, return to left needle. Pass the next stitch beyond over the purled stitch and off the needle. Do the same with the next stitch beyond, and then return the stitch to the right needle again.

△ These two Purl Decreases form a pair, and give the same angle on the front as the Knit pair.

For design effect of all four Decreases *see* Fig. 294.

The centre stitch always remains vertical in the middle of all four Decreases.

FOUR DOUBLE DECREASES AS IN FIG. 295.

S.1, K.2 tog., p.s.s.o. (Right Diagonal.)

Slip 1 stitch. Knit the next 2 stitches together. Insert the left needle through the slipped stitch and pass it over the stitch and off the needle.

K.R. (Knit Reverse). (Left Diagonal.)

S.1, K.1, p.s.s.o., ret. L.N., p.n.s.o. Slip 1 stitch, knit the next and pass the slipped stitch over. Transfer the stitch to left needle and insert right needle into stitch beyond and pass this over the stitch and off the needle. Ret. R.N.

△ These two Knit Decreases form a true pair.

S.I, P.I, ret. L.N., p.n.s.o., ret. R.N., p.s.s.o. (Right Diagonal.)

Slip 1 stitch. Purl the next. Slip the next purlwise and return to left needle again. (This will turn it.) Transfer purled stitch to left needle and lift the "turned" stitch over this and off the needle. Return to right needle and pass the first slipped stitch over.

P.2 tog. REVERSE. P.2 tog., ret. L.N., p.n.s.o. (Left Diagonal.)

Purl 2 stitches together. Transfer resulting stitch to left needle, and pass the next stitch beyond over this and off the needle.

△ These two Purl Decreases form a pair, and give the same angles on the front as the Knit pair.

For design effect of these four Decreases *see* Fig. 295.

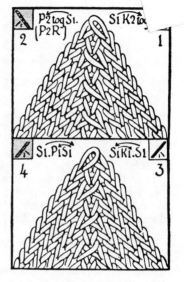

FIG. 295.

DOUBLE DECREASE AS IN FIG. 296.

CENTRAL CHAIN DECREASE. S.2, K.I, p.2.s.s.o.

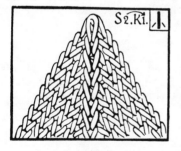

FIG. 296.

Insert the needle knitwise into 2 stitches as though to knit them together, and slip them both off the needle. Knit the next stitch beyond, and then pass the 2 slipped stitches over this knitted stitch and off the needle. Middle stitch central and vertical.

Also known as DOUBLE CENTRAL DECREASE.

For design effect of this Decrease *see* Fig. 296.

KEY

THE ORNAMENTAL PAIRING OF DECREASES. *Fig. 297.*

This chart will be found of great value to designers, as it gives in brief all the different methods of Decreasing, correctly paired, and as detailed on the previous pages.

△ The Signal drawings again indicate the diagonal made by the upper stitch of the Decrease on the FRONT of the Fabric: the solid black signals when worked on the front of the fabric, and the lined signals when worked on the back.

It will be seen that P.2 tog. when knitted on the back of the fabric, will give the same diagonal on the front, as K.2 tog., while the Purl Reverse (P.R.) will give the same effect on the front as S.1, K.1, p.s.s.o.

In Round Knitting, these Decreases made on the back of the fabric are not necessary, but modern methods of knitting are mainly concerned with the making of Single Fabrics, so these Decreases made in back rows are very necessary in order to obtain continuity of line in the planning of elaborate patterns. *See* Fig. 140.

The technique is decidedly more difficult because it is reversed, just as the actions of making a Knit Stitch are reversed when making a Purl Stitch.

The true motion of Knitting is circular, and not to and fro. This is an adaption, to which all reverse actions are an expediency.

SMOOTH PAIRING

When the upper stitches are paired so that they lean towards each other as a pyramid, the Pairing is smooth and regular. △ All the Decreases shown in this diagram (Fig. 297) are smoothly paired.

REVERSE PAIRING

When the order is reversed so that the angles of each slope outwards instead of inwards, the Pairing is Reversed or Rough, as the stitches of the Decrease will now lie at an opposite angle to the fabric.

Both have their particular value in design. Compare Figs. 180 and 181.

ORNAMENTAL PAIRING OF DECREASES

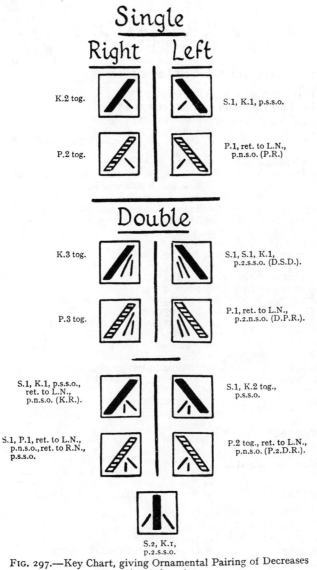

FIG. 297.—Key Chart, giving Ornamental Pairing of Decreases
(at a glance).

ABBREVIATIONS

K.	= Knit.
K.1	= Knit 1 stitch.
K.1 B.	= Knit 1 stitch through the back. This will cross it.
K.1 (2 Throws)	= *See* page 87 and 107.
P.	= Purl.
P.1	= Purl 1 stitch.
P.1 B.	= Purl 1 stitch through the back. This will cross it.
P.1 (2 Throws)	= *See* pages 87 and 107.
S.1	= Slip 1 stitch from the left to the right needle without knitting it.
P.S.S.O.	= Pass Slip Stitch Over.
P.2.S.S.O.	= Pass 2 Slip Stitches Over.
P.N.S.O.	= Pass next Stitch Over.
(K.1 over 1)	= *See* Fig. 69.
(P.1 over 1)	= *See* Fig. 70.
(K.2 over 2 Back)	= *See* Fig. 78.
(K.2 over 2 Front)	= *See* Fig. 79.
(K.3 over 3 Back)	= *See* Fig. 78.
(K.3 over 3 Front)	= *See* Fig. 79.
(K.B. 3 over 3 Back)	= *See* page 67.
(K.B. 3 over 3 Front)	= *See* page 67.
( ) 3 times	= Repeat directions in brackets 3 times, or as many as figure denotes.
P.w.	= Purlwise (S.1, P.w.).
K.w.	= Knitwise (S.1, K.w.).
Ret. L.N.	= Return to left needle.
Ret. R.N.	= Return to right needle.
F. of F.	= Front of Fabric.
B. of F.	= Back of Fabric.
S.S.	= Stocking Stitch.

INCREASES

(*See* page 290 for full descriptions.)

M.1 (B.)	= Make 1 stitch using Bar Increase.
M.1 (L.)	= Make 1 stitch using Lifted Increase.
M.1 (L.a.)	= Make 1 stitch using Lifted Increase.
M.1 (R.c.)	= Make 1 stitch using Crossed Raised Increase.
M.1 (R.o.)	= Make 1 stitch using Raised Open Increase.
O.	= Over (*see* page 292).
O.2	= Double Over.
O.(C.)	= Over before a Crossed Knit Stitch or Crossed Purl Stitch.
O. (Rev.) or O. (R.)	= Over Reversed (*see* Fig. 289.)

DECREASES

(*See* page 295 for full descriptions.)

K.2 tog.	= Knit 2 stitches together.
P.2 tog.	= Purl 2 stitches together.
K.2 tog. B.	= Knit 2 stitches together through the back of the stitches.
S.1, K.1, p.s.s.o.	= Slip 1, knit 1 and pass slipped stitch over.
P.R.	= Purl Reverse (*see* Decreasing, Fig. 293).
K.3 tog.	= Knit 3 stitches together.
P.3 tog.	= Purl 3 stitches together.
D.S.D.	= Double Slip Decrease (*see* page 297).
D.P.R.	= Double Purl Reverse (*see* page 298).
S.1, K.2 tog., p.s.s.o.	= Slip 1 stitch, knit 2 stitches together, pass slipped stitch over.
C.C.D.	= Central Chain Decrease (*see* Fig. 296).
S.2, K.1, p.2.s.s.o.	= Slip 2 stitches off together, knit one, pass 2 slipped stitches over.
K.R.	= Knit Reverse Decrease.
P.R.	= Purl Reverse Decrease.

FRENCH KNITTING TERMS

Abbreviations as used in knitting directions are given in brackets.

French.	English.
A l'endroite.	On the front or right side of the fabric.
A l'envers.	On the back of the fabric.
Abreviations du Tricot.	Knitting abbreviations.
Aiguille.	Needle.
Aiguille droite (aig. dr.).	Right needle.
Aiguille gauche (aig. gche.).	Left needle.
Ainsi de suite.	All alike (and so on).
Augmentation (Augm.).	Make a stitch.
Augm. d'une Maille levée.	Make 1 (Raised Increase).
Augm. dans une Maille.	Knit into front and back of stitch.
Augm. invisible.	Make 1 (Lifted). Invisible Increase.
Bord en chainette.	Chain edge (selvedge).
Bord Perle.	All edge stitches knitted.
Ce point s'exécute avec un multiple de 12 m., plus 2 m.l.	Cast on a multiple of 12 stitches, plus 2 edge stitches.
Chaine de Mailles.	Edge stitches.
Diminutions.	The Decreases.
Double jeté à l'endroite (dble. jeté end.).	Double Over (O.2).
Fermeture des Mailles.	To Cast off. Finish.
Glisser une Maille.	Slip a stitch.
Jeté à l'endroit (Jeté endre).	Make an Over as before a Knit Stitch.
Jeté à l'envers (Jeté env.).	Over as before a Purl Stitch.
l'Aller et retour.	Knit a row and Purl back again.
Maille (M.).	Stitch.
Maille a l'endroit (M. endr.).	Knit Stitch.
Maille a l'envers (M. env.).	Purl Stitch.
Maille lisière (m.l.).	Edge Stitch.
Maille à l'endroit Torse.	K. into back of stitch to make Crossed Stitch.
Maille à l'envers Torse.	Purl into back of stitch.
Maille glissée à l'endroit.	Slip knitwise.
Maille glissée à l'envers.	Slip purlwise.
Montage cylindrique sur 4 aiguilles.	Casting-on round knitting, 4 needles.
Montages des Mailles.	The Casting-on.
Montage tricote avec 2 aiguilles.	Casting-on with 2 needles.

French.	English.
Montage tricote avec 1 aiguille.	Casting-on with 1 needle.
Monter les Mailles.	To Cast on.
Point.	Stitch.
Point de côtes 1 et 1.	1 and 1 Rib.
Point de côtes 2 et 2.	2 and 2 Rib.
Point Jarretière.	Garter Stitch.
Point Jersey.	Stocking Stitch.
Rabattre.	p.s.s.o.
Rabattre tout les Mailles.	To Cast off.
Rang (rg.).	A row.
Rang enverse.	Purl row.
Remaillage sur on bord.	Rejoin. Pick up the edge stitches, or the cast-on edge.
Tour (tr.).	A round.
Tricoter.	To Knit.
*Tricoter à l'endroit.	Knit on the front of the fabric a Knit row.
*Tricoter à l'envers.	Knit on the back of the fabric a Purl row.
Un rang de m. a l'endroite.	A row of Knit stitches.
Un range de m. a l'envers.	A row of Purl stitches.
Un surjet simple (1 surj. sple.).	S.1, K.1, p.s.s.o.
Un surjet double (1 surj. dble.).	S.1, K.2, p.s.s.o.
Une diminution à droite (1 dim. a dr.).	K.2 tog.
Une diminution à gauche (1 dim. a gche.).	P.2 tog.

NOTE.—Stitches are called "Front" and "Back" stitches, instead of Knit and Purl stitches. Also Front rows and Back rows for Knit rows and Purl rows.

GERMAN KNITTING TERMS

Ab wiederholen.	Repeat from.
Abbildung.	Picture, illustration.
Abheben.	To slip.
Abketten der Maschen.	To cast off.
Abnehmen.	To Decrease.
Abnehmen durch Uberziehen.	Decrease (S.1, K.1, p.s.s.o.).
1 Abnehmegang.	1st Decreasing Round.
Anschlagen.	To cast on.
Arbeit.	Work.
Auf der Rückseite durchweg links stricken.	All back rows Purl.
Auffassen der Randmaschen.	Pick up the edge stitches.
Auflegen.	Over as before a Knit Stitch.
Auflegen, 1 Masche abheben, 1 Masche rechts und uberzeihen.	Over, Slip, K.1, p.s.s.o.
Daruber.	Over that.
Doppelter Kreuzanschlag.	Double cross cast-on.
Doppelumschlag.	Double Over.
Ende der Reihe.	End of row.
Eine Masche abheben.	Slip 1 stitch.
Eine Masche (ungestricket) abheben.	Slip a stitch without knitting it.
Farbe.	Colour.
Farbwechsel.	Change of colour.
Gang.	A Round (as in stocking-making).
Geschlossnen Arbeit.	Closed or Round Knitting.
Gestrickt.	Knitted.
Glatte Masche.	Smooth or Knit Stitch.
Hohlmaschen.	Hole Stitch.
im Wechsel.	In change or alternatively.
Links abnehmen.	P.2 tog.
Masche.	Stitch.
Masche links.	Purl (or left) stitch.
Masche rechts.	Knit (or right) stitch.
2 Maschen rechts zusammenstricken.	Knit 2 tog.
Maschenglied.	Stitch on the needle.
Maschenzahl teilbar durch.	Stitch number divisible by.
Offene Arbeit.	Open or Flat knitting on 2 needles.
Randmasche.	Edge Stitch.
Rechts abnehmen.	(K.2 tog.).
Rechtsmuster.	Stocking Stitch.
Reihe.	Row.
Ruckseite.	Back. Reverse or Wrong side.

Runde.	A round.
Spitzen muster.	Point or Lace Pattern.
Stricken.	Knitting.
Uberziehen.	Overdraw (p.s.s.o.).
Umschlag.	Over as before a Purl Stitch.
Verdrehte Masche.	Crossed Knit Stitch.
Zahl.	Number.
Zopfmuster.	Cable Stitch or Pattern.

NOTE.—Stitches are called " Right " and "Left" (Rechts and Links) stitches instead of Knit and Purl stitches. Also Right rows and Left rows, instead of Knit rows and Purl rows.

TEXTURE INDEX

Choose at a glance a suitable fabric for the purpose required. This Index is not given in any arbitrary sense, as the knitter will quickly find other and more individual uses for the different fabrics, but it will provide a first basis of thought.

BEDSPREADS

Bell-and-Rope Pattern.
Candle-light Pattern.
Dimple Shale and Rib Pattern.
Feather Pattern.
Garden-Plot Square.
Heavy Double Basket Pattern.
Hexagon Medallion.
Maltese Cross Medallion.
Parquet Cloqué.
Scale Pattern.
Square Medallion.
Windmill Medallion.

BERET AND BONNET FABRICS

Circular Medallion.
Dimple Eyelet.
Floral Medallion.
Hexagon Medallion.
Maltese Cross Medallion.
Octagon Medallion.
Pentagon Medallion.
Picot Diamond Eyelet Pattern.
Picot Lacis.
Picot Knots.
Pin Check.
Purse Stitch.
Windmill Medallion.

BORDER ENCLOSURES (HORIZONTAL)

Bluebell Stitch.
Crested Garter Insertion Stitch.
Crossed Elongated Stitch.
Double Crested Garter Insertion.
Double Elongated Stitch.
Eyelet Beading.
Elongated Crossed Garter.
Elongated Stocking Stitch.
Embossed Ruching.
Gauge Pattern.
Indian Cross Stitch.

Reverse Eyelet.
Ribbon Brioche.
Tunisian Stitch (Horizontal).
Welts.

BOYS' KNICKER FABRICS

(Extra Strong Fabrics.)

Close Stitch.
Corn-on-the-Cob Stitch.
Double Rose Fabric.
Heel Stitch.
Hopsac Stitch.
Pin Check.
Plaited Four Stitch.
Rose Fabric.
Tunisian Stitch (Oblique).
Woven Rib.

CLOQUÉ OR EMBOSSED FABRICS

(Suitable for Soft Furnishings, Cushions, Cot or Pram Spreads, etc.)

Basket Pattern.
Bell-Ringer's Peal Pattern.
Bell-and-Rope Pattern.
Bric-à-brac Cloqué Pattern.
Butterfly Cloqué.
Cable Rib.
Chenille Tuft.
Corrugated Fabric.
Detached Oval Cluster.
Embossed Ruching.
Escalator Pattern.
Fuchsia Pattern.
Parquet Cloqué Pattern.
Picot Knots.
Pinnacle Crêpe Pattern.
Scale Pattern.
Waved Embossed Ribbing.
Welting, Fantastic.

LACE AND LACY FABRICS

Beach-Leaf Lace.
Bell-Ringer's Peal Pattern.
Bell-and-Rope Pattern.
Bluebell Stitch.
Bramble Stitch.
Broderie Anglaise Motif.
Broken Key Pattern.
Cane Stitch.
Cat's Eye Pattern.
Chevron Lace Stitch.
Dimple Shale and Rib Pattern.
Drooping Elm-Leaf.
Elongated Crossed Garter Stitch.
Elongated Stocking Stitch.
Embroidery Eyelet Diamond.
Eyelet Diamond Pattern.
Eyelet Diamond Picot Pattern,
Eyelet Rib.
Faggot Diamond Pattern.
Faggot Stitch Insertions.
Falling-Leaf Pattern.
Feather Pattern.
Gate and Ladder Pattern.
Grand Eyelet Lace.
Honeycomb Slip Stitch.
Horseshoe Imprint Pattern.
Lace Diadem Eyelet Pattern.
Lace Faggot Stitch.
Long-Ladder Pattern.
Laburnum Stitch.
Little Windows.
Miniature-Leaf Pattern.
Ogee Lace Pattern.
Old Shale Pattern.
Open Star Stitch.
Picot Eyelet Diamond.
Pine Trees Pattern.
Purse Stitch.
Ruffer Feather Pattern.
Spider Stitch.
Spot-Ladder Motif Pattern.
Trellis Faggot Pattern.
Zig-zag Lace Faggot and Horse-
  shoe.
Zig-zag Faggot Trellis.
Zig-zag Faggot Trellis and Rib
  Fantastic.

PLEATING

Knife Pleating.
Pennant Pleating.

PRAM COVERS

Bell-Ringer's Peal Pattern.
Bell-and-Rope Pattern.
Bluebell Stitch.
Brioche Stitch.
Candle-light Pattern.
Chevron Fantastic.
Coral Loop Stitch.
Dimple Shale and Rib.
Double English Brioche.
Feather Pattern.
Grand Eyelet Lace.
Indian Cross Stitch.
Laburnum Stitch.
Miniature-Leaf Pattern.
Parquet Cloqué.
Ribbon Brioche Stitch.
Ribbon Eyelet.
Scale Pattern.
Syncopated Brioche.
Waved Embossed Ribbing.
Welting Fantastic.

SCARVES (SINGLE)

(If vertical fabrics are chosen, use
fine yarns, and knit very wide, as
for Shetland scarves.)

Brioche Stitch.
Diagonal Knitting.
Moss Stitch.
Old Shale Pattern.
Purse Stitch.
Syncopated Brioche Stitch.
Welts.

SCARVES (ROUND)

Chevrons, Little.
Spot Eyelet.
Stocking Stitch.
Sugar-Stick Ribbing.

SEMI-SPORTS

Basket Patterns.
Brioche Stitch.
Butterfly Cloqué.
Butterfly Slip Stitch.
Diagonal Rib (2 and 2).
Dimple Eyelet.
Fancy Chevron, Broad.
Fancy Cross Garter Stitch.

Feather Pattern.
Garter Welt.
Giant Check.
Grecian Plait Stitch.
Horseshoe Imprint Pattern.
Knotted Rib.
Moss Stitch.
Plaited Brioche.
Rib-Welt Patterns.
Rice Stitch.
Ribbing, Uneven.
Rose Fabric.
Shadow Plaited Stitch.
Shadow Rib Diagonal.
Syncopated Brioche Stitch.
Threaded Cross Stitch.
Waffle Stitch.
Wager Welt.
Welts, Even.
Wheat-Ear Rib.
Zig-zag Checks.
Zig-zag Plaited Rib.

SHAWLS

(* = Reversible Fabrics.)

*Brioche Stitch.
*Cane Stitch.
Dimple Shale and Rib Pattern.
*Grand Eyelet Lace.
Old Shale Pattern.
*Purse Stitch.
Ribbing Fantastic.
*Ribbon Brioche.
*Syncopated Brioche.

SLIPPER FABRICS

Chevron, Little.
Feather Pattern.
Knotted Rib.
Macaroni Rib.
Plaited Basket Stitch.
Ribbon Brioche.
Syncopated Brioche Stitch.
Tunisian Stitches.

SOCK TOPS (CHILDRENS)

Picot Hem.
Tunisian Stitch (Horizontal).
Welts.

SOCKS OR STOCKINGS

Heel Stitch.
Ribbing.
Stocking Stitch.

SMOCKING

Clustering Tie Stitch.

SPORTS FABRICS

Broken Ribbing.
Butterfly Drop Motif.
Cable Ribs.
Checks.
Corrugated Garter Stitch.
Double Basket, Fine Pattern.
Double Basket, Heavy Pattern.
Double Moss Stitch.
Double Plaited Basket Stitch.
Escalator Pattern.
Garter Stitch.
Grecian Plait Stitch.
Harris Tweed Patterns.
Herringbone Slip Stitch.
Hopsac Stitch.
Macaroni Stitch.
Miniature Cross Over Rib.
Pinnacle Crêpe Pattern.
Plaited Basket Stitch.
Plaited Four Stitch.
Plaited Brioche Stitch.
Plaited Ribs.
Threaded Cross Stitch.
Travelling Diagonal Crossed Rib.
Waved Ribbon Rib.
Waved Ribbon Rib, in Cross
    Knit Stitch.
Welt Fabrics.
Welts, Uneven.
Wheat-Ear Rib.
Zig-zag Knotted Rib.

TAILORED FABRICS

Brocade Patterns.
Bias Repeat Pattern.
Bias Chevrons.
Chessboard Check.
Chevron, Fantastic.
Chevron, Little.
Cross Cord Rib.
Diagonal Rib and Check.
Diagonal Rib, Fancy.
Double Diamond Pattern.

Eyelet Rib.
Fancy Cross Garter Stitch.
Little Chevrons.
Raindrop Stitch.
Ribbing, Uneven.
Rice Stitch.
Single Diamond.
Spot Eyelet.
Spot Pattern.
Spot Pattern Cross Motif.
Stocking Stitch.
Threaded Cross Stitch.
Wager Welt (Reverse Side).

THICK FABRICS AND EDGINGS

Brioche Stitch.
Close Stitch.
Corrugated Fabric.
Double Plaited Basket Stitch.
Heel Stitch.
Herringbone Slip Stitch.
Hopsac Stitch.
Plaited Four Stitch.
Ribbon Brioche.
Woven Rib.

TIES

(For Round Knitting.)

Stocking Stitch.
Sugar-Stick Ribbing.

TOWEL FABRICS

(To be knitted in White Cotton.)

Filet Lace Edging.
Filet Lace Insertion.
Garter Stitch.
Moss Stitch.
Waffle Stitch.

TWO-COLOUR FABRICS

Butterfly Cloque.
Corn-on-the-Cob Stitch.
Elongated Crossed Slip Stitch.
Elongated Slip Stitch.
Hexagonal Pattern.
Over Check.
Pin Check.

UNDERGARMENT FABRICS

Broken Key Pattern.
Candle-light Pattern.
Faggot Diamond Pattern.
Falling-Leaf Pattern.
Old Shale Pattern.
Ribbed Patterns.
Spot Eyelet.
Stocking Stitch.

INDEX

A CATALOG OF SELECTED

DOVER BOOKS

IN ALL FIELDS OF INTEREST

A CATALOG OF SELECTED DOVER
BOOKS IN ALL FIELDS OF INTEREST

THE ART NOUVEAU STYLE, edited by Roberta Waddell. 579 rare photographs of works in jewelry, metalwork, glass, ceramics, textiles, architecture and furniture by 175 artists—Mucha, Seguy, Lalique, Tiffany, many others. 288pp. 8⅜ × 11¼.
23515-7 Pa. $8.95

AMERICAN COUNTRY HOUSES OF THE GILDED AGE (Sheldon's "Artistic Country-Seats"), A. Lewis. All of Sheldon's fascinating and historically important photographs and plans. New text by Arnold Lewis. Approx. 200 illustrations. 128pp. 9⅜ × 12¼.
24301-X Pa. $7.95

THE WAY WE LIVE NOW, Anthony Trollope. Trollope's late masterpiece, marks shift to bitter satire. Character Melmotte "his greatest villain." Reproduced from original edition with 40 illustrations. 416pp. 6⅛ × 9¼.
24360-5 Pa. $7.95

BENCHLEY LOST AND FOUND, Robert Benchley. Finest humor from early 30's, about pet peeves, child psychologists, post office and others. Mostly unavailable elsewhere. 73 illustrations by Peter Arno and others. 183pp. 5⅜ × 8½.
22410-4 Pa. $3.50

ISOMETRIC PERSPECTIVE DESIGNS AND HOW TO CREATE THEM, John Locke. Isometric perspective is the picture of an object adrift in imaginary space. 75 mindboggling designs. 52pp. 8¼ × 11.
24123-8 Pa. $2.50

PERSPECTIVE FOR ARTISTS, Rex Vicat Cole. Depth, perspective of sky and sea, shadows, much more, not usually covered. 391 diagrams, 81 reproductions of drawings and paintings. 279pp. 5⅜ × 8½.
22487-2 Pa. $4.00

MOVIE-STAR PORTRAITS OF THE FORTIES, edited by John Kobal. 163 glamor, studio photos of 106 stars of the 1940s: Rita Hayworth, Ava Gardner, Marlon Brando, Clark Gable, many more. 176pp. 8⅜ × 11¼.
23546-7 Pa. $6.95

STARS OF THE BROADWAY STAGE, 1940-1967, Fred Fehl. Marlon Brando, Uta Hagen, John Kerr, John Gielgud, Jessica Tandy in great shows—*South Pacific, Galileo, West Side Story*, more. 240 black-and-white photos. 144pp. 8⅜ × 11¼.
24398-2 Pa. $8.95

ILLUSTRATED DICTIONARY OF HISTORIC ARCHITECTURE, edited by Cyril M. Harris. Extraordinary compendium of clear, concise definitions for over 5000 important architectural terms complemented by over 2000 line drawings. 592pp. 7½ × 9⅜.
24444-X Pa. $14.95

THE EARLY WORK OF FRANK LLOYD WRIGHT, F.L. Wright. 207 rare photos of Oak Park period, first great buildings: Unity Temple, Dana house, Larkin factory. Complete photos of Wasmuth edition. New Introduction. 160pp. 8⅜ × 11¼.
24381-8 Pa. $7.50

LIVING MY LIFE, Emma Goldman. Candid, no holds barred account by foremost American anarchist: her own life, anarchist movement, famous contemporaries, ideas and their impact. 944pp. 5⅜ × 8½. 22543-7, 22544-5 Pa., Two-vol. set $13.00

UNDERSTANDING THERMODYNAMICS, H.C. Van Ness. Clear, lucid treatment of first and second laws of thermodynamics. Excellent supplement to basic textbook in undergraduate science or engineering class. 103pp. 5⅜ × 8.
63277-6 Pa. $3.50

SMOCKING: TECHNIQUE, PROJECTS, AND DESIGNS, Dianne Durand. Foremost smocking designer provides complete instructions on how to smock. Over 10 projects, over 100 illustrations. 56pp. 8¼ × 11. 23788-5 Pa. $2.00

AUDUBON'S BIRDS IN COLOR FOR DECOUPAGE, edited by Eleanor H. Rawlings. 24 sheets, 37 most decorative birds, full color, on one side of paper. Instructions, including work under glass. 56pp. 8¼ × 11. 23492-4 Pa. $3.50

THE COMPLETE BOOK OF SILK SCREEN PRINTING PRODUCTION, J.I. Biegeleisen. For commercial user, teacher in advanced classes, serious hobbyist. Most modern techniques, materials, equipment for optimal results. 124 illustrations. 253pp. 5⅜ × 8½. 21100-2 Pa. $4.50

A TREASURY OF ART NOUVEAU DESIGN AND ORNAMENT, edited by Carol Belanger Grafton. 577 designs for the practicing artist. Full-page, spots, borders, bookplates by Klimt, Bradley, others. 144pp. 8⅜ × 11¼. 24001-0 Pa. $5.00

ART NOUVEAU TYPOGRAPHIC ORNAMENTS, Dan X. Solo. Over 800 Art Nouveau florals, swirls, women, animals, borders, scrolls, wreaths, spots and dingbats, copyright-free. 100pp. 8⅛ × 11. 24366-4 Pa. $4.00

HAND SHADOWS TO BE THROWN UPON THE WALL, Henry Bursill. Wonderful Victorian novelty tells how to make flying birds, dog, goose, deer, and 14 others, each explained by a full-page illustration. 32pp. 6½ × 9¼. 21779-5 Pa. $1.50

AUDUBON'S BIRDS OF AMERICA COLORING BOOK, John James Audubon. Rendered for coloring by Paul Kennedy. 46 of Audubon's noted illustrations: red-winged black-bird, cardinal, etc. Original plates reproduced in full-color on the covers. Captions. 48pp. 8¼ × 11. 23049-X Pa. $2.25

SILK SCREEN TECHNIQUES, J.I. Biegeleisen, M.A. Cohn. Clear, practical, modern, economical. Minimal equipment (self-built), materials, easy methods. For amateur, hobbyist, 1st book. 141 illustrations. 185pp. 6⅛ × 9¼. 20433-2 Pa. $3.95

101 PATCHWORK PATTERNS, Ruby S. McKim. 101 beautiful, immediately useable patterns, full-size, modern and traditional. Also general information, estimating, quilt lore. 140 illustrations. 124pp. 7⅞ × 10¾. 20773-0 Pa. $3.50

READY-TO-USE FLORAL DESIGNS, Ed Sibbett, Jr. Over 100 floral designs (most in three sizes) of popular individual blossoms as well as bouquets, sprays, garlands. 64pp. 8¼ × 11. 23976-4 Pa. $2.95

AMERICAN WILD FLOWERS COLORING BOOK, Paul Kennedy. Planned coverage of 46 most important wildflowers, from Rickett's collection; instructive as well as entertaining. Color versions on covers. Captions. 48pp. 8¼ × 11. 20095-7 Pa. $2.25

CARVING DUCK DECOYS, Harry V. Shourds and Anthony Hillman. Detailed instructions and full-size templates for constructing 16 beautiful, marvelously practical decoys according to time-honored South Jersey method. 70pp. 9¼ × 12¼. 24083-5 Pa. $4.95

TRADITIONAL PATCHWORK PATTERNS, Carol Belanger Grafton. Cardboard cut-out pieces for use as templates to make 12 quilts: Buttercup, Ribbon Border, Tree of Paradise, nine more. Full instructions. 57pp. 8¼ × 11. 23015-5 Pa. $3.50

CHILDREN'S BOOKPLATES AND LABELS, Ed Sibbett, Jr. 6 each of 12 types based on *Wizard of Oz, Alice,* nursery rhymes, fairy tales. Perforated; full color. 24pp. 8¼ × 11. 23538-6 Pa. $2.95

READY-TO-USE VICTORIAN COLOR STICKERS: 96 Pressure-Sensitive Seals, Carol Belanger Grafton. Drawn from authentic period sources. Motifs include heads of men, women, children, plus florals, animals, birds, more. Will adhere to any clean surface. 8pp. 8½ × 11. 24551-9 Pa. $2.95

CUT AND FOLD PAPER SPACESHIPS THAT FLY, Michael Grater. 16 colorful, easy-to-build spaceships that really fly. Star Shuttle, Lunar Freighter, Star Probe, 13 others. 32pp. 8¼ × 11. 23978-0 Pa. $2.50

CUT AND ASSEMBLE PAPER AIRPLANES THAT FLY, Arthur Baker. 8 aerodynamically sound, ready-to-build paper airplanes, designed with latest techniques. Fly *Pegasus, Daedalus, Songbird,* 5 other aircraft. Instructions. 32pp. 9¼ × 11¼. 24302-8 Pa. $3.95

SIDELIGHTS ON RELATIVITY, Albert Einstein. Two lectures delivered in 1920-21: *Ether and Relativity* and *Geometry and Experience.* Elegant ideas in non-mathematical form. 56pp. 5⅜ × 8½. 24511-X Pa. $2.25

FADS AND FALLACIES IN THE NAME OF SCIENCE, Martin Gardner. Fair, witty appraisal of cranks and quacks of science: Velikovsky, orgone energy, Bridey Murphy, medical fads, etc. 373pp. 5⅜ × 8½. 20394-8 Pa. $5.50

VACATION HOMES AND CABINS, U.S. Dept. of Agriculture. Complete plans for 16 cabins, vacation homes and other shelters. 105pp. 9 × 12. 23631-5 Pa. $4.50

HOW TO BUILD A WOOD-FRAME HOUSE, L.O. Anderson. Placement, foundations, framing, sheathing, roof, insulation, plaster, finishing—almost everything else. 179 illustrations. 223pp. 7⅞ × 10¾. 22954-8 Pa. $5.50

THE MYSTERY OF A HANSOM CAB, Fergus W. Hume. Bizarre murder in a hansom cab leads to engrossing investigation. Memorable characters, rich atmosphere. 19th-century bestseller, still enjoyable, exciting. 256pp. 5⅜ × 8. 21956-9 Pa. $4.00

MANUAL OF TRADITIONAL WOOD CARVING, edited by Paul N. Hasluck. Possibly the best book in English on the craft of wood carving. Practical instructions, along with 1,146 working drawings and photographic illustrations. 576pp. 6½ × 9¼. 23489-4 Pa. $8.95

WHITTLING AND WOODCARVING, E.J Tangerman. Best book on market; clear, full. If you can cut a potato, you can carve toys, puzzles, chains, etc. Over 464 illustrations. 293pp. 5⅜ × 8½. 20965-2 Pa. $4.95

AMERICAN TRADEMARK DESIGNS, Barbara Baer Capitman. 732 marks, logos and corporate-identity symbols. Categories include entertainment, heavy industry, food and beverage. All black-and-white in standard forms. 160pp. 8⅛ × 11. 23259-X Pa. $6.00

DECORATIVE FRAMES AND BORDERS, edited by Edmund V. Gillon, Jr. Largest collection of borders and frames ever compiled for use of artists and designers. Renaissance, neo-Greek, Art Nouveau, Art Deco, to mention only a few styles. 396 illustrations. 192pp. 8⅜ × 11¼. 22928-9 Pa. $6.00

THE BOOK OF WOOD CARVING, Charles Marshall Sayers. Still finest book for beginning student. Fundamentals, technique; gives 34 designs, over 34 projects for panels, bookends, mirrors, etc. 33 photos. 118pp. 7¾ × 10⅝. 23654-4 Pa. $3.95

CARVING COUNTRY CHARACTERS, Bill Higginbotham. Expert advice for beginning, advanced carvers on materials, techniques for creating 18 projects—mirthful panorama of American characters. 105 illustrations. 80pp. 8⅜ × 11. 24135-1 Pa. $2.50

300 ART NOUVEAU DESIGNS AND MOTIFS IN FULL COLOR, C.B. Grafton. 44 full-page plates display swirling lines and muted colors typical of Art Nouveau. Borders, frames, panels, cartouches, dingbats, etc. 48pp. 9⅜ × 12¼. 24354-0 Pa. $6.00

SELF-WORKING CARD TRICKS, Karl Fulves. Editor of *Pallbearer* offers 72 tricks that work automatically through nature of card deck. No sleight of hand needed. Often spectacular. 42 illustrations. 113pp. 5⅜ × 8½. 23334-0 Pa. $2.25

CUT AND ASSEMBLE A WESTERN FRONTIER TOWN, Edmund V. Gillon, Jr. Ten authentic full-color buildings on heavy cardboard stock in H-O scale. Sheriff's Office and Jail, Saloon, Wells Fargo, Opera House, others. 48pp. 9¼ × 12¼. 23736-2 Pa. $3.95

CUT AND ASSEMBLE AN EARLY NEW ENGLAND VILLAGE, Edmund V. Gillon, Jr. Printed in full color on heavy cardboard stock. 12 authentic buildings in H-O scale: Adams home in Quincy, Mass., Oliver Wight house in Sturbridge, smithy, store, church, others. 48pp. 9¼ × 12¼. 23536-X Pa. $3.95

THE TALE OF TWO BAD MICE, Beatrix Potter. Tom Thumb and Hunca Munca squeeze out of their hole and go exploring. 27 full-color Potter illustrations. 59pp. 4¼ × 5½. (Available in U.S. only) 23065-1 Pa. $1.50

CARVING FIGURE CARICATURES IN THE OZARK STYLE, Harold L. Enlow. Instructions and illustrations for ten delightful projects, plus general carving instructions. 22 drawings and 47 photographs altogether. 39pp. 8⅜ × 11. 23151-8 Pa. $2.50

A TREASURY OF FLOWER DESIGNS FOR ARTISTS, EMBROIDERERS AND CRAFTSMEN, Susan Gaber. 100 garden favorites lushly rendered by artist for artists, craftsmen, needleworkers. Many form frames, borders. 80pp. 8¼ × 11. 24096-7 Pa. $3.50

CUT & ASSEMBLE A TOY THEATER/THE NUTCRACKER BALLET, Tom Tierney. Model of a complete, full-color production of Tchaikovsky's classic. 6 backdrops, dozens of characters, familiar dance sequences. 32pp. 9⅜ × 12¼. 24194-7 Pa. $4.50

ANIMALS: 1,419 COPYRIGHT-FREE ILLUSTRATIONS OF MAMMALS, BIRDS, FISH, INSECTS, ETC., edited by Jim Harter. Clear wood engravings present, in extremely lifelike poses, over 1,000 species of animals. 284pp. 9 × 12. 23766-4 Pa. $8.95

MORE HAND SHADOWS, Henry Bursill. For those at their 'finger ends,'' 16 more effects—Shakespeare, a hare, a squirrel, Mr. Punch, and twelve more—each explained by a full-page illustration. Considerable period charm. 30pp. 6½ × 9¼. 21384-6 Pa. $1.95

DECORATIVE NAPKIN FOLDING FOR BEGINNERS, Lillian Oppenheimer and Natalie Epstein. 22 different napkin folds in the shape of a heart, clown's hat, love knot, etc. 63 drawings. 48pp. 8¼ × 11. 23797-4 Pa. $1.95

DECORATIVE LABELS FOR HOME CANNING, PRESERVING, AND OTHER HOUSEHOLD AND GIFT USES, Theodore Menten. 128 gummed, perforated labels, beautifully printed in 2 colors. 12 versions. Adhere to metal, glass, wood, ceramics. 24pp. 8¼ × 11. 23219-0 Pa. $2.95

EARLY AMERICAN STENCILS ON WALLS AND FURNITURE, Janet Waring. Thorough coverage of 19th-century folk art: techniques, artifacts, surviving specimens. 166 illustrations, 7 in color. 147pp. of text. 7⅞ × 10¾. 21906-2 Pa. $8.95

AMERICAN ANTIQUE WEATHERVANES, A.B. & W.T. Westervelt. Extensively illustrated 1883 catalog exhibiting over 550 copper weathervanes and finials. Excellent primary source by one of the principal manufacturers. 104pp. 6⅛ × 9¼. 24396-6 Pa. $3.95

ART STUDENTS' ANATOMY, Edmond J. Farris. Long favorite in art schools. Basic elements, common positions, actions. Full text, 158 illustrations. 159pp. 5⅜ × 8½. 20744-7 Pa. $3.50

BRIDGMAN'S LIFE DRAWING, George B. Bridgman. More than 500 drawings and text teach you to abstract the body into its major masses. Also specific areas of anatomy. 192pp. 6½ × 9¼. (EA) 22710-3 Pa. $4.50

COMPLETE PRELUDES AND ETUDES FOR SOLO PIANO, Frederic Chopin. All 26 Preludes, all 27 Etudes by greatest composer of piano music. Authoritative Paderewski edition. 224pp. 9 × 12. (Available in U.S. only) 24052-5 Pa. $6.95

PIANO MUSIC 1888-1905, Claude Debussy. Deux Arabesques, Suite Bergamesque, Masques, 1st series of Images, etc. 9 others, in corrected editions. 175pp. 9⅜ × 12¼. (ECE) 22771-5 Pa. $5.95

TEDDY BEAR IRON-ON TRANSFER PATTERNS, Ted Menten. 80 iron-on transfer patterns of male and female Teddys in a wide variety of activities, poses, sizes. 48pp. 8¼ × 11. 24596-9 Pa. $2.00

A PICTURE HISTORY OF THE BROOKLYN BRIDGE, M.J. Shapiro. Profusely illustrated account of greatest engineering achievement of 19th century. 167 rare photos & engravings recall construction, human drama. Extensive, detailed text. 122pp. 8¼ × 11. 24403-2 Pa. $7.95

NEW YORK IN THE THIRTIES, Berenice Abbott. Noted photographer's fascinating study shows new buildings that have become famous and old sights that have disappeared forever. 97 photographs. 97pp. 11⅜ × 10. 22967-X Pa. $6.50

MATHEMATICAL TABLES AND FORMULAS, Robert D. Carmichael and Edwin R. Smith. Logarithms, sines, tangents, trig functions, powers, roots, reciprocals, exponential and hyperbolic functions, formulas and theorems. 269pp. 5⅜ × 8½. 60111-0 Pa. $3.75

HANDBOOK OF MATHEMATICAL FUNCTIONS WITH FORMULAS, GRAPHS, AND MATHEMATICAL TABLES, edited by Milton Abramowitz and Irene A. Stegun. Vast compendium: 29 sets of tables, some to as high as 20 places. 1,046pp. 8 × 10½. 61272-4 Pa. $19.95

THE PRINCIPLE OF RELATIVITY, Albert Einstein et al. Eleven most important original papers on special and general theories. Seven by Einstein, two by Lorentz, one each by Minkowski and Weyl. 216pp. 5⅜ × 8½.   60081-5 Pa. $3.50

PINEAPPLE CROCHET DESIGNS, edited by Rita Weiss. The most popular crochet design. Choose from doilies, luncheon sets, bedspreads, apron—34 in all. 32 photographs. 48pp. 8¼ × 11.   23939-X Pa. $2.00

REPEATS AND BORDERS IRON-ON TRANSFER PATTERNS, edited by Rita Weiss. Lovely florals, geometrics, fruits, animals, Art Nouveau, Art Deco and more. 48pp. 8¼ × 11.   23428-2 Pa. $1.95

SCIENCE-FICTION AND HORROR MOVIE POSTERS IN FULL COLOR, edited by Alan Adler. Large, full-color posters for 46 films including *King Kong, Godzilla, The Illustrated Man*, and more. A bug-eyed bonanza of scantily clad women, monsters and assorted other creatures. 48pp. 10¼ × 14¼. 23452-5 Pa. $8.95

TECHNICAL MANUAL AND DICTIONARY OF CLASSICAL BALLET, Gail Grant. Defines, explains, comments on steps, movements, poses and concepts. 15-page pictorial section. Basic book for student, viewer. 127pp. 5⅜ × 8½.
21843-0 Pa. $2.95

STORYBOOK MAZES, Dave Phillips. 23 stories and mazes on two-page spreads: *Wizard of Oz, Treasure Island, Robin Hood*, etc. Solutions. 64pp. 8¼ × 11.
23628-5 Pa. $2.25

PUNCH-OUT PUZZLE KIT, K. Fulves. Engaging, self-contained space age entertainments. Ready-to-use pieces, diagrams, detailed solutions. Challenge a robot; split the atom, more. 40pp. 8¼ × 11.   24307-9 Pa. $3.50

THE HUMAN FIGURE IN MOTION, Eadweard Muybridge. Over 4500 19th-century photos showing stopped-action sequences of undraped men, women, children jumping, running, sitting, other actions. Monumental collection. 390pp. 7⅞ × 10⅞.   20204-6 Clothbd. $18.95

PHOTOGRAPHIC SKETCHBOOK OF THE CIVIL WAR, Alexander Gardner. Reproduction of 1866 volume with 100 on-the-field photographs: Manassas, Lincoln on battlefield, slave pens, etc. 224pp. 10⅝ × 8¼.   22731-6 Pa. $6.95

FLORAL IRON-ON TRANSFER PATTERNS, edited by Rita Weiss. 55 floral designs, large and small, realistic, stylized; poppies, iris, roses, etc. Victorian, modern. Instructions. 48pp. 8¼ × 11.   23248-4 Pa. $1.95

AUTOBIOGRAPHY: The Story of My Experiments with Truth, Mohandas K. Gandhi. Boyhood, legal studies, purification, the growth of the Satyagraha (nonviolent protest) movement. Critical, inspiring work of the man who freed India. 480pp. 5⅜ × 8½.   24593-4 Pa. $6.95

ON THE IMPROVEMENT OF THE UNDERSTANDING, Benedict Spinoza. Also contains *Ethics, Correspondence*, all in excellent R Elwes translation. Basic works on entry to philosophy, pantheism, exchange of ideas with great contemporaries. 420pp. 5⅜ × 8½.   20250-X Pa. $5.95

Prices subject to change without notice.
Available at your book dealer or write for free catalog to Dept. GI, Dover Publications, Inc., 31 East 2nd St. Mineola, N.Y. 11501. Dover publishes more than 175 books each year on science, elementary and advanced mathematics, biology, music, art, literary history, social sciences and other areas.